# A DOCUMENTARY
# HISTORY OF ENGLAND

*J. J. Bagley and P. B. Rowley*

—— I ——

1066–1540

PENGUIN BOOKS

Penguin Books Ltd, Harmondsworth, Middlesex, England
Penguin Books Inc., 7110 Ambassador Court, Baltimore, Maryland 21207, U.S.A.
Penguin Books Australia Ltd, Ringwood, Victoria, Australia

—

First published 1966
Reprinted 1968

—

—

Made and printed in Great Britain
by Hazell Watson & Viney Ltd,
Aylesbury, Bucks
Set in Linotype Granjon

PELICAN BOOKS

A767

# A DOCUMENTARY HISTORY OF ENGLAND
## VOLUME I   1066–1540

*Advisory Editor: Professor J. H. Plumb*

John J. Bagley was educated at Cowley School, St Helens, and the University of Liverpool. He graduated in 1930 and since then, apart from war-time service in the R.A.F., he has been teaching and studying history. He was formerly a schoolmaster at Rochdale and Upholland and is now Reader in History in the Extra-Mural Department of the University of Liverpool. He considers himself lucky that he had a grounding in the history of Medieval England from three such tutors as G. W. Coopland, May McKisack, and the late R. R. Betts.

John Bagley has published biographies of Margaret of Anjou and Henry VIII, histories of Lancashire and Upholland Grammar School, a social history, *Life in Medieval England*, and *Historical Interpretation: Sources of English Medieval History, 1066–1540*. Since the war he has developed a particular interest in the history of the north-western counties. He is vice-president and ex-editor of the *Transactions of the Historic Society of Lancashire and Cheshire*, general editor of *A History of Cheshire*, and a Fellow of the Royal Historical Society.

Peter B. Rowley (*right*) was born in 1931 and received his early education at Queen Elizabeth Grammar School, Wakefield. He proceeded, on an Open Exhibition in Classics, to Hertford College, Oxford, where he read Classical Moderations and the Final Honours School of Literae Humaniores. After five years of administrative work with the Church Commissioners for England, he served for three years as Assistant Secretary at Birkbeck College, University of London; and is now Librarian in the Department of Adult Education and Extra-Mural Studies, University of Liverpool.

# Contents

## *Acknowledgements*

The translation on pp. 138-51 is taken from Lynn Thorndike's *The Sphere of Sacrobosco and its Commentators* (copyright © The University of Chicago, 1949), published by the University of Chicago Press, to whom we wish to make acknowledgement. Figure 1 (p. 139) is reproduced from A. C. Crombie's *Augustine to Galileo* (1952) by courtesy of Heinemann Educational Books Ltd.

# To the Reader

OUT of the thousands of documents that have come down from the five centuries between 1066 and 1540, we have chosen a handful. We venture to think that each of these few possesses particular significance, but since the list represents our personal choice we do not expect that you will be able to give it your full approval. Without doubt you would have preferred this instead of that, and to at least two or three of our items you would never have given a moment's serious thought. Yet our choice was not made arbitrarily. We reluctantly put aside such 'descriptive' documents as Domesday Survey, the monastic chronicles, and the Paston letters. Instead we looked for documents which played a major part in forming our national institutions, or which, by their lasting influence on men's thoughts and actions, helped to shape life in medieval England, or which portray an aspect of society which was current over a long period of time. We took as wide a view of medieval history as we could, so that our chosen documents cover theological and scientific beliefs as well as legal and government administration, economic change as well as political speculation.

All but two of our documents were originally written in Latin or French. Our translation attempts to reproduce the original text as closely as is consistent with intelligibility and a reasonably modern idiom. We have eliminated archaisms, but we have retained necessary technical terms and explained them either in square brackets in the text, or in the glossary at the end of the book.

Since it is possible that you will wish to consult a number of the Latin or French texts for yourself, we have told you something of their history and referred you to books in which they can be found. But for general works on the period we can do no better than advise you to consult the bibliographies which Lady Stenton and Dr A. R. Myers compiled for Volumes 3 and 4 of the *Pelican History of England*.

*Liverpool, June 1965*

J.J.B.
P.B.R.

# 1. *The Rule of St Benedict*

EVERY county in Great Britain contains architectural and archaeological evidence of medieval monasticism. The Yorkshire dales, the valley of the Tweed, and many a single site display substantial ruins. At a number of once important houses, such as Vale Royal in Cheshire or Croxton in Leicestershire, the aerial photograph and the archaeologist's spade are necessary to reveal what is left of the foundations, but, in contrast, the medieval cathedral monasteries and certain Oxford and Cambridge conventual houses are still in daily use. Simply to see the hundreds of sites plotted on such a map as the Ordnance Survey *Map of Monastic Britain* is to realize what an important role monasteries played in the life of medieval England: to study the cartularies of the different houses and to list the lands that eventually belonged to them is to understand why they were a major factor in developing the wealth of the country.

Christian monasticism is almost as old as the Church itself. In the early years of the fourth century St Anthony and St Pachomius founded monasteries in Egypt, and two generations later St Basil established a monastery in Pontus in Asia Minor. The disturbed years which followed the break-up of the Roman Empire witnessed many other foundations, but there was little permanence or uniformity in these early monasteries. None of them achieved a form of government and pattern of daily life which the others were prepared to adopt. Some measure of discipline was established by insisting that monasteries should be subject to episcopal jurisdiction, but the most lasting remedy for confusion was the gradual but, eventually, widespread acceptance of the guiding principles and regulations put forward by St Benedict of Nursia, who, in the first half of the sixth century, founded a number of monasteries, including the famous Monte Cassino set high in the mountains between Rome and Naples. These principles and regulations, known as the Rule of St Benedict, moulded medieval monasticism into a regular form: they still guide the corporate activities of most monastic brotherhoods today. It would be difficult to exaggerate the direct and indirect influence the Rule has had during more than fourteen centuries. Tens of thousands have lived by it, and hundreds who have been influential in the secular church, in universities and schools, and even in government and administration have lived under its discipline for some part of their lives.

Despite his careful explanations of many details, St Benedict did not intend his Rule to provide the answer to all monastic problems – in his own words it was a 'little Rule for beginners' – but he put it forward as a practical foundation upon which communities could build their own superstructure. He divided the active hours of each monastic day into three parts, and advocated that monks should spend one in praise and prayer in church, another in study and contemplation, and the third in manual work. He considered that monks should live a simple life. They had no need of anything beyond the minimum of clothes, furniture, and tools, and even these should belong to the community and not to individual members. They should eat sparingly and abjure all luxuries. But St Benedict did not approve of excessive asceticism. Too severe a mortification of the flesh achieved little good. 'Because of the weaker brethren,' he said, 'let everything be done in moderation.'

St Benedict did not found an *order* of monks. His Rule made each abbot an elected benevolent despot over his particular community: 'he is held to supply Christ's place in the monastery' for he is called by his name, 'Abba, Father.' God had guided the community to choose him, therefore the members must obey him as if his instructions were those of God. No abbot could claim supremacy or exercise powers of inspection over another: within his own frontiers each reigned supreme. At his election the abbot undertook to rule in the fear of God and by the Rule, and to take heed of the opinions and wishes of all the brethren. But, even if he neglected to do this, his decisions and interpretations were still binding and his word still indisputable law. Thus over the years the Rule suffered many different interpretations. Not only did climate and local conditions dictate regional differences, but also each abbey built up its own traditions, which ultimately it recorded in its 'Customs'.

Augustine and the monks who landed in Kent in 597 introduced St Benedict's Rule into England. Within the next hundred years they and their successors built monasteries at Canterbury, Rochester, Winchester, Peterborough, and a dozen other centres. From northern houses such as Hexham and Jarrow, Benedictine influence spread into the Celtic church and as the seventh century passed into the eighth the monastic ideal was inspiring increasing enthusiasm throughout England. But it was not to last. The Norse landing on Lindisfarne in 793 initiated almost two centuries of destruction, and not until the second half of the tenth century, the days of Dunstan, Ethelwold, and Oswald, was it possible to put fresh life into the old foundations and establish new houses at Cerne, Bury St Edmunds, Coventry, and half a dozen other centres.

The first of the medieval monastic 'reformations' came from Cluny in Burgundy. This community, founded in 910, reinterpreted the Benedictine Rule chiefly by extending the hours spent in worship, reducing virtually to nothing the time given to manual work, and deciding that to adorn the church as richly as possible was to make a right use of monastic wealth. The duke of Aquitaine, the founder, succeeded in freeing Cluny from episcopal supervision. The community acknowledged no authority but that of Rome, and, spurred on by a fervent desire to convert others to its new version of monastic life, it used its special privileges to found and control many houses. The abbot of Cluny claimed supremacy. By appointing the head of each affiliated abbey and daughter priory, by making regular visitations, and by periodically convening at Cluny a general congregation of the abbots or priors of all Cluniac houses, he succeeded in establishing the first monastic order. But Cluniac enthusiasm of the tenth and eleventh centuries did far more than this. It helped to strengthen papal authority, revise canon law, and bring more centralization into western Christendom. It encouraged churchmen, artists, and musicians to give thought to liturgy, church design, and decoration, and it played a part in making possible the administrative reforms of Gregory VII.

Cluny won limited success in England. It inspired the brief tenth-century monastic revival, but it was not until after the Norman Conquest that the first Cluniac priories – Lewes, Much Wenlock, Bermondsey, and others – were founded. Early twelfth-century Englishmen gave a much more enthusiastic welcome to the new critics of Cluny, the Cistercians, who were practising and preaching a very different interpretation of St Benedict's Rule. In 1098 a group of dedicated but critical monks had left the Cluniac house of Molesme to make a fresh start a hundred miles further south, at Cîteaux in the valley of the Saône. They had restored study and manual work to the daily routine, insisted upon more frugal and more solitary living than they had had at Cluny, and, during the next few years under the influence of Stephen Harding and St Bernard, evolved a puritanical form of monastic living which had a surprisingly wide appeal. The Cistercians explained their view of the Rule of St Benedict in two documents, the Charter of Love (*Carta Caritatis*) and the Constitutions of 1119. They wished to found their houses in deserted and neglected areas, and use the daily toil of all their members, from abbots to novices, to develop waste into useful land. They exalted Chapter 48 of the Rule: 'Idleness is the enemy of the soul. Therefore the brothers should work with their hands at fixed times of the day, and at other fixed times should read sacred works.' The Cistercians rejected the rich food and soft raiment of the contemporary, degenerate Cluniacs, forbade meat to be eaten in the frater, and insisted upon a strict observance of fasts. The gold and silver ornaments which decorated every Cluniac church they considered superfluous and distracting. Wooden crosses, iron candlesticks, plain glass, and simple vestments satisfied practical needs and did not take their attention away from meditation and prayer. The Cluniacs had made their novitiate so short and easy that it served no useful purpose, but the Cistercians, following the Rule more closely, insisted that all their novices should endure a full, exacting novitiate before they were considered worthy of full admission to the order. Even the lay brothers, whom the Cistercians recruited to help with the manual work, lived under strict discipline. They fasted, observed silences, and took the vows of poverty, chastity, and obedience.

Once St Bernard had become the abbot of Clairvaux, one of the first four daughter houses of Cîteaux, the Cistercian movement spread rapidly throughout Western Europe. It founded its first English houses at Waverley in Surrey in 1128 and at Rievaulx and Fountains in Yorkshire in 1131 and 1132. In 1147 it incorporated the minor order of Savigny, and so took over Furness, the important abbey situated in the wild country to the north of Morecambe Bay. Eventually the Cistercians possessed almost eighty English houses, many of which developed new agricultural areas and made considerable contributions to the valuable English wool trade. The Cistercian order insisted upon strict uniformity.

Despite the difficulties of medieval travel, the general chapter of Cistercian abbots, which met annually at Cîteaux, instituted a system of inspection which succeeded in enforcing the rules of the order remarkably well. No individual house could vary the accepted interpretation of the Rule: the sequence of services, labour, and study was the same everywhere. Cistercian buildings had to conform to a master plan, and archaeological evidence shows that any part of the buildings that did not conform had to be pulled down and rebuilt. 'Twelve monks at least with a thirteenth as abbot' constituted the permitted minimum allowed to found a new house, and every Cistercian church had to be dedicated to the Virgin. Throughout the twelfth century the Cistercians maintained their astringent influence upon monasticism. After that, accumulation of wealth and manifold secular responsibilities induced changes which inevitably led to a decline of asceticism and a less strict interpretation of the Benedictine Rule.

The Carthusians were other rebels against the Cluniac view of monasticism, but they worked out a third distinctive way of life still based upon the Benedictine Rule. They emphasized the need for solitude and silence: in Chapter 6 of his Rule, St Benedict had written, 'Since silence is of such importance, permission to speak should only rarely be given even to the more advanced disciples.' The Carthusians interpreted the word *rarely* severely. They felt manual work to be inappropriate for monks, and strictly limited the occasions of corporate worship in the church. Consequently Carthusian monks lived hermits' lives most of the time. They ate little and for days on end spoke to no one. They devoted their life to study and the contemplation of God. As one would expect, such an exacting life appealed to comparatively few men in each generation. St Bruno founded the order in 1084, but the first English Charterhouse, Witham in Somerset, did not come into existence for another hundred years. By 1300 there were only another three foundations in England, and during the fourteenth century another five. Yet Carthusian influence cannot be measured by the small number of its houses. During the later Middle Ages when all other orders relaxed the severity of their rules, the Carthusians still maintained the ascetic life of the first generations of their order. Almost alone they defied the government of Henry VIII when it tried to force all English monasteries to assent to the separation from Rome.

The late-eleventh- and twelfth-century enthusiasm for monasteries inspired many groups of canons, secular clergy, to adopt a conventual life. They took vows of chastity, poverty, and obedience and exchanged their service to the laity for communal prayer and contemplation. But instead of using the Rule of St Benedict as their guide, they adopted the Rule of St Augustine. In origin, this was advice written in the early fifth century, a hundred years before St Benedict, by St Augustine of Hippo to a group of nuns, but it had been adapted to suit monks. Its principles were similar to those of the Benedictine Rule. Augustine, like Benedict, demanded implicit obedience to a superior: 'Obey him who is set over you as if he were your father; obey much more the one who has supreme responsibility for you all.' He assumed that all who became members of a community would surrender individual wealth: 'Do not call anything your own, but let all things be held in common. He that is in authority over you should distribute food and clothing, not equally to all, because you are not all equal, but to each of you according to need.' Augustine required monks to be celibate, but he did not anticipate that they would shut themselves away from the world for ever: 'We do not forbid you, when walking, to look at a woman; but it is sinful to lust for them, or to wish them to lust for you . . . . And do not claim that your minds are chaste if your eyes are not, for an unchaste eye is the messenger of an unchaste heart.' The canons of Barnwell, near Cambridge, claimed that St Augustine's Rule was both 'simple and easy, so that unlearned men and children can walk in it without stumbling' and 'deep and lofty, so that the wise and strong can find in it matter for abundant and perfect contemplation. An elephant can swim in it and a lamb can walk in it safely.' But in practice the Augustinian Rule was found to be too general a document to stand alone, and from the first the Canons Regular had to supplement it with more precise regulations, which inevitably were based upon regulations which one or other order of Benedictine monks had found beneficial. Because of the Rule they professed to follow, the main order of canons took the name of Augustinian, or Austin, canons, but life in their houses did not differ much from life in houses following the Rule of St Benedict. The Premonstratensian canons, the most important of a number of breakaway orders, deliberately aped the Cistercians. Through their annual chapter and methods of inspection, they achieved a Cistercian-like uniformity, and followed a daily timetable similar to that in use in Cistercian houses. But the Augustinians preferred their houses to be much more independent. In pre-Cluny style they allowed each abbey to run its own life and adopt regulations of its own. The only outside control was that exercised by the bishop on his periodic visitations.

The Augustinian canons founded about two hundred houses in England, but most of them were small. They tended to congregate in East Anglia and between London and the Channel coast. Their first houses, at Canterbury, Huntingdon, Colchester, and Cambridge, were either centred on thriving churches or were converted houses of secular canons. But gradually the canons broke their ties with parish and diocesan work. New houses were built at Aldgate, Barnwell, Oxford, and many other places so that their communities could live a full conventual life. The Premonstratensians, St Norbert's order, built their first English monastery in Lincolnshire in 1143. They founded another score during the next two generations, and like the Cistercians, their Benedictine prototypes, they chose remote, discouraging sites.

Nunneries, as monasteries, followed the Rule of either Benedict or Augustine, but usually life in the nunneries was not so strictly controlled as in twelfth-century monasteries. When Gilbert of Sempringham founded his little order in Lincolnshire in the first half of the twelfth century, he considered that the Augustinian Rule was too harsh for the nuns in his double houses. He decreed that they should live by the Benedictine Rule. But that was probably because he had reinforced the Augustinian Rule incumbent on his monks by stricter regulations taken from the Cistercians and the Premonstratensians. As we have seen, the severity or laxity of either Rule depended upon who was putting it into practice. The interpretation was more decisive than the text.

*

The widespread popularity and influence of St Benedict's Rule is reflected in the very large number of early manuscripts of the Rule which survive; there are few texts, the Bible apart, which can rival this number. Amongst these surviving manuscripts there are two distinct traditions. The more authentic text is probably preserved in a group of Frankish manuscripts of the ninth century, of which St Gall 914, the *Sangallensis*, dating from *c.* A.D. 820, is the best known. The Frankish manuscripts derive from a lost copy of the Rule, known as the Aachen exemplar, which was sent to Charlemagne in A.D. 787 by the then abbot of Monte Cassino, to serve as a model for use in monasteries of the Empire. By doubtful tradition, this copy was said to have been taken from St Benedict's autograph of the Rule. The manuscripts belonging to this tradition, which is the one followed in the present translation, give the text of the Rule in a mixture of classical and vulgar Latin.

In the 'rival text', the vulgarisms have been removed and the Latin is more consistently classical. The manuscript known as *Oxoniensis* is the oldest surviving example of this 'revised version', and also the oldest surviving copy of the Rule. It is preserved in the Bodleian Library at Oxford, where it is MS. Hatton 48, and is believed to have been written in England about A.D. 700.

An excellent modern edition of the Rule, suitable for the general reader, is by Abbot Justin McCann, *The Rule of Saint Benedict* (1952). This edition has the Latin text of the 'authentic' version, but with the more difficult vulgarisms as footnotes, together with a facing translation, introduction, and notes. There is a critical edition of *S. Benedicti Regula Monasteriorum* by Abbot Cuthbert Butler, 3rd ed. (Freiburg, 1935): under the same title, Dom Benno Linderbauer (Bonn, 1928) and Dom Philibert Schmitz, *S. Benedicti Regula Monachorum*, 2nd ed. (Maresdous, 1955) print the text of the 'authentic' version. For St Benedict and Benedictine monachism generally, see Justin McCann, *Saint Benedict*, rev. ed. (1958); J. Chapman, *Saint Benedict and the Sixth Century* (1929); and Cuthbert Butler, *Benedictine Monachism*, 2nd ed. (1924).

The standard general surveys of monastic activity in England up to the time of the dissolution of the monasteries are by Dom David Knowles, *The Monastic Order in England, 943–1216*, 2nd ed. (1963), and *The Religious Orders in England*, 3 vols. (1948–59). For one example of the customs or sets of ordinances which the individual houses needed to supplement the rules of their orders, see also his edition and translation of *Lanfranc's Monastic Constitutions* (1951) for the Benedictine community of Christ Church, Canterbury.

The *Regularis Concordia*, with which the name of Archbishop Dunstan is associated, and which served as a pattern of Benedictine monachism in England in the tenth century and afterwards, has been edited and translated by Dom Thomas Symons (1953).

Eileen Power, *Medieval English Nunneries* (1922), is the best account of the female communities. For the Carthusians, see E. M. Thompson, *The Carthusian Order in England* (1930); and for the Premonstratensians, H. M. Colvin, *The White Canons in England* (1951). There is a translation of the *Carta Caritatis* of the Cistercians in *English Historical Documents*, vol. II (1953), ed. D. C. Douglas and G. W. Greenaway.

## 1. THE RULE OF ST BENEDICT

*Prologue*

Listen, my son, to the precepts of your master and hear them in your heart; receive with gladness the charge of a loving master and perform it fully, so that by the hard road of obedience you may return to him from whom you strayed along the easy paths of disobedience. To you, then, who, renouncing your own will, enlist with your true sovereign, Christ the Lord, and take up the strong and shining weapons of obedience, I now direct my words.

My first and most important charge to you is this: that whatever you set out to achieve in the way of goodness, you shall ask the Lord most earnestly in your prayers to bring it about, so that he who has deigned to count us amongst the number of his children shall never have cause to grieve for our misdeeds. For we should give him such obedience always, out of the store of goodness which he has set within us, that he will never like an angry father disinherit his sons, nor, in irritation with our sins, condemn us to everlasting punishment, as a dread lord his most unworthy servants who have refused to follow him to glory. . . .

And if we would escape the pains of hell and come to everlasting life, we must make haste and do those things which will serve us for eternity, now whilst there is still time and we are in this body and can still accomplish all these things as dwellers in the light.

We must therefore establish a school of the Lord's service, and it is our hope in this establishment to prescribe nothing harsh or burdensome. But if, at the dictates of justice, some degree of strictness is applied for the preservation of brotherly love or the correction of faults, do not lose heart because of this and flee from the way of salvation. For the entry to such a way must needs be narrow, but as our faith increases and we are confirmed in the monastic life, our hearts enlarge and we run easily along the way of God's commandments, with a love of such sweetness that words cannot express it. And so, keeping Christ always as our master and remaining steadfast to his teaching in the monastery until death, we may share in his passion by our suffering and become worthy, in this way, to share his kingdom. Amen.

## 1. *The Different Kinds of Monks*

There are four well-defined categories of monks. First, there are the *Coenobites*, that is, those who live in a monastery, soldiering under a rule and an abbot.

Then there is the second kind, that of Anchorites or Hermits. I do not mean those who take to the solitary life in the first flush of religious conversion, but men who have served a long probation in a monastery and have studied alongside many others to fight against the devil, each bearing up the other with comfort and encouragement. They have learned their lesson and go forth from the ranks of the brothers well-equipped to face single combat in the desert; they have the strength now to stand alone and do not need the moral support of others, but with God as their ally they are able to fight, single-handed and unsupported by a comrade's arm, against the sins of the flesh and the mind's evil thoughts.

The third kind of monks, and a most loathsome one, is that of the *Sarabaites*. They have not been tried, as gold is tried in the furnace, by any rule or test of discipline, but they are pliable as lead and still keep faith with the world in their actions; and by the very way they wear their hair, they are marked out as false to God. They live two or three together, or one man alone, without a shepherd, penned up in their own sheep-folds and not in the Lord's. . . .

The fourth kind of monks is that of the *Gyrovagi*. They spend their whole lives wandering from one province to another, staying for three or four days at a time in any cell that offers lodging, always on the move and never at rest; they are slaves to their own wills and ensnared by gluttony, and, all things considered, worse than the *Sarabaites*.

It is better not to speak of the deplorable 'lives in religion' which all these men lead, but to pass over them in silence. Let us therefore dismiss them from our consideration and proceed, with God's help, to give rules to the surpassingly healthy strain of the *Coenobites*.

## 2. *What Qualities an Abbot should have*

An abbot who is worthy to govern a monastery should suit his actions to the name *superior* which he bears; and he should remember always what *abbot* signifies. For when he is called by this name, he is held to supply Christ's place in the monastery, since *abbot* is another name for Christ, as in this passage of the apostle : *You have received the spirit of the adoption of sons, wherein we cry, Abba, Father.*[1] And so the abbot ought not, either in his teaching, or in his government, or in his commands, to exceed the warrant which he has in the precepts of the Lord; but his commands and teaching shall be instilled into the minds of his disciples like the leaven of divine justice. Let the abbot remember always that at the dread Judgement of God, both his own teaching and the obedience of his disciples will

1. This sentence is based on Romans, VIII, 15. Similarly, the many other quotations used in the Rule are all based on the Scriptures, but they are not necessarily exact quotations from the Vulgate. Sometimes two halves of the same quoted sentence have widely different origins.

surely pass under review; and he may be certain that the blame for any loss of value which the master finds in the sheep will be laid at the shepherd's door. But if the shepherd has devoted every care to a restless and wayward flock and has spared no effort to cure their distempers, he will be absolved from responsibility for them at the Judgement of the Lord. . . .

Therefore, when anyone assumes the name of abbot, he should govern his disciples through teaching of two kinds, making known to them all that is good and holy both by his precept and by his example; but especially by his example. To the more capable disciples he should expound the Lord's commands verbally; but to those of harder hearts and simpler understanding, he should exemplify the divine precepts in his own conduct. If he has taught his disciples that something is against the divine law, he should demonstrate by his own conduct that it must not be allowed in practice. . . .

The abbot shall make no distinction of persons in the monastery, nor love one more than another, unless he is found better in virtue or obedience. The free-born monk shall not be set above the former slave, merely because he is free-born, but only if there is some other good reason. In which case, and in all others where justice requires it and the abbot sees fit, he shall change any man's position. But otherwise let each one keep his proper place, since, slave and free-born alike, we are all one in Christ and are all equally servants in the army of the one Lord. *For there is no respect of persons with God*, and only for this reason are we set apart in his sight, if we are found better than others in virtue and humility. . . .

The abbot in his teaching should always follow that rule of the apostle, when he says: *Reprove, rebuke, exhort*. Which is to say, that he should adapt his approach to circumstances; at one time using fear, and at another gentle persuasion, alternating between the severity of a master and a father's loving kindness. He should sternly reprove the undisciplined and unruly: but the obedient, meek, and patient he should exhort towards a greater proficiency in virtue. We warn him to rebuke and chastise the careless and contemptuous. And let him not blind himself to the faults of offenders, but as soon as they are rooted and begin to grow, let him do his utmost to cut them out, being mindful of the fate of Eli, the priest of Shiloh. The better characters and those with a good understanding he shall punish for a first and second offence by verbal admonition: but he shall restrain the bad and hardened cases, the proud and the disobedient, by scourging and by corporal punishment at the very onset of their wrong-doing, knowing the Scripture: *A fool is not corrected by words*; and again: *Beat your son with the rod, and you will deliver his soul from death. . . .*

### 3. *Summoning the Brothers to Council*

Whenever there is important business to be transacted in the monastery, the abbot shall call the whole community together and place the facts before them. And having heard the advice of the brothers, he shall turn the matter over in his own mind and act accordingly as he thinks best. We have said that all should be called upon for their advice for this reason, that the Lord often reveals what is best to a junior member. The brothers, therefore, shall give their advice, but with all humility and deference, and they shall not presume to defend their views heatedly. Rather, the matter shall rest upon the abbot's good judgement, and once he has decided on the best course to follow, let all obey him. However, just as it befits the disciples to obey their master, so it is seemly that he, for his part, should be impartial and far-seeing in all his administration. . . .

When matters of minor importance in the monastery's concerns are to be transacted, the abbot shall take the advice of seniors only, accordingly as it is written: *Be advised in everything you do, and you will not then repent of your actions. . . .*

### 7. *Humility*

Holy Scripture calls out to us, brethren, saying: *Whoever exalts himself shall be humbled, and whoever humbles himself shall be exalted. . . .* And so, brethren, if we wish to attain that highest peak of humility and quickly scale those heavenly heights to which we climb by the humility of our earthly life, we must make an ascent of our actions and raise upon them that ladder of Jacob's dream, on which he was shown angels passing up and down; by the figure of whose ascending and descending we understand no other significance, but this one surely, that we descend by exalting ourselves, but by our humility we rise. And this ladder which we speak of as being raised is our life here on earth which, for the humbled in heart, God raises up until it reaches heaven. We represent our body and soul as the two sides of this ladder, on either side of which our holy calling has set various rungs of humility and discipline for us to climb.

The first rung of humility's ladder is for a brother to keep the fear of God constantly before his eyes and never for one moment to lose it from his sight; and for him to be ever mindful of all God's commandments, and of how hell will burn, because of their sins, those who scorn God. Let him turn over constantly in his soul the life everlasting that is prepared for those who fear God, and, keeping himself hourly free from sins and faults, both of thought, word, hand, foot, and self-will, and also from the desires of the flesh, let him reflect that he is hourly watched by God from heaven and that his actions are everywhere regarded by the divine gaze and are reported to God each hour by the angels. . . .

We must beware of evil desire, since death lies close to the door of delight; for which reason we are commanded by Scripture, to *go not after lusts*. Therefore, considering that *the eyes of the Lord behold the good and evil* . . . we should be heedful, brethren, of what the prophet says in the psalm and take care lest God, at some particular hour, should see us sinking into evil and losing our profit and, although he forgives us this time because he loves us and hopes for our amendment, should say to us in the future: *These things you did, and I was silent.*

The second stage of humility is for a brother not to be enamoured of his own will, nor to delight in the fulfilment of his desires, but to imitate by his actions these words of the Lord: *I came not to do my own will, but the will of Him who sent me.* . . .

The third stage of humility is for him to submit himself, from love of God, in all obedience to his superior, taking Christ as his example, of whom the apostle says: *He was made obedient even unto death*.

The fourth stage of humility is for him to bear with patience and a quiet mind any difficulties or set-backs, or even wrongs, which may arise to confront him in this obedience, without his becoming tired or a deserter; for the Scripture says: *He who perseveres to the end shall be saved*. . . .

The fifth stage of humility is for him to confess humbly to his abbot all evil thoughts that enter his heart, and all his secret sins, without concealing anything. . . .

The sixth stage of humility is for a monk to rest contented with anything, however cheap and nasty it may be, and, in everything that he is set to do, to rate himself a poor, unworthy workman, saying to himself with the prophet: *I am reduced to nothing and am all ignorance; I am become in Thy sight as a beast of burden, and yet am I always with Thee*.

The seventh stage of humility is for him to proclaim by his tongue that he is the lowest of all and the least in value; and not only to say this, but to believe it also, humbling himself and saying with the prophet: *But I am a worm and no man; I am reviled by all men and scorned by the people*. . . .

The eighth stage of humility for a monk is to do nothing except what is recommended by the common rule of the monastery and the example of his seniors.

The ninth stage of humility for a monk is to restrain his tongue from speech and to maintain his silence unbroken, except to answer a question; because, as we learn from Scripture, *sin must be present in a wealth of words*, and *the talkative man does not prosper upon the earth*.

The tenth stage of humility is for him not to be easily moved and prompt to laugh, for it is written that *the fool lifts up his voice in laughter*.

The eleventh stage of humility for a monk is to speak mildly and without laughter, humbly and seriously, in words that are few and to the point, and without raising his voice. . . .

The twelfth stage of humility for a monk is not only to be

humble in his heart, but at all times to show this humility to those who see him, by his outward bearing also. This is to say that whether he is at the work of God [*opus dei*, i.e. worshipping in church], in the oratory, in the monastery, in the garden, on the road, in the fields, or wherever he is, whether walking, standing, or sitting, his head shall be always bowed and his eyes shall be fixed on the ground, as he thinks of himself as on trial each hour of the day for his sins, and reflects upon the dread judgement which he will shortly have to face; repeating over and over again within his heart these words which the publican, with his eyes downcast, said in the Gospel: *Lord, I a sinner am not worthy to raise my eyes to heaven.* ...

Having climbed all these rungs on the ladder of humility, the monk will shortly come to that perfect love of God which casts out fear. Then, as the result of constant practice, he will begin to do naturally, as it were, and without effort, all those things which formerly he could not contemplate without dread; no longer from fear of hell, but from love of Christ, with a strength that has grown from long practice and his delight in virtue. Such gifts, through the Holy Spirit, will the Lord deign to show forth in His workman, now that his faults and sins have been washed away.

## 8. *The Divine Office at Night*

In winter, that is from 1 November up to Easter, the brothers shall rise at the eighth hour of the night, as common sense requires, since this will give them a little extra sleep beyond midnight and allow them to rise with their digestions settled. The time that follows after the Night Office shall be employed by those brothers who are not yet fully masters of the psalms and lessons, in perfecting their knowledge.

From Easter to 1 November, the times shall be so arranged that Matins, which are to be said at dawn, follow straight after the Night Office,[1] with only sufficient interval between them to

1. The Night Office was technically held in the middle of the night; but practice varied considerably. The custom of each house as well as the season of the year determined the timing of the service. St Benedict refers to the Night Office as *Vigils* or the *Night*

give the brothers time to go out and satisfy the needs of nature.

## 16. *How God's Work* [*Opus Dei*] *is to be done through the Day*

The prophet says: *Seven times a day have I praised thee*. We will match this sacred number of seven if we perform our bounden duty at the hours of Matins, Prime, Terce, Sext, Nones, Vespers, and Compline. For these are the day hours of which he said: *Seven times a day have I praised thee*.

The same prophet refers to the Night Office when he says: *At midnight I rose to give thee praise*.

At these times, therefore, shall we return praise to our Creator *for the judgements of his justice*, namely at Matins, Prime, Terce, Sext, Nones, Vespers, and Compline; and let us rise up in the night to give him praise.

## 17. *How Many Psalms are to be said at these Hours*

We have already settled the order in which psalms are to be sung at the Night Office and at Matins. Let us now look at the hours which follow.

At Prime, let three psalms be said, one by one, each with its own Gloria, and, before the psalms begin, the proper hymn for the hour, preceded by the versicle, *O God, incline unto my aid*. Then, after the three psalms have been said, there shall be recited the lesson, versicle, and Kyrie eleison, and so the service ends.

The same order of service shall be followed at Terce, Sext, and Nones; namely, versicle and proper hymn, three psalms, lesson, versicle, and Kyrie eleison, which complete the service. These services shall be sung; with antiphons, where the community is a sizeable one, but straight through and without separation into parts, where the community is small.

*Laud*, and to the office which follows it at daybreak as *Matins*, but in the later terminology of the Roman Catholic church these two offices became known as *Matins* and *Lauds* respectively.

Vespers shall consist of the singing of four psalms with antiphons and, after the psalms, the reciting of the lesson; next shall follow the responsary, hymn of St Ambrose, versicle, canticle from the Gospels, and Kyrie eleison; the whole ending with the Lord's Prayer.

Compline shall consist of three psalms, spoken straight through without an antiphon; and there shall then follow the proper hymn, lesson, versicle, and Kyrie eleison, with the blessing to bring the service to an end.

## 32. The Tools and other Property of the Monastery

The abbot shall appoint brothers, on whose lives and characters he may depend, to be responsible for the safe-keeping and return after use of the tools, clothing, and other property belonging to the monastery. He shall commit articles to their care as he thinks fit, and shall keep an inventory of them so that, despite the changes which occur from time to time amongst the brothers who are set in charge, he may know for himself what he has issued and what has been returned. If anyone is slovenly or careless with the property of the monastery, he shall be reproved and if he does not then amend his ways, let him be punished according to the Rule.

## 33. Whether Monks should have Personal Possessions

The sin of personal possession, above all others, should be cut out by its roots from the monastery. None of the brothers shall presume to give or receive anything except at the abbot's direction, or to have anything whatever of his own, neither a book, nor writing tablets, nor a pen: they shall have nothing at all, for they may not even dispose of their own bodies and wills, but must look to the father of the monastery for all their needs. They shall not be allowed to have anything except by the abbot's gift or consent. *Let all things be common to all, nor let anyone say that anything is his own*, or act as though it were. Should anyone be detected in the indulgence of this most pernicious vice, he shall be cautioned once and for a second time, and if he still does not reform, he shall be punished.

## 34. *Whether All should share equally in the Necessities of Life*

We should act in accordance with the account of Scripture, where *distribution was made to every man according as he had need*. We do not intend by this that special regard shall be paid to persons (which God forbid!) but that there shall be consideration for infirmities. He who needs less shall, under this method of distribution, give thanks to God and not be resentful; and he whose needs are greater shall be humble for his infirmity and not become proud because of the consideration which he receives; and in this way all the members will be at peace. Above all, let not the evil of discontented murmuring, whatever the cause, appear in any word or outward sign. Any of the brothers found guilty on this score shall be severely disciplined.

## 40. *The Allowance of Drink*

Each man *has his proper gift from God, one after this manner and another after that*, and we are therefore somewhat reluctant to prescribe how much others should eat and drink. However, we believe that a daily allowance of one hemina [1] of wine for each man is sufficient: but although we have set this amount, out of regard for the weakness of feebler brothers, let those to whom God has given the strength of abstinence know that they will receive their proper reward.

If, however, the situation of the monastery, or the hard work required from the brothers, or the intense heat of summer, call for an increased allowance, the superior shall grant it at his discretion, but he shall be careful always lest surfeit or drunkenness creep up on them. We read, it is true,[2] that wine is not at all

1. Probably about half a pint.
2. In the *Apophthegmata*, or *Sayings of the Fathers*, a product of fourth-century Egyptian monachism.

a drink for monks, but in these present times it is impossible to persuade them of this. Let us, however, agree on this point at least, that we will not drink to satiety, but more sparingly, since *wine makes apostates of even the wise.* . . .

## 48. *The Daily Manual Labour*

Idleness is the enemy of the soul. Therefore the brothers should work with their hands at fixed times of the day, and at other fixed times should read sacred works. We believe that appropriate periods are allowed for both these activities in the arrangement which follows.

From Easter until 14 September, the brothers shall go out in the morning and engage in whatever work has to be done, from the first hour until almost the fourth. From the fourth hour until about the sixth, they shall be free for reading. After the sixth hour, when they have eaten, they shall rise from table and rest in their beds, maintaining a complete silence. If any of them wishes to read to himself during this period, he shall read so as not to disturb the others. *Nones* shall be sung a little early, in the middle of the eighth hour, and afterwards they shall again work at what has to be done, until Vespers. . . .

From 14 September up to the beginning of Lent, they shall be free for reading right up to the second hour, when Terce shall be sung; and from then until Nones they shall all work at their appointed tasks. When the first summons to Nones is given, they shall lay aside their work and make themselves ready by the time the second summons is sounded. After the evening meal, which follows Nones, they shall be free for reading or to learn the psalms.

In the days of Lent they shall be free for their reading from early morning until the end of the third hour, and from then on until the end of the tenth hour they shall work at their appointed tasks. At the beginning of Lent, each of them shall be issued with one of the separate parts of the Bible,[1] which he is to read

1. *Singulos codices de bibliotheca* could alternatively be translated as 'a book each from the library': but the term *bibliotheca* was anciently applied to the Bible because of its separation into nine

through from beginning to end over the Lenten period. It is naturally of great importance that at these times when the brothers are free for reading, two senior brothers shall be assigned to go the rounds of the monastery and make sure that none of the brothers, from laziness, is spending his free time idly or in gossip, not only to the neglect of his own reading and self-improvement, but to the distraction of others as well. If they come across such an offender (which God forbid!) he shall be rebuked once and for a second time, and if he still does not reform, he shall receive such punishment as is prescribed by the Rule that the others shall have cause to fear. And the brothers shall not seek one another's company at times that are unsuitable.

On Sundays they shall all be free for reading, except those to whom duties of one kind and another are allocated. If there is anyone so slothful or lacking in diligence that he cannot, or will not, apply himself to reading and study, let him be given some work to do, to prevent his being idle. Brothers whose strength is low or their health delicate, however, should receive consideration from the abbot because of their weakness; and they shall only be given such manual or skilled work to do as will keep them occupied, without calling for such strenuous efforts on their part that they are borne down under the weight, or driven from the monastery.

## 53. *The Reception of Guests*

All guests who arrive at the monastery shall be received as Christ, and so will He one day say to them: *I was a stranger and you took me in. . . .*

The abbot shall give the guests water for their hands, and the whole community shall join with him in washing the feet of all guests, and in afterwards reciting the verse: *Lord, we have received thy mercy in the midst of thy temple*. They shall employ the greatest care and solicitude in the reception of poor people and pilgrims; for in them is Christ most truly received. As for the rich, the fear which they inspire is in itself sufficient to give them respect.

---

volumes, of which one, for example, would contain the Prophets, and another the Gospels.

Let the kitchen which serves the abbot and the guests of the monastery be set apart, so that when guests, of whom there are always some in the monastery, arrive at all hours the brothers shall not be disturbed. . . .

A brother who has the fear of God in his heart shall be set in charge of the guest house, where a sufficient number of beds shall be made up ready. This is God's house, and it shall be efficiently administered by brothers who know the work.

Let none of the brothers associate or speak with the guests, unless they are specially instructed to do so. If they should meet or see a guest, they shall greet him humbly, as we have said, and ask for his blessing, and then go on their way, explaining that they are not allowed to have conversation with a guest.

## 63. *The Order of Precedence in the Community*

Let the brothers maintain in the monastery an order of seniority determined by the relative dates of their reception into the community, or by the merits of their own lives where the abbot has so determined. . . . The brethren shall receive the kiss of peace, take communion, and lead the singing of the psalms according to the order which the abbot has decided, or to which their age in the habit entitles them. Under no circumstances whatever shall age decide their order, nor affect it, for Samuel and Daniel were only boys when they passed judgement on their elders. . . .

The juniors shall honour their seniors, and the seniors shall love their juniors. When they address one another they may not use the personal name alone, but a senior shall call his junior *Brother*, and the junior shall call his senior *Nonnus*, which means *Reverend Father*. The abbot, since he is held to supply Christ's place in the monastery, shall be called *Lord* and *Abbot*, not by any presumption of his own, but out of love and honour of Christ. The abbot shall think upon this and by his conduct show himself worthy of such honour.

Whenever brothers meet, the junior shall ask the senior for his blessing; and when a senior passes by, his junior shall rise and make room for him to sit, nor presume to sit down beside him, except by his bidding. And so, *in honour preferring one another*, will they fulfil the Scriptural command. . . .

## 64. *The Appointment of an Abbot*

This principle shall apply to every appointment of an abbot, that he shall be made abbot who is chosen unanimously in the fear of God by the whole body of the community; and if there is no unanimity, the appointment shall be made on the choice of that part of the community, however small, which has been guided by the soundest counsel.

The person to be appointed as abbot shall be chosen for his wise learning and for the goodness of his life, even though he was the last to join the community and is the least senior of them all. If it should happen that the community is given to wickedness (which God forbid!) and they have all from the same motive unanimously fixed their choice as abbot upon some-one who connives at their wickedness, and their misdoing is somehow made known to the bishop of their diocese or to neighbouring bishops or Christian people, these latter shall prevent the success of their wicked conspiracy and place a worthy steward in the house of God. . . .

The person appointed as abbot shall constantly reflect upon the weight of the burden which he has shouldered, and the nature of Him to whom he must account for his stewardship. He shall know that it is his duty rather to profit the brothers than to preside over them; and for this reason, he should be learned in the divine law and know how to draw from it lessons both old and new. And he shall be sober, chaste, and merciful. He shall always *exalt mercy above judgement*, so that he himself may obtain mercy. He shall hate wickedness, but love the brothers, and when he administers correction, he shall be careful not to go too far, lest in trying to scrape off the rust he shatter the vessel. Let him always mistrust his own frailty, and remember that the bruised reed must not be broken.

We do not intend by this that he should allow faults to flourish, but that he shall cut them out carefully and with loving care for his patients, treating each one as his case requires, as we have previously said. He shall be more concerned to make himself loved than feared. He shall not be violent in his nature, nor given to anxiety; nor extreme in his opinions and obstinate; nor jealous or over-much given to suspicion, because otherwise he will never be at peace. Before he gives a command, he shall weigh it carefully and consider its effects; and whatever task he appoints, whether God-directed or mundane, let him be discreet and moderate, remembering the discretion of holy Job, who said: *If I cause my flocks to be driven at too hard a pace, they will all die in a single day.* And so, following this and other examples of discretion, which is the mother of all virtues, he shall so moderate all that he asks of the brethren that the strong are not completely drained of their enthusiasm, nor are the weaker brothers caused to break ranks and flee. . . .

## 73. *This Rule does not constitute the Whole of Righteousness*

We have written this Rule so that by its observance in monasteries we may show ourselves to have made some progress in virtue and a beginning in the religious life. But for those who would press forward to the perfect state of the religious life, there are the teachings of the holy fathers, by observing which a man will be led to the peak of perfection. For what page, or what sentence even, of divine authority in the Old or New Testament is not a most sure guide for human conduct? What book of the holy Catholic fathers does not ring out this message, that the road is straight which leads to our Creator? What else for good-living and obedient monks but means to virtue are the Conferences of the Fathers, their Institutes and Lives, and the Rule of our holy father Basil? But we, who are idle and disobedient and live our lives badly, find in them only discomfiture and a cause for shame. Whoever you are, therefore, who would make good progress along the road to the heavenly country, conform yourself exactly, with Christ's help, to this little rule for beginners; and from this beginning, under God's protection, you will at length attain to those great heights of wisdom and virtue which we have described.

## 2. *The Coronation Charter of Henry I, 1100*

*Norman* and *feudal* are almost interchangeable. The one word evokes the other. Yet the Normans did not introduce feudalism into England. After the battle of Hastings, William the Conqueror found himself ruler of a country which was already feudal, even though some of its traditions and customs were new to him. Certain features of English government attracted the Norman king. He particularly admired the unity of the administration, the acknowledged rights and privileges of the crown, and the recognized status of the king as *God's thegn*, His pre-elected deputy on earth. These characteristics William determined to keep in his own version of feudalism, which was an amalgam of what, from his point of view, was best in feudal Normandy and feudal England. By 1087, the year in which he died, William had considerably systematized English administration. He had reserved to the crown some 1,400 manors, which gave him an income equal to about a quarter of the national income and about twice that enjoyed by Edward the Confessor. The rest of the land he had distributed to tenants in chief, who, he planned, would provide him with soldiers and war equipment whenever he required them. He had tied together landholding and service more securely than in Anglo-Saxon times, so that already there existed, partly imported from Normandy, accepted rules and traditions, which governed relations between crown and baronage.

The Conqueror replaced the Anglo-Saxon witan with the *curia regis*, a feudal assembly in which his major tenants in chief sat both by right and by obligation. Without the cooperation of his chief landholders no feudal king could rule efficiently, so it was deemed both right and prudent that he should take notice of his tenants' advice and respect their rank and privileges. Nevertheless, the Norman kings claimed and exercised supreme authority. Their decisions had the force of law, and their coronation by the archbishop, the deputy of the pope, exalted them above the most powerful of their barons. Each Easter, Whitsuntide, and Christmas, the three outstanding festivals of the church, the archbishop virtually reconsecrated the king before his people. Feudal lawyers did not find it easy to define exactly what was meant by *rex dei gratia*, but all agreed that the title gave the king a special status among men. He represented God on earth: 'as God's image, the king is worthy of love, reverence, and worship', wrote John of Salisbury early in Henry II's reign. Yet, in the very same passage of *Policraticus*, John justified the taking up of arms against a tyrant: 'not only is it lawful to slay the tyrant, but also it is right and just to do it. He that takes the sword deserves to perish by the sword.' But men of the eleventh and twelfth centuries did not confuse tyranny with firm government. They knew from experience that a weak and vacillating king brought nothing but disaster. It was, they believed, the king's business to rule, and not, as William's eldest son, Robert Curthose, did, give way to threats and a show of force. He should exact obedience from all his subjects both great and small. He should uphold the rule of law, and from the ravages of the bully and the criminal protect those too weak to defend themselves.

The Conqueror fulfilled most, but not all, of these exacting requirements. In the words of *Anglo-Saxon Chronicle E*, 'he was gentle to those good men who loved God, but severe beyond measure towards those who resisted his will . . . he was held in much reverence . . . he was very stern and full of wrath, so that no one dared do anything against his wish . . . the rich protested and the poor grumbled [at the forest laws] but he was so sure of himself that he took no notice; they must do all that the king willed if they wished to live, keep their estates, hold their possessions, or maintain their rights.' William Rufus, the Conqueror's successor, did not win either the approval or the implicit obedience that his subjects had given to his father. He could hardly have claimed for the crown more authority than his father had done, but he quarrelled bitterly with the church and outraged his tenants' sense of justice. Above all, he turned influential opinion against him by parading his personal feelings of anti-clericalism. Much of his father's tyranny had been forgiven – especially by the clerks who wrote the chronicles – because he had respected the dignity and privileges of clerics and shown himself enthusiastic about the rebuilding of churches and the founding of monasteries.

The principle of primogeniture established itself but slowly in England. Before the reign of Henry II, a new king was always of the blood royal, but not necessarily the eldest son of his predecessor. He claimed to be 'elected' by his 'subjects', and this was true in the very restricted sense that a sufficient number of barons had to support him if he were to make his reign effective. The Conqueror, himself an illegitimate son, willed that Normandy, his hereditary fief, should pass to his eldest son, Robert, but that England, his conquest, should go to his favourite son, William. This division of estates could not help but divide the loyalties of the Anglo-Norman barons, so that when Robert attempted to reunite his father's dominions, he found powerful allies in England. In the midlands Hugh de Grentmesnil, William of Eu, and several other tenants in chief took up his cause, and in Kent and Sussex Robert of Mortain and his brother, Bishop Odo of Bayeux, whom the dying Conqueror had released from jail, led a serious revolt on his behalf. For many weeks in 1088 it looked as if William Rufus might easily lose his throne. To encourage his tenants, he issued a statement that he intended to observe the laws of Edward the Confessor – a promise vague enough not to be dangerous later on – and, to keep the loyalty of his English subjects, he spoke of removing restrictions and discriminations. Fortunately for the new king, Hugh Lupus of Chester, William de Warenne, and other powerful barons remained loyal, and the lackadaisical Robert failed to support the rebels who had declared for him. The pro-Robert revolt collapsed, and Rufus, unmindful of his promises, settled down to enjoy his inheritance.

Duke Robert was soon in grave difficulty himself. Debts compelled him to sell the western portion of Normandy to his younger brother Henry, and in the rest of his duchy he found it impossible to keep law and order. Early in 1191 Rufus led an army across the Channel to exploit the political chaos. With an extensive use of bribes he had already created a friendly fifth column, and he easily occupied Normandy east of the Seine. Robert had no option but to come to terms, and to join William in driving Henry out of the Cotentin peninsula and the district of Avranches. The rest of the decade was just as full of war and political scheming: campaigns first against the Scots and then against the Welsh, renewed fighting in Normandy, the suppression of a baronial revolt led by Robert de Mowbray, the purchase of Normandy for three years to enable Robert to go crusading, designs to conquer Vexin and Maine on the frontiers of Normandy, each followed one another in rapid succession. And in the midst of this turbulence, Rufus's life came to an abrupt, unexpected end in the New Forest. Walter Tirel shot the arrow, but Rufus's brother, Henry, gained most from the death. Soon after the Normandy campaign of 1191 Henry had been reconciled to the king, and ever after had remained outwardly loyal. He was a member of the hunting party in the New Forest, and once he knew that William had died, he acted with such vigour and boldness that some people suspected that he had planned the 'accident'. Within the space of three days he took charge of the treasury at Winchester, and had himself 'elected' and crowned king at Westminster. After that he had to consolidate his position, and protect it against the counter-attacks which Duke Robert and other possible contenders might mount against it. The coronation charter formed an important bastion in his defences.

The barons did not disapprove of Rufus because he went to war. Like all medieval aristocrats they had been brought up to regard fighting as their profession and war as a natural and honourable part of life. They held their land by military service, and looked to their king to wage successful war against his enemies. In their opinion, however, Rufus proved himself a tyrant by breaking solemn promises and by flouting their established rights. He showed no mercy to offenders. Whether he hanged them or not, he confiscated their lands or fined them heavily. He did not allow inheritance to become automatic; he selected the heir and made him pay a heavy relief in order to inherit his father's estates. He used his rights of wardship and marriage to the full, restricted his tenants' rights to dispose of their wealth as they wished, extended the forests and imposed the forest laws with vigour. In everything he did he brought home to his barons and their subtenants that all his subjects held land and enjoyed privileges at the king's pleasure, and since he was constantly pressing for more money in order to reward his favourites, pay his mercenaries, and bribe potential allies, everyone in the kingdom felt the burden of his rule.

Leaders of the church were particularly indignant. The king and his right-hand man, Ranulf Flambard, treated churchmen no differently from other landholders. They refused to exempt church lands from geld as the Conqueror had done, and they handled a vacant bishopric, abbey, or parish as they would handle a secular fief which had fallen to a son under age or to an unmarried daughter – that is, they drew the revenue from the estates until the successor was ready to take over, and then exacted a substantial relief before recognizing his entitlement. Ranulf enjoyed this money-raising. He was a cleric himself – he occupied the rich see of Durham – but that did not prevent him from prolonging vacancies, particularly of rich livings, or from justifying new exactions by some questionable feudal theory. For four years after the death of archbishop Lanfranc, Rufus and Ranulf plundered the estates of the archbishopric of Canterbury. They would certainly not have ceased then had not Rufus been taken ill, and, thinking himself dying, tried to make amends: 'he was advised to think of the well-being of his soul,' wrote Eadmer, 'open the dungeons, release the prisoners, forgive debts, and restore liberty to the churches by appointing priests, especially to Canterbury'. He released 'the common mother of the whole kingdom from her state of widowhood' by appointing Anselm to the vacant see. Anselm protested that as a monk he had no understanding of secular matters, but indeed, in William's eyes, he proved to be a refractory and obstinate archbishop. Protracted disputes over the extent of land belonging to Canterbury and over the taxation of clerics led to a major quarrel about the archbishop's loyalty to Pope Urban II. In 1097, without seeking William's permission to leave the country, Anselm journeyed from Canterbury to Rome. The king declared the Canterbury estates forfeit, and they were still in his hands in 1100 when he was killed.

Henry I's reason for publishing his coronation charter, therefore, was to reassure the barons that he did not intend to behave as outrageously as his brother William had done. He sent a copy of the charter to each shire, for much the same purpose as nowadays the leader of Her Majesty's Opposition puts his programme before the voters on the eve of an election. He disapproved of what had gone before, promised better things in the future, and, by stating in some detail what he intended to do, made his bid for the support of the barons. In general he undertook to rule by the law of Edward the Confessor as amended by the Conqueror: clause 1 agreed to respect the freedom of the church, and clauses 2–11 listed the offences which Rufus had committed against feudal tradition and which Henry promised to put right. It need hardly be stated that during the course of his reign Henry failed to observe his own charter. Indeed, he committed as many feudal offences as ever his brother had done: just as heartlessly he took the revenue from vacant bishoprics and abbacies, for considerable fines he permitted clergy to break the new law of celibacy, and his succession of wars, chiefly in Normandy, compelled him continually to press his subjects for money. In his defence he would probably have echoed his brother William's question to Lanfranc, 'Who is there who can fulfil everything that he has promised?' But because he was more capable and tactful than either of his brothers, Henry succeeded where they had failed.

Thus, the coronation charter is no guide to the policy which Henry followed. But it is important in two other respects. It sets out what the Anglo-Normans considered to be correct, legal relations between crown and barons, and it established a precedent which had considerable influence throughout and beyond the twelfth century. Stephen, Henry's successor, issued two charters. The first, a short one probably published in 1135, announced to his people that he had granted 'to all my barons and vassals of England all the liberties and good laws which Henry, king of the English, my uncle, granted to them'; the second, a longer one witnessed by a large number of bishops and earls in 1136, he obviously modelled on Henry I's charter. In 1154 Henry II also followed precedent and sealed a coronation charter: '. . . I have granted and restored, and by this present charter confirmed, to God and to the holy church, and to all my earls, barons, and vassals, all concessions, gifts, liberties, and privileges, which King Henry, my grandfather, granted and conceded to them.' By the end of the century Henry I's charter had acquired a halo of legend, so that the barons who compelled John to accept the Great Charter saw themselves as restoring the machinery of government to the ideal which the wise Henry Beauclerc had proclaimed at the beginning of his reign.

*

Copies of the charter were sent to each county, but none of these originals survive; by a doubtful tradition, Matthew Paris relates that all the exemplars were later withdrawn, except for those at York, Canterbury, and St Albans. However, the text of the charter survives in twenty-eight different versions derived from the various originals. They were collated by F. Liebermann, *Die Gesetze der Angelsachsen*, vol. 1 (Halle, 1898), 521 ff., and 'The Text of Henry I's Coronation Charter', in *Trans. Royal Hist. Soc.*, n.s., VIII (1894), 21–48. The present translation follows Liebermann's text for the main body of the charter, with the preamble taken from the Rochester copy, and the list of witnesses from the copy sent to Worcestershire. The names of witnesses and of the persons named in the preamble of the different versions vary according to the particular county to which the originals were sent. There is no warrant in any of the early versions for the conventional separation of contents into preamble, fourteen clauses, and a sealing clause.

W. Stubbs, *Select Charters*, 9th ed., revised by H. W. C. Davis (1913), 117–19, prints the text of the Rochester copy of the charter, but with the preamble of the Worcestershire copy. *Statutes of the Realm*, Record Commissioners (1810–28), vol. I., Charters, 1, prints a text made up from the Rochester copy and the two versions given in the *Red Book of the Exchequer*, fo. 163 v., edited by Hubert Hall in the Rolls Series (1896).

For the significance of the coronation and the coronation oath, see P. E. Schramm, trans. L. G. Wickham Legg, *A History of the English Coronation* (1937); and two articles by H. G. Richardson, 'The English Coronation Oath', in *Trans. Royal Hist. Soc.*, 4 ser., XXIII (1941), 129–58 although covering mainly a later period; and 'The Coronation in Medieval England', in *Traditio*, XVI (1960), 111–202 – a more technical treatment.


## 2. THE CORONATION CHARTER OF HENRY I, 1100

Henry, by the grace of God king of the English, sends greeting to all his barons and faithful subjects, both French and English.

(1) Know that, by God's mercy and the common counsel of the barons of the kingdom of England, I have been crowned king of the said kingdom.

And whereas the kingdom was oppressed by wrongful exactions, I have made it my first care, out of reverence for God and the love which I bear towards you all, to make God's Holy Church free : to the effect that I will not sell nor set out at farm [lease] any of its estates, nor during the vacancy of any see, following the death of an archbishop, bishop, or abbot, will I take anything from the church demesne or from his tenants, in the period before a successor is installed.

Further, I put an end to all those evil customs by which the kingdom of England has been wrongfully oppressed, and which are set out in separate sections below.

(2) If any of my barons or earls, or any other of my tenants dies, his heir shall not buy back his estate, as was the practice in my brother's time, but he shall relieve [enter into possession of] it by paying the lawful and just relief.

In the same way, my barons' own tenants shall relieve their holdings from their lords on payment only of the lawful and just relief.

(3) If any of my barons or any other of my tenants wishes to give in marriage his daughter, sister, niece, or other female relative, he shall speak to me in the matter. But I will take nothing from him as the price of my consent, nor will I forbid the marriage, unless he wishes to give her in marriage to one of my enemies.

If any of my barons or other of my tenants dies leaving a daughter as his heir, I will give her in marriage, together with her estate, after taking counsel with my barons.

And if a man dies leaving a widow but no children, his widow shall have her dowry and marriage portion, and I will not give her in marriage except in accordance with her wishes.

(4) And if a man dies leaving a widow and children who are under age, the widow shall have her dowry and marriage portion, so long as she remains chaste as the law requires, and I will not give her in marriage except in accordance with her wishes; and the guardianship of the estate and of the children shall be given to the widow or some relative, whoever has the greater right.

I charge my barons to act similarly towards the sons, daughters, and widows of their tenants.

(5) I altogether forbid that common mintage, which has been taken in every county and city contrary to the practice of King Edward's reign, shall be levied in future.

If a counterfeiter or anyone else is taken with false money in his possession, then let the justice which he deserves be done to him.

(6) I remit all penalties under legal proceedings instituted by my brother, and all debts owing to him; but this does not apply to my own proper dues or to sums agreed to be paid in respect of another man's inheritance, or in respect of property which would, in stricter justice, have belonged to another.

I further remit any pledge which anyone has given to obtain his inheritance, and all reliefs agreed for rightful inheritances.

(7) If any of my barons, or any other of my tenants begins to fail in health and makes a gift or disposition of his personal estate, I grant that the terms of such gift shall be observed. But

if he has been prevented by death in battle or by the failure of his powers from making such gift or disposition of his estate, his wife or children or relatives or vassals shall apportion it, for his soul's sake, as seems best to them.

(8) If any of my barons or any other of my tenants is in forfeit [subject to fine] for an offence, he shall not pledge himself at mercy [be compelled to pay] to the full extent of his personal estate, as was done in the time of my father and my brother, but he shall make amends according to the gravity of the offence, as was the practice before my father's time, in the time of my other predecessors. But if he has been convicted of treason or a crime, then let him make just amends.

(9) I remit all murder fines incurred before that day on which I was crowned king; for murders committed in future, only the just and proper penalties shall be imposed in accordance with the law of King Edward.

(10) With the common consent of my barons, I have kept the forests in my own hands exactly as my father held them.

(11) I grant of my own gift that knights who hold their estates by the performance of military service, equipped with the hauberk, shall have their demesne lands exempt from all gelds and liability to provide work-service, so that, in proportion as they are relieved of this heavy burden, they may provide themselves so much more effectively with horses and arms, and so be suitably equipped and ready for my service and the defence of my realm.

(12) I establish a firm peace in the whole of my kingdom and order that it be kept for the future.

(13) I restore to you the law of King Edward, with the reforms made to it by my father with the counsel of his barons.

(14) If anyone has appropriated anything of mine or of another's property since the death of King William, my brother, let him return the whole of it forthwith, and no punishment will be inflicted upon him. But if he keeps back anything of such spoils in his possession and the charge is proved against him, he will answer to me severely.

In witness whereof, Maurice bishop of London, William bishop elect of Winchester, Gerard bishop of Hereford, Earl Henry, Earl Simon, Walter Giffard, Robert de Montfort, Roger Bigot, Eudo the steward, Robert fitz Hamon, and Robert Malet. At Westminster, when I was crowned. Farewell.

# 3. *The Assizes of Clarendon and Northampton,* *1166 and 1176*

JUST as it is no slight on Sir Robert Peel to say that he won his reputation as a forward-looking statesman by putting into law other men's ideas, so it does not damage Henry II's claim to be considered a major reformer to discover that almost all the innovations popularly associated with his name had been tried out by one or more of his predecessors. He was not the first English king to employ professional, itinerant justices, to use juries, or to issue writs to bring particular cases into his own court. He certainly did not initiate a new legal code, or envisage anything more than amendments to the existing law. His was a common-sense, practical approach to urgent problems of administration. The recent civil war between the factions of Stephen and Matilda had weakened royal government, and had encouraged many men, noble and common, to hold the law in scant respect. Henry II considered that his chief task was to restore the full authority of the crown, to increase its revenue, and to give surer protection to life and property throughout the kingdom. He had no blue-print or master plan to work to: one necessary step inevitably led him to take another. From the practices and experiments of his forebears he chose those items which he thought would serve his ends. If they proved their worth he developed them, and, as the years went by, coordinated them into an administrative routine.

Most stages of the new procedure seem to have been introduced merely by the king giving his judges verbal instructions. The archives contain hardly any documents which formally authorized innovations, but occasionally Henry, with the acquiescence of his council, issued an assize, or ordinance, which put particular practices into more permanent form. The Assize of Clarendon was the first of these edicts. Together with its revision, ten years later at Northampton, it enables us to study the progress of Henry's administrative and judicial reforms.

Both these assizes are lists of instructions, which the king gave to his judges before they set out to travel round the circuit of shires assigned to them. Not surprisingly they contain clauses which had immediate but only temporary importance. For example, in 1166 Henry directed his judges to enforce the cruel order, recently issued at Oxford, forbidding householders to give shelter to any member of the Catharan sect, a group of German heretics, and in 1176 he instructed them to make sure that the castles of those barons who had recently rebelled against him were properly razed to the ground. But the historical importance of these two documents lies not in such transient clauses, but in those which reveal the initiation of long-lasting judicial routines and practices.

Clauses 4, 5, and 6 of the Assize of Clarendon and almost every clause of the Assize of Northampton suggest that royal justices travelling on circuit – i.e. itinerant justices or justices in eyre (modern French *errer*, to wander) – had become a regular practice in the decade between 1166 and 1176. Two contemporary chroniclers, Ralph de Diceto, dean of St Paul's, and the unknown author of *The Deeds of Henry II* – almost certainly Roger of Hoveden – confirm this deduction. Both record that at the Northampton council of January 1176 Henry II divided England into six circuits and appointed three judges for each circuit, and three years later, according to the second chronicler, he amended this arrangement to four circuits each served by five or six judges. Kings other than Henry II had helped to establish this system. Occasionally, William I had sent specially appointed judges to hear pleas in the shire courts, and, when he had done so, he had expected all important landholders from a wide area round the court to attend. Henry I had used itinerant justices more freely. He had sent them on circuit from one shire to another to supervise administrative matters, hear appeals from shire and manor courts, and give judgement in the most important criminal and civil cases. Stephen and Henry II continued Henry I's practice, but Henry II arranged that his judges should visit the shires far more frequently and regularly. By writ his ministers instructed the sheriff to summon a full attendance at the court. All freeholders were to be present in person or represented by a suitable deputy. Each borough in the shire sent twelve burgesses and each vill its reeve and four other householders. It was a major occasion, on which a large body of the king's subjects could witness royal justice in action in the very area where the crime was committed or the civil dispute originated. In the twelfth century these royal courts did not destroy the traditional shire and hundred courts, but as time increased the number of cases which came before them, they gradually made the lesser courts redundant.

Royal judges used a jury, a legal device long associated with the crown. When the Conqueror's judges had heard pleas in the shire court, they had relied on a jury of local men to determine the facts. The commissioners who had been charged with gathering information for Domesday Survey had put their questionnaires before local juries, and both Henry I and Stephen had continued the tradition of establishing facts by summoning juries of men most likely to be informed about them. Henry II developed this practice. The first clause of the Assize of Clarendon ordered judges to use local juries to find out whether there were any accused or suspected robbers, murderers, or thieves in the district, and the first clause of the Assize of Northampton shows that Henry was prepared to put to the ordeal immediately anyone who was accused by sworn juries of twelve knights or freemen from the hundred or of four men from each vill. Furthermore, in clauses 4 and 5 of the same edict, he gave instructions that judges were to use a jury to establish the facts in disputes between individuals and in cases involving rightful inheritance. Steadily juries became an accepted part of criminal and civil judicial administration. Clause 9 of the Constitutions of Clarendon, a statement of procedure governing disputes between church and state, had already decreed in 1164 that twelve lawful men, 'in the presence of the king's justice', should be the means of deciding whether an estate was held in frankalmoign [free alms] or by ordinary feudal tenure, and about 1190 the author of *Concerning the Laws and Customs of the kingdom of England* showed that the sworn jury was by then the accepted means of settling all cases of disputed holding of land. Some juries, of the type from which the grand jury evolved, 'presented' offenders to the king's justices. Others provided the court with necessary local evidence and information; others again determined guilt or innocence. The function of these new jurors was quite different from that of the oath-helpers or compurgators of Anglo-Saxon law, who could only swear or refuse to swear that the accused was innocent of the crime. Moreover, the accused, who previously had to find his oath-helpers, now took no part in the choice of jurors. The sheriff nominated juries to serve in criminal courts, and, in civil cases concerning land, the two disputants nominated four knights to select the twelve local men from whom the king's judges would hear evidence.

Ordeal and jury existed side by side in Henry's legal administration. The church blessed and supervised the ordeals. It taught that God revealed guilt when the water 'refused to receive' the accused man, or when the burnt hand of the accused woman did not heal quickly, or when the accused knight, or his champion, failed to defeat his opponent. But there were many sceptics — the king among them. The Assizes of Clarendon and Northampton both show that Henry II mistrusted verdict by ordeal and placed greater store on the previous record and the popular reputation of the accused. Clause 1 of the Assize of Northampton confirmed clause 14 of the Assize of Clarendon: when the ordeal by water has declared the accused to be innocent, 'he shall find sureties and may then remain in the kingdom', but if the accused stands condemned by the common report of 'the county and the competent local knights', notwithstanding the verdict of the ordeal, 'he shall leave the kingdom within forty days'. Dislike of ordeals continued to grow, so that by the end of John's reign, condemned at last by the church at the Fourth Lateran Council, they ceased to be used in English courts. Fortunately, thanks to Henry II's foresight and common sense, they were hardly missed. For years the established and familiar jury system had been winning favour as a more acceptable alternative.

The use of the jury had been one of the factors which had enhanced the reputation of the royal courts, for most suitors confidently expected that they would receive better justice there than elsewhere. This attitude of mind made it easier for Henry II to expand the scope of his courts' jurisdiction. As everyone else did, he too looked upon justice as a possession and as a source of revenue, and periodically he issued an assize which invited suitors to bring particular kinds of cases to be heard before his judges. Very shortly the acceptance of the royal invitation became so automatic that it was generally held that the royal courts alone had jurisdiction in these particular matters. The Assize *Utrum*, embodied in the Constitutions of Clarendon, brought before the justices all disputes concerning the holding of land in free alms. The Assize of *Novel Disseisin*, which was probably issued at the same council as the Assize of Clarendon, decreed that if a freeholder had been recently dispossessed, or disseised, of his land he could have his case heard by a jury in the king's court irrespective of his lord's wishes. In feudal eyes this was revolutionary indeed, but with the ordinance known as the Grand Assize, Henry II widened this tenant-right to cover all disputes about the holding of land. He issued another two assizes concerning possession. Clause 4 of the Assize of Northampton seems to have been the origin of the Assize *Mort d'Ancestor*, which upheld the right of the heir to succeed without question to the estates held by a tenant at the time of his death, and on another occasion, probably a little later, Henry issued the Assize of *Darrein Presentment* which, in the case of a disputed advowson of a church, ruled that he who had presented the incumbent on the last occasion should continue to do so until the king's judges had deemed otherwise. In all these civil actions, the assizes directed that the judges should use a local jury to discover the truth.

According to the Assize of Clarendon, men and women accused of murder, robbery, theft, or the sheltering of anyone who had committed such felonies had to await trial by the king's judges. The Assize of Northampton added to the list two more criminal offences – forgery and arson. No matter who was his lord, anyone accused of these crimes must be tried in a royal court. The sheriff could arrest him, his lord could go bail for him, but neither could determine the case or, more pointedly, seize the accused's possessions. The sheriffs were to keep in jail accused men and women who could not provide a surety, but they could take a prisoner and the chief witnesses before the king's judges in another county, if that would quicken justice without upsetting the timetable of the judge's circuit. To bring particular cases before his own courts the king issued writs, and as time passed he used an increasing number of writs against the courts of sheriffs and tenants in chief.

It is fortunate that there has survived the legal commentary *Concerning the Laws and Customs of the kingdom of England*, for, written about 1190 by an unknown lawyer, traditionally said to be Ranulf de Glanville, it gives us a detailed account of English legal practice at the end of Henry II's reign. By contrasting it with a similar document, *The Laws of Henry I*, written earlier in the twelfth century, it is possible to estimate the progress made as a result of Henry II's reforms. 'Glanville' quotes the text of the different writs which were used to summon different categories of litigants before the king's judges, and explains most carefully how the three possessory assizes worked out in practice and how the judges determined which alternative, trial by battle or grand assize, they would use in cases of dispute about the holding of land. He defines aids, reliefs, and other feudal incidents, and describes the procedure by which itinerant justices tried and punished the various classes of criminals brought before them. 'Glanville's' list of the crimes which belonged to the king's court is longer than the list given in the Assizes of Clarendon and Northampton – treason, sedition, concealment of treasure trove, murder, manslaughter, arson, robbery, rape, forgery, and, significantly, 'other pleas of a similar kind'. Gradually royal justice was taking to itself all serious pleas, both civil and criminal, and leaving to the shire, hundred, and manor courts only petty offences against public order, breaches of manor custom, and minor, local disputes between individuals.

*

There is no official document entitled *The Assize of Clarendon*, but the traditional text is preserved, along with the real or purported texts of other early legislation from the time of Canute onwards, in two collections of the late twelfth or early thirteenth centuries. One of these collections is a manuscript in the Bodleian Library at Oxford, where it is catalogued MS. Rawlinson C 641. The Latin text of the Assize of Clarendon which it contains was printed by

W. Stubbs, *Select Charters* (1913), 170–73, and has been followed in the present translation. The other collection, known as *Liber de Legibus Angliae*, was incorporated by Roger of Hoveden (or Howden) into his *Chronica*, ed. W. Stubbs, Rolls Series (1868–71), vol. II, 215–52.

The Assize of Northampton survives only in the version of Roger of Hoveden, *Chronica* (op. cit.), vol. II, 89–91, and *Gesta Regis Henrici Secundi*, ed. W. Stubbs, Rolls Series (1867), vol. I, 108–11, reprinted in *Select Charters*, 179–81, and followed in the present translation.

The numbering of the paragraphs in both assizes is conventional.

For a discussion of the two assizes, see H. G. Richardson and G. O. Sayles, *The Governance of Medieval England* 1963), especialy app. 4, and *Law and Legislation from Æthelberht to Magna Carta* (1966), pp. 88–131.

The respective parts played by local courts and officers, local juries, and royal justices in preserving law and order through the country can be studied in Helen Cam, *The Hundred and the Hundred Rolls* (1930) and *Liberties and Communities in Medieval England* (1944); and in W. A. Morris, *The Frankpledge System* (1910), *The Early English County Court* (1926), and *The Medieval English Sheriff to 1300* (1927). There is a good study of the Assize of Clarendon by N. D. Hurnard, 'The Jury of Presentment and the Assize of Clarendon', in *Eng. Hist. Rev.*, vol. LVI (1941), 374–410.

## 3. THE ASSIZE OF CLARENDON, 1166

This is the beginning of the Assize of Clarendon, made by King Henry II with the assent of the archbishops, bishops, abbots, earls, and barons of all England.

1. In the first place, King Henry aforesaid, in consultation with all his barons, has decreed that, for the preservation of peace and the maintenance of justice, declarations shall be made for every

county and for every hundred by twelve of the more competent men of a hundred and by four of the more competent men of each vill, sworn on oath to reply truthfully to this question, whether anyone, within their hundred or vill, has been accused or publicly suspected of robbery, murder, or theft, or of harbouring men guilty of such crimes, since the lord king's accession; these declarations are to be made at the instance and in the presence of the sheriffs, or at the instance and in the presence of the justices.

2. And if the existence of a charge or suspicion of robbery, murder, or theft, or of harbouring men guilty of such crimes since the lord king came to the throne, is formally attested against anyone by these twelve men, he shall be arrested and shall take an oath, that he has committed no robbery, murder, or theft of property to a greater value than five shillings to his knowledge, and has not harboured men guilty of such crimes, since the lord king came to the throne; and this oath shall be tested by the ordeal of water.

3. And if, within three days of a man's arrest, his lord or the lord's steward or the lord's men apply for his release on bail, he shall be bound over pending trial, with his chattels as security.

4. And when it happens, upon the arrest of a robber, murderer, or thief, or of the harbourers of such criminals, following a formal attestation of the charge or suspicion against them, that the justices are not shortly expected in the county where the arrest was made, the sheriffs shall send word of their arrest to the nearest justice, by some informed messenger. Thereupon the justices will send word back to the sheriffs, telling them where they wish the prisoners to be brought before them; and on receipt of these instructions, the sheriffs shall bring the prisoners before the justices, along with two competent men from the hundred or vill where the arrest was made, charged with the official record of the county and hundred as to the reason for the arrest; and there let the prisoners stand trial.

5. And no one shall hold court and jurisdiction over men arrested under the procedure of this assize, that is, following the formal attestation of a charge or suspicion against them, nor shall anyone have charge of their chattels, except the lord king, in his

own court and before his own justices; and the lord king shall have all their chattels. But where arrests are made otherwise than on a formal attestation, then let the customary and due procedures be followed.

6. The arresting sheriffs shall bring their prisoners before a justice without formal summons from him, but merely on the receipt of instructions where to bring them, as was said before; and where delivery is made to them of robbers, murderers, or thieves, or the harbourers of such criminals, following their arrest, whether on a formal attestation or otherwise, they shall immediately receive such prisoners into their custody, and make no delay.

7. Jails are to be built in each county where none exist, in a borough or one of the king's castles, at the king's expense and with timber taken from a nearby wood of the king, or from some other wood, under the supervision of the king's servants. The sheriffs can then ensure the close keeping of prisoners in these jails by the officers normally assigned to guard prisoners, and by their own servants.

8. It is the lord king's further pleasure that all men shall be present at the county courts to act as attestors, and that no one shall withhold his presence and testimony on the grounds that he is exempt, or because he has previously exercised his own jurisdiction within his own soke.

9. No one within a castle, or outside a castle, or even within the honour of Wallingford, shall prevent the sheriffs from entering his court or territory to take views of frankpledge and to see that all men are pledged. . . .[1]

10. No inhabitant of a city or town shall maintain or receive guests in his house, or on his land, or in his soke, unless he guarantees to produce them before a justice, if they should be required, or unless they are frankpledged.

1. The remainder of this clause, in the Latin, reads *et ante vice-comites mittantur sub libero plegio*, which literally means *and they shall be sent before the sheriffs under free pledge*. There is no generally accepted interpretation of the meaning of this phrase.

11. No one living within or without a city, borough, or castle, and not even the inhabitants of the honour of Wallingford, shall prevent the sheriffs from entering their lands or sokes to arrest persons accused or under suspicion of robbery, murder, or theft, or of harbouring others guilty of such crimes, or outlaws, or men accused of forest offences; but it is the king's will rather that they help the sheriffs to arrest such men.

12. If anyone of known bad character and disrepute is taken with the proceeds of a robbery or theft upon him, and has no warranty for the goods, he shall be summarily punished; but if nothing is known against the man on whom such property is found, he shall explain how it came into his possession, and the truth of his statement shall be tested by the ordeal of water.

13. If anyone has confessed before competent witnesses, or before the hundreds, to robbery, murder, or theft, or to the harbouring of men guilty of these crimes, but later takes it upon himself to retract his confession, he shall not proceed to trial, but shall be dealt with summarily.

14. The king further wills that if anyone is brought to trial who is of an extremely bad character and is declared by many competent witnesses to be most notorious, then even if he comes unscathed through the ordeal, he shall nevertheless abjure the lands of the king and within eight days cross over the sea, unless the wind delays him, in which case he shall cross with the first fair wind. He shall remain abroad, an outlaw, and shall not return, except by the lord king's mercy; and if he returns otherwise, he shall be arrested as an outlaw.

15. The lord king forbids any waif, that is, a vagrant or a stranger, to be lodged anywhere except in a borough, and there he shall only be lodged for one night, unless he has an excuse to stay longer because of the sickness of himself or his horse.

16. And if, without excuse, he stays longer than one night, he shall be arrested until his lord comes and bails him out or until he has given adequate security himself; and the host shall be similarly arrested.

17. If robbers, murderers, or thieves, or the harbourers of men guilty of such crimes, or outlaws, or offenders against the law

of the king's forests, flee from one county to another, and the sheriff of the first county sends word of this to the sheriff of the county into which they have fled, he shall arrest them; and if he learns for himself, or is told, that such men have fled into his county, he shall similarly arrest them and keep them in custody, until they have given him adequate security.

18. Each sheriff shall draw up a full list of fugitives from his county, at a meeting of the county court; and he shall bring the written list of names before the justices immediately upon their arrival, so that search may be made for the fugitives over all England, and their chattels taken for the king's need.

19. It is the king's will that, as soon as the sheriffs receive word of the coming of the itinerant justices and are summoned to appear before them with their counties, they shall gather their counties together and seek out all those who are newly come amongst them since this present assize; and when they have sought out such persons, they will release them on bail to appear before the justices, or they will keep them in custody until the justices arrive, and thereupon they will bring before them all the newcomers to the county.

20. The lord king forbids that any man of low degree shall be received as a monk, canon, or friar by any body of monks, or canons, or by any religious house, until his character is known; unless he is suffering from a fatal illness.

21. The lord king also forbids that anyone in the whole of England shall receive into his land or soke, or into a house of which he is master, any adherent of those renegades who were excommunicated and branded at Oxford. Anyone who harbours them will be completely at the king's mercy, and the house in which they were harboured shall be carried outside the town and burned. Each sheriff will swear to uphold this provision, and he will secure the same oath from his officers, and from all knights and freeholders of his county.

22. The lord king wills that this assize be observed in his kingdom for so long as he pleases.

## THE ASSIZE OF NORTHAMPTON, 1176

These are the assizes made at Clarendon and afterwards confirmed at Northampton.

1. If a man is indicted before the lord king's justices for murder, theft, or robbery, or for harbouring men guilty of these crimes, or for forgery or arson, on the sworn testimony of twelve knights of the hundred, or of twelve competent freemen if there are no knights present, and on the sworn testimony of four men from each vill of the hundred, he shall submit to the ordeal of water, and if he fails in this ordeal, he shall lose a foot. At Northampton it was further provided, in the interests of a stricter justice, that he should lose his right hand also, as well as a foot, and that he should abjure the kingdom and leave it as an exile within forty days. But if he bears the ordeal, he shall find sureties and may then remain in the kingdom, unless the county, and the competent local knights, have together indicted him for murder or other base felony. If this is the manner of his indictment, then even if he has come safely through the ordeal of water, nevertheless he shall leave the kingdom within forty days and take his chattels with him, saving the right of his lords; and he shall abjure the kingdom, being at the lord king's complete mercy.

This assize shall operate from the time when the assize was made at Clarendon right up to the present, and for the future for so long as the king pleases, in cases of murder, treason, arson, and all the other crimes before specified, but not in cases of petty theft and robbery committed in time of war, as for example of horses, cattle, and other property of lesser value.

2. No one shall provide a stranger with lodging in his house, in a borough or town, for longer than one night, unless he is prepared to accept full responsibility for him, or unless his guest can give good reason for staying longer. The host of the house shall acquaint his neighbours with the reason given, and when the guest leaves, he shall do so in the day time, in full view of the neighbours.

59

3. If anyone is arrested with the proceeds of murder, theft, robbery, or counterfeiting, or of any other felony which he has committed, upon him, and confesses to his crime in the presence of the reeve of the hundred or borough, and in the presence of competent witnesses, he cannot subsequently, when he appears before the justices, retract his confession; and if he confesses to such a crime in their presence, although the proceeds were not found upon him, he shall be similarly bound by his confession when he comes before the justices.

4. When a freeholder dies, his heirs shall continue to hold his fee in the same seisin as their father held it on the day of his death; and they shall have his chattels, with which to execute his will. Afterwards, they shall seek out their lord and pay him the relief and whatever else is due to him from the fee.

If the heir is a minor, the lord of the fee shall receive his homage and remain his guardian until he comes of age. If the heir has other lords, they shall receive his homage and he shall render to each of them what is due.

The dead man's widow shall have her dowry and those of her husband's chattels which belong to her.

If the lord refuses to the heirs that seisin of the dead man's fee which they demand as their right, the lord king's justices shall cause recognizance to be made by twelve competent witnesses of the dead man's seisin of the fee on the day of his death; and whatever seisin they declare him to have held, the justices shall make restoration to the heirs accordingly.

If anyone is found guilty in breach of these provisions, he shall be at the royal mercy.

5. The justices of the lord king shall call for similar recognizances in cases of forcible ejection which have occurred since the lord king's first coming into England after the conclusion of peace between him and his son.

6. The justices shall receive oaths of fealty to the lord king, before the end of Easter or the end of Pentecost at the latest, from all men, namely, from earls, barons, knights, and freeholders, and even from rural labourers, as a condition of their remaining in the kingdom. Anyone who is not prepared to

swear his fealty shall be arrested as an enemy of the lord king. The justices shall also require from those who have not yet performed acts of homage and allegiance to the lord king that they shall come to them within such time as they shall prescribe, and do homage and allegiance before them to the king as their liege lord.

7. The justices shall also administer justice and the redress of wrongs in all matters concerning the lord king and his crown, under the authority of the lord king's writ, or the writs of those who are in his stead; unless values of more than one half of a knight's fee are involved, or unless the matter in dispute is so weighty that it cannot be settled without the lord king being present, or is of such nature that the justices refer it to him, or to others who are in his stead, because of their own doubt. They shall, however, apply themselves to the limit of their powers, in their efforts to procure the lord king's advantage.

They shall also conduct, in the counties through which they travel, the assize concerning malignant thieves and malefactors of the land, which has been established by the counsel of the king, and of his son, and of his subjects.

8. The justices shall see to it that where castles have been demolished, they have been wholly demolished, and that those which have still to be demolished, are well and truly razed. If they fail in this, the king will wish to have the judgment of his court upon them, as scorners of his command.

9. The justices shall inquire of escheats, churches, and lands in the lord king's gift, and of female wards who are his to give in marriage.

10. The bailiffs of the lord king shall answer to the Exchequer for the revenues of the assize and for all profits which they take from their bailiwicks, except for such profits as accrue to the sheriff's office.

11. The justices shall also inquire into the custody of castles, discovering which men are liable for guard duty, at which castle, and for what period; and they shall send the results of these inquiries to the lord king.

12. As soon as a thief is arrested, he shall be delivered to the

sheriff for custody: but if the sheriff is absent, let him be taken to the nearest castellan for him to guard until he can deliver him to the sheriff.

13. The justices shall cause inquiry to be made, according to the custom of the land, concerning which men have left the kingdom; and unless such men are willing to return within a set period of time and stand their trial in the lord king's court, they shall be outlawed; and the justices shall bring the names of outlaws to the Exchequer twice a year, at Easter and Michael-mas, and immediately afterwards the names shall be sent to the lord king.

# 4. *The Assize of the Forest, 1184*

THE Anglo-Saxons were so few in number that they found England too spacious for their needs. Virgin woodlands and unused, largely unexplored moors and heaths covered extensive stretches of the country. Now and again a pioneering family would venture with its sheep or cattle into the edges of these uninhabited lands, or clear a small acreage and bring it under the plough, but, for the most part, only occasional hunting excursions disturbed the wild life that lived there. Hunting animals and birds for food is, of course, as old as primitive man, but by the last century of Anglo-Saxon England, if not before, hunting for sport had become a royal and aristocratic privilege. Edward the Confessor appointed wardens to protect game in the forests of the royal estate, and Canute, who recognized the right of his noblemen to preserve their own hunting areas, issued a stern warning against any interference with the royal hunt:

Let everyone abstain from my hunting: on pain of the full fine, take heed where I will have no trespassing on my hunting.

William the Conqueror, however, introduced into England continental ideas about maintaining extensive royal forests and keeping the hunting of bigger game as a zealously guarded prerogative of the king. The writer of *Anglo-Saxon Chronicle E* thought it was one of William's idiosyncrasies that he should protect the red deer and wild boars with such care and 'love the stags as much as if he had been their father', but William's sons and Angevin descendants turned out to be no less enthusiastic and possessive. They all kept – some even widened – the boundaries, or metes, of the royal forest, and enforced a code of forest law modelled upon the oppressive laws which the Carolingians had developed in France in the ninth century. From the Conquest onwards, English law defined *forest* as those parts of the country which the king reserved for hunting. By no means did William I restrict the forest to his own demesne lands or to areas of woodland and waste: he included most of Essex and much of Hertfordshire, Sussex, and Hampshire as well as large parts of more distant counties in the north and west. Henry I made new forests. Stephen, anxious to win support, promised in his charter of 1136 that he would 'restore and surrender to the churches and the kingdom' all Henry's additions, and 'reserve for my own use' only those forests 'which William, my grandfather, and William, my uncle, established and maintained'. But Henry II not only re-claimed Henry I's forests, but also added extensions of his own, so that by the end of his reign about one third of England was subject to forest law. Writing at this time, the author of *The Dialogue of the Exchequer* explained that the well-wooded counties, where 'there are hiding-places and rich pasture for wild animals', were the counties of royal forest, and that the forest was the 'sanctuary of kings and their chief pleasure'. There they could lay aside their cares, and 'for a short while breathe the pure air of freedom'. Shortage of money, however, compelled Richard I and John to sell demesne land and forest rights in several counties, but their successors quickly recovered most of these alienated royal rights. Edward I and Edward III were both ardent upholders of forest law, and not until Tudor times did the crown significantly amend its attitude.

The professed object of the forest law was the preservation of 'the beasts of the forest', which to the Norman kings meant the wild boar, and red, fallow, and roe deer. In 1338 the court of king's bench officially excluded roe deer from legal protection, and as the years advanced, wild boars became scarce. But red and fallow deer multiplied exceed-ingly. For centuries they supplied the royal household with a steady supply of venison, and yet in the sixteenth century topographical writers usually commented upon the large herds of deer to be found in many parts of England. Polydore Vergil wrote that 'almost everywhere a man may see clauseres and parks paled and enclosed and fraught with venerie [deer]', and William Harrison estimated that in Kent and Essex there must have been a hundred enclosed parks, 'wherein great plenty of fallow deer is cherished and kept'. Inside the royal forests the law protected trees, bushes, heather, and bracken, the food or vert of the deer, as carefully as the animals themselves. On pain of heavy fines it forbade men to turn deer pasture into arable land or to graze cattle and sheep in the wrong place or at the wrong season of the year. It prohibited men who lived inside the forest boundaries – and this, of course, could include large village communities as well as isolated cottagers – from carrying bows and arrows or owning dogs which had not been 'lawed' by having their claws cut to prevent them from hunting. Anyone caught poaching venison, either inside or outside the forest, could be castrated and blinded, and collective fines or confiscations of property were frequently levied to avenge unexplained dead deer. The law also protected forest timber, and made provision for rearing a good supply of sparrow hawks and goshawks for the royal falconers. To a privileged tenant the king would occasionally grant rights of free warren so that he could hunt foxes, hares, rabbits, pheasants, and partridges on his own estates. But rights of warren did not include deer hunting.

Forest laws and forest administration called for a hierarchy of officials. The humblest were the woodwards, or gamekeepers. The agisters collected from those who lived in the forest rents and fees for the privilege of grazing their cattle, and occasionally their sheep or goats, on specified forest pastures, and for allowing their pigs to roam the forests in the autumn to feed on the mast, the fruit of the oak, beech, and other forest trees. Forest law forbade any farm animals to be pastured in the forest during the fortnight before and the fortnight after midsummer's day, the fence month, when the deer were fawning. Anyone who ignored this regulation, or cut down a tree, or encroached upon the vert, or broke any other of the many laws of the forest would be summoned to appear before the verderer in the court of attachment. This court met every forty days. It dealt summarily with minor offences, and referred others either to the swanimote, usually held two or three times a year, or to the high court of the justices in eyre of the forest, which only met once every three years. The chief executive officer in the forest was the master forester. It was his responsibility to see that his foresters in fee, or subwardens, carried out the king's orders, both general and particular. He inspected assarts and vaccaries, saw that the king's need of timber or venison was promptly met, and held in custody or on bail offenders waiting trial by the king's justices. Henry II appointed a chief justice of the forest. Henry III appointed two such officials, and after 1239 it became customary for one to be responsible for the forests south of the Trent and the other for forests north of the Trent. For the triennial, and later septennial, forest eyre, other judges sat with the chief justice. They examined the evidence presented by the regarders, the twelve knights in every area charged with making a pre-eyre survey of the forest and its administration, and then heard the more serious cases which the master forester and the verderers brought before the court. Evidence from the pipe rolls supports the view that the justices in eyre usually levied heavy fines on convicted offenders rather than have them mutilated as the law prescribed. Indeed, from the end of the twelfth century onwards, it is increasingly clear that the crown looked upon the forests not so much as a hunting ground as a necessary source of revenue. Rents, fees, and fines had become more important than game: however indifferent he might be about hunting, no king could relax the forest law because he could not afford to lose the income it gave him.

The Assize of the Forest is a contemporary statement of forest law as it existed in the second half of the twelfth century. It is the earliest forest-law text which has survived, but it was not new law in 1184. Rather it was a re-enactment and possible expansion of the existing law, which almost certainly dated back to the reign of Henry I if not to that of the Conqueror. We owe the text to Roger of Hoveden, who, if we accept that he was the author of *The Deeds of Henry II*, incorporated three versions of the assize in his writings.

No one but the king thought the forest laws justified: barons, clergy, freemen, and villeins all considered them hateful and restricting. The major tenants in chief found it irksome that their rights of warren, which they maintained as jealously as the king maintained the forest laws, did not include the right of hunting deer whenever they wished to do so. All ranks in the church disliked the law which, for forest offences, expressly denied them benefit of clergy, and the lesser landholders and their villeins usually had little choice but to suffer in bitter silence when the sacrosanct deer strayed from the coverts and woodland pastures into their growing crops. Whenever circumstances permitted, the king's subjects protested. The writer of *Anglo-Saxon Chronicle E* spoke out bluntly against the Conqueror for not heeding the complaints of the rich and the lamentations of the poor against the forest laws: 'he cared not for the rancour of them all; they had to obey the king's will entirely if they wished to live or hold their land.' There is gentler, ironic protest in the following passage from *The Dialogue of the Exchequer*:

The organization of the forests . . is separate from the other judgments of the kingdom and is subject only to the will of the king or of some officer appointed specially for this purpose.

Indeed it observes its own laws, which, it is said, derive not from the common law of the land but from the will and whim of the king. So that whatever has been done according to it may be said to be not *absolutely* just, but *just according to the law of the forest*.

The barons who prepared the text of Magna Carta insisted, in clauses 47 and 48, that recent extensions of the forest should be abolished and that an official inquiry should be held immediately into the way the forest law was being administered. Two years later William the Marshal issued the Charter of the Forest in the name of the infant Henry III. The seventeen clauses of this charter were the barons' way of implementing the official inquiry promised in Magna Carta. They turned back the clock as far as 1154, first by declaring that all new forests made outside the king's demesne by Henry II, Richard, and John should be disafforested, and secondly by trying to restore forest administration to what it had been before Henry II's reign. They redefined the rule about the lawing of dogs, severely curtailed the perquisites that the foresters could claim, restricted the number of swanimotes to three a year decreeing that only the officers of the forest need attend, and declared that every freeman had the unchallengeable right to pasture his cattle as he wished on his own land within the metes [bounds] of the forest, to allow his pigs to roam the woods, and, provided that it did not injure his neighbour's rights, to make a mill, fishpond, or drain, keep eyries of hawks, falcons, eagles, or herons, or extend his arable land. The eleventh clause of the charter dinted, if it did not break, the royal monopoly of deer hunting:

Any archbishop, bishop, earl, or baron who shall pass through our forests shall be allowed to take one or two deer in the presence of the forester should he happen to be present. If the forester is not there, let the hunter sound his horn lest he seem to do it by stealth.

During Henry III's minority commissioners were appointed to visit counties and, with the help of local juries, define the areas to be disafforested, but once Henry III had declared himself of full age the fight back began. He rescinded many disafforestations made on the authority of the charter, and claimed that where Henry II had restored the forests of Henry I he had not been making new afforestations. The extent of the forest and the exactions made by forest law continued to be a bone of contention between the king and the nobility. Whenever the king was under extraordinary baronial pressure, he was ready to pay lip service to the Charter of the Forest and promise perambulations and reforms. But once he recovered full independence, he forgot his promises and often revoked his concessions. In 1297, Edward I confirmed Magna Carta, but he left out the disafforestation clauses, and hedged round his promises to reform with so many conditions that no one believed him to be serious. Nevertheless, in 1327, Isabella and Mortimer accepted the boundary adjustments defined by Edward I's perambulations, and although the crown continued to enforce the law, creating local outcries and individual hardships, from Edward III's reign onwards the severity of forest law and the abuses of forest administration ceased to be the major, widespread grievances they had been during the previous two centuries. Not until James I and Charles I tried to reclaim large tracts of disafforested land and restore the lapsed laws did royal forests again become a subject of national complaint.

*

There is no contemporary document of the Assize of the Forest, but the traditional text is preserved in Roger of Hoveden, *Chronica*, ed. W. Stubbs, Rolls Series (1868–71), vol. II, 243–4; vol. IV, 63–4. The version of the assize in *Gesta Regis Henrici Secundi et Ricardi I*, ed. W. Stubbs,

Rolls Series (1867), vol. I, 323–4, contains only clauses 1–3 and 5–6.

The present translation follows the Latin text of the assize printed in W. Stubbs, *Select Charters* (1913), 186–8, and as appendix IV, clix–clxiv, in his edition of the *Gesta* (op. cit.), vol. II. The preamble and sections 1–12 represent the version of Hoveden's *Chronica*; the remaining clauses, 13–16, do not appear in Hoveden, but were collated by Stubbs from two Elizabethan versions of the assize, BM. MS. Vespasian F, iv, and John Manwood's *Treatise and Discourse of the Laws of the Forest* (1598). For a discussion of the text of the assize, see H. G. Richardson and G. O. Sayles, *The Governance of Medieval England* (1963), app. 4.

The best accounts of the forests and their administration, and of the forest laws, are still those by C. Petit-Dutaillis, *Studies and Notes Supplementary to Stubbs's Constitutional History* (1930), 147–251; and by G. J. Turner in his introduction to *Select Pleas of the Forest*, Selden Society (1901). There is a popular treatment by J. C. Cox, *The Royal Forests of England* (1905), and a detailed local study by R. Cunliffe Shaw, *The Royal Forest of Lancaster* (1956).

## 4. THE ASSIZE OF THE FOREST, 1184

This is the English assize of the Lord King Henry, son of Matilda, which he has made for the protection of his forest and forest game, with the advice and approval of the archbishops and bishops, and of the barons, earls, and nobles of England, at Woodstock.

(1) In the first place, he forbids anyone to offend against him in any particular touching his forests or his forest game; and he desires that no one shall place confidence in the fact that he has hitherto been moderate in his punishment of offenders against his forests and forest game, and has taken from them only their chattels in satisfaction for their offences. For if anyone

offends against him in the future and is convicted for his offence, the king will have from him the full measure of justice which was exacted in the time of King Henry, his grandfather.

(2) He forbids that anyone shall have bows, arrows, hounds, or harriers in his forests, except by licence from the king or other duly authorized person.

(3) He forbids any owner of a wood within King Henry's forest to sell or give away anything out of the wood to its wasting or destruction: but he allows that they may take freely from their woods to satisfy their own needs, provided that they do so without wasting, and under the supervision of the king's forester.

(4) The king has commanded that all owners of woods within the boundaries of a royal forest shall appoint suitable foresters to their woods and go surety for them, or else find other suitable sureties capable of making satisfaction for any offences which the foresters may commit in matters that concern the lord king. The owners of woods which are outside the forest regard [a triennial survey by twelve knights, cf. (7)] but in which the king's game is protected shall only have such men as foresters or keepers of their woods as have sworn to uphold the lord king's assize and to protect his game.

(5) The lord king commands his foresters to keep a watchful eye upon the forest holdings of knights and other owners of woods inside the boundaries of a royal forest, to make sure that these woods are not destroyed. If, despite their surveillance, the woods are destroyed, the owners of the woods may be well assured that satisfaction will be taken from no one else, but from their own persons or estates.

(6) The lord king has commanded that all his foresters shall take an oath to uphold to the letter, and to the full extent of their powers, this assize which he has made for the protection of his forests, and not to obstruct the knights and other worthy owners when they seek to exercise within their own woods those rights which the king has allowed them.

(7) The king has commanded that in every county where he has game, twelve knights shall be appointed as custodians of his game and of his vert [greenwood] and generally to survey the

forest; and that four knights shall be appointed to agist [oversee the pasturing of cattle in] his woods and to control and receive the dues from pannage [the feeding of swine]. The king forbids anyone to allow cattle to be pastured in his own woods, where these lie within the boundaries of a forest, before the agisting of the lord king's woods, which takes place during the fifteen days before and the fifteen days after Michaelmas [15 September–14 October].

(8) The king has commanded that where any of the demesne woods of the lord king are destroyed and the forester in charge of them is unable to account satisfactorily for their destruction, he shall not be fined, but shall answer with his own body [i.e. be imprisoned and maybe mutilated].

(9) The king forbids any clerk in holy orders to offend against him in respect of his forests or of his forest game. He has given strict instructions to his foresters that they shall not hesitate to lay hands upon such persons, if they find them offending, in order to restrain them and secure their arrest; and he will cover them fully in their actions by his personal warrant.

(10) The king has commanded that surveys shall be made of old and new assarts [forest clearings] and of purprestures [encroachments] and of forest damage generally, and that each item of damage shall be separately recorded.

(11) The king has commanded that earls, barons, knights, freeholders, and all men shall come when summoned by his master forester to hear the pleas of the lord king concerning his forests and to conduct his other business in the county court. If they fail to attend, they will be at the lord king's mercy [they will be fined].

(12) At Woodstock, the king commanded that for a first and second forest offence a man shall give safe pledges [for his future good conduct], but that for a third offence no further pledges shall be taken from him, nor shall he be allowed any other manner of satisfaction, but he shall answer with his own body.

(13) The king commands that all males over twelve years of age who live within an area where game is protected shall take

an oath for the protection of the game. Clerks in holy orders with lay holdings within the area shall not be exempt from taking the oath.

(14) The king commands that wherever his wild animals are protected, or have customarily enjoyed protection, mastiffs shall be lawed [have the claws and three toes of their forefeet cut to prevent their being used for hunting].

(15) The king commands that no tanner or bleacher of hides shall be resident in his forests, except in a borough.

(16) The king absolutely forbids that anyone in future shall hunt wild animals by night, with a view to their capture, in areas where his wild animals are protected or outside these areas in places where they are often to be found or where protection was formerly applied [the purlieus of the forest], on penalty of one year's imprisonment or the payment of a fine and ransom at the king's pleasure; or that anyone, at the risk of incurring this same penalty, shall set traps for the king's wild animals, using dead or living animals as bait, anywhere within the king's forests and woods, or within areas which used to form part of a forest, but were later disafforested by the king or his progenitors.

## 5. Borough Charters – London, Liverpool, and Manchester

MEDIEVAL England was predominantly an agricultural country. At least nine tenths of its inhabitants lived in villages and hamlets, and by their own labour produced almost all the necessities their community required. The remainder lived in towns sited for the most part in the eastern and south-eastern counties. Domesday Survey mentions sixteen cities and about a hundred boroughs, but even inside these relatively urban areas the burgesses busied themselves with their crofts, gardens, and orchards. Outside the borough boundaries they farmed the open fields and grazed their cattle and sheep on the common pasture. London, by far the most populous of medieval boroughs, was no exception. William fitz Stephen, who wrote his well-known description of London in the middle years of Henry II's reign, was proud of his city's agricultural and pastoral amenities. On the north side, he tells us, were well-watered, pleasant meadows. The city's ploughed fields yielded bumper crops, and every week at Smithfield there was both a sale of horses and a country market, at which Londoners could buy such items as ploughs, mares with their foals, herds of cows, and flocks of sheep.

Despite their significance as centres for craftsmen and despite the slowly-growing volume of their trade, the other towns of medieval England were considerably more rural than London. They were, of course, all small communities. From the slender evidence available, it has been calculated that London had about 20,000 inhabitants at the end of the eleventh century, and rather more than 30,000 a hundred years later. These figures are far bigger than those of any other English town. Domesday Survey shows that in Edward the Confessor's reign the numbers of houses in York, Norwich, and Lincoln, the three largest boroughs outside London, were approximately 1,500, 1,300, and 1,200 respectively. Oxford and Thetford had something approaching 1,000 houses, Chester half that number, and boroughs like Warwick or Canterbury no more than 200 or 300. No population figures have survived, but it might be reasonable to assume that on average three or four adults and adolescents would be living in each of these small, wooden houses. Numerous children were born, but comparatively few survived.

Most boroughs in Norman and Angevin England had grown out of the English burhs of the ninth and tenth centuries. Burhs were strong points strategically placed in the English system of defence against the Danish invaders. Some of them were based on old Roman sites, some developed from existing commercial and administrative centres, and others were built anew. They were royal creations, and though the baronage and the church later acquired rights and revenues in many boroughs, the crown controlled the development of most of them. By offering plots of land for a money rent, it encouraged craftsmen and traders to work alongside the garrison soldiers. It used picked burhs as local government centres: both the hundred courts and the shire courts, which had administrative as well as judicial duties, met inside burh defences, and several burhs were chosen as provincial minting-places. Naturally, the people of the district found the local burh the most convenient centre for buying and selling, and the itinerant traders, who carried their goods from one market to another, welcomed the security which a garrison town could give them. To some of the bigger towns – London above all, York, Rochester, Norwich, and others with easy access to the sea – came increasing numbers of traders from Scandinavia, the Low

Countries, German cities, and northern France, so that in the middle of the eleventh century it looked as if many English boroughs had a promising future immediately ahead.

William the Conqueror and his sons, however, showed no respect or sympathy for the pride and aspirations of burgesses. They were interested first in the military occupation of England, and then in the maintenance of royal authority and military strength. William I did not hesitate to destroy whole quarters of towns in order to throw up his motte-and-bailey castles on the best strategic sites, and none of the Norman kings were eager to recognize the corporate privileges and partial self-government which the boroughs had begun to accumulate during the previous century. Of course they readily exploited the boroughs as sources of revenue. They increased – frequently doubled or trebled – traditional fees, rents, and tolls, and left it to the sheriff of the county to collect the money and deliver it twice a year, Easter and Michaelmas, to the royal treasury. Town revenues were bound to vary from year to year, but the crown let the sheriff pocket the profit from the good years and suffer the losses from the bad. It stipulated the sum – the farm – it expected from each borough, and left the sheriff to collect it. During the reign of William I, London's farm was £300, which was considerably greater than any other borough's – than, for example, York's £100 or Thetford's £76. Stafford's £7 and Reading's £5 are representative of a number of surprisingly small farms. Some farms moved up substantially and a few moved down a little during the next hundred years.

Both the twelfth and thirteenth centuries witnessed considerable growth in local and in overseas trade. Increasing surpluses of corn, butter, cheese, meat, and hides were offered for sale to home and foreign buyers. English wool sold well across the Channel, steady demand stimulated iron, coal, lead, and tin mining, and profits were often spent on foreign goods which varied from French wines to Italian silks, from Scandinavian furs to Asian spices. The boroughs were the vehicles for this trade, and as the burgesses saw their wealth increasing, their community growing, and their town becoming more imposing with new houses, churches, and public buildings, it was natural that they should wish to have a greater voice in their own destiny. In particular they resented being considered merely a part of the county. They wanted to rid themselves of the sheriff and his men, and to account to the king directly for the farm of the borough. London and Lincoln made the first successful moves in 1130–31. According to the pipe roll of 1130, the earliest to survive, the burgesses of Lincoln offered a farm of '200 marks' worth of silver and four of gold' if 'they might hold the city of the king in chief'. Henry I appears to have accepted the offer. A few months later he satisfied Londoners by issuing the following charter :[1]

Henry, by the grace of God king of the English, sends greeting to the archbishop of Canterbury and to the bishops and abbots, and to the earls, barons, justices, and sheriffs, and to all his faithful subjects, both French and English, throughout England. Know that I have granted to my citizens of London that they shall hold Middlesex at farm for a composite payment of £300 annually, for themselves and their heirs from me and my heirs, with full power to the citizens to appoint as sheriff whomsoever they please of their own number, and as justice anyone or whomsoever they please of their own number to look after the pleas of my crown and the proceedings to which they give rise; no one else shall be justice over these men of London. And the

1. The Latin text of the charter is printed by F. Liebermann, *Die Gesetze der Angelsachsen*, vol. I (Halle, 1898), 524–6, and by W. Stubbs, *Select Charters* (1913), 129–30. There is an article by H. G. Richardson, 'Henry I's Charter to London', in *Eng. Hist. Rev.*, vol. XLII (1927), 80–87.

citizens shall not plead outside the city walls for any plea; and they shall be exempt from payment of scot, Danegeld, and murder-fine, nor shall any of them be forced to prove his innocence at law in a trial by combat. And if any citizen is impleaded in a crown plea, let him assert his standing as a citizen of London by an oath which shall be judged within the city. Let no one be billeted within the city walls, nor lodging be provided for any of my household or that of another, by force. And let all men of London and all their goods be free and exempt from payment of toll, passage, lastage, and all other dues throughout the whole of England and in all the seaports. And let the churches and barons and citizens have good and peaceful possession of their sokes [areas of jurisdiction] with all their dues, so that dwellers within the sokes shall pay dues to no one but those to whom the sokes belong, or to the officials whom they have placed there in charge. No man of London shall be fined at mercy more than his wer, namely 100 shillings; I speak here of proceedings in which the imposition of a monetary fine is appropriate. And let there be no miskenning in the hustings nor in the folkmoot, nor in any other proceedings within the city; and the hustings shall meet once a week, namely on Monday. I will see to it that my citizens have their lands, securities and the repayment of their debts, both within the city and outside; and if they complain to me about lands, I will do them right according to the law of the city. If anyone takes a toll or customs duty from citizens of London, let the citizens of London take, within the city from what belongs to that borough or town where the toll or duty was levied, as much as the man of London paid in toll; and a further sum may be taken as damages. And let all debtors to the citizens discharge their debts, or prove in London that the debts are not owing; if they do not either discharge the debts or come to refute them, then the citizens to whom they are in debt may make their distraint within the city from the borough, town, or county in which the debtor lives. And the citizens shall have their hunting chases with as full and good a right as their ancestors ever had them, namely in the Chilterns, Middlesex, and Surrey. In witness whereof, the bishop of Winchester, Robert fitz Richard, Hugh Bigot, Alfred de Totnes, William d'Aubigny, Hubert the king's chamberlain, William de Montfiquet, Hugulf de Tani, John Belet, and Robert fitz Siward. Given at Westminster.

Henry I died four or five years after granting London these privileges, and from 1135 to 1154 England suffered the disastrous effects of baronial warfare. In their anxiety to win the support of Geoffrey de Mandeville, the hereditary constable of the Tower, both Matilda and Stephen ignored Henry's charter, and prevented the Londoners from exercising their newly-acquired right of electing their own sheriff. To both factions barons mattered far more than burgesses, and during this period several boroughs passed from royal to baronial control because neither Matilda nor Stephen hesitated to alienate a borough and its revenues if they thought that the sacrifice would help to bribe a particular nobleman to fight on their side.

Henry II's accession in 1154 put an end to the civil war, but the new king mistrusted burgesses who wanted self-government. In exchange for an initial payment and an increased farm, he was prepared now and again to lease them the farm, *firma burgi*, but the independence displayed by communes in Flanders and France set him against granting them any permanent privilege of freedom from shrieval control. The usual concessions his charters conceded to burgesses were to have a gild merchant and to be free from tolls in other borough markets and fairs. He treated London quite severely. Although he granted the citizens a new charter, which stipulated judicial concessions, such as quittance from the collective murder-fine and from trial by battle, and commercial privileges, such as freedom from toll throughout England, he kept the appointment of the sheriff in his own hands and he raised the farm to over £500.

It was only when Richard and John came to the throne that the boroughs found it relatively easy to buy self-government and commercial freedom. Both kings were eager for money, Richard in order to fight his crusade, and John to carry out his adventures abroad and to curb his barons at home. Charter-mongering was one way of increasing revenue, and usually boroughs were eager to buy. As early as 1190 London bought from William Longchamp, one of the two justiciars of the crusading Richard, both its previously-held right of electing its own sheriffs and the refixing of the farm at the old figure of £300. For a further payment of 1,500 marks (or £1,000 since a mark was worth 13s. 4d.) Richard confirmed these privileges when he returned to England for a few months in 1194, and as soon as John succeeded his brother as king, the Londoners paid another 3,000 marks to have these rights confirmed again, this time in perpetuity. John had posed as a friend of the Londoners once before. In 1191, when he was count of Mortain and was conspiring to win the city from the Longchamp faction, he had publicly approved of London declaring itself a *commune*. He never used that emotive word again, but from 1191 the Londoners were busy establishing their city administration under a mayor and council of men whom for the moment they called *échevins* instead of the traditional *aldermen*. They devised a communal seal and claimed to be a collective tenant in chief. Henry fitz Ailwin, the first mayor, and his council of *échevins* met serious difficulties in establishing their authority, but the political strife of 1215 eventually gave them the opportunity of full recognition. Yet another charter, granted by John in May, gave the citizens of London the corporate right to elect their mayor annually. He announced his grant in the following words:

Know that we have granted and by this our present charter confirmed to our barons of the city of London that they may elect for themselves each year from their own number a mayor, who shall be faithful to us, discreet and fit to govern the city; and when he has been elected, let him be presented to us, or to our justiciar if we are absent, and swear his faith to us. And they may, if they so wish, remove the mayor from office at the end of a year and elect another in his place, or they may keep the same man as mayor, provided that he is presented to us or to our justiciar in our absence.

A month later Magna Carta included the mayor among the twenty-five barons whom it appointed to see the agreement carried out, but it went no further than John's charter in conceding to the city the right to be free of royal control. Indeed medieval London never did achieve the independent status of Ghent, Rouen, and other continental communes.

Almost all the other English boroughs had ambitions less than London's. They were content if they could exclude the sheriff's men, farm their own taxes, and have their own court, merchant gild, market, and fair. For such privileges they were prepared to pay a fair sum, and if they could proffer the money, Richard, John, and Henry III were usually ready to listen to their petitions. The charter which Henry III granted to the burgesses of the little borough of Liverpool in 1229 is a typical example of the scores of borough charters which these three kings issued. Liverpool dates its foundation from 1207 when John, in a letters patent, invited 'his faithful people' to take burgages in the new borough, but Henry's is the first Liverpool charter. He used the fashionable legal term *liber burgus*, which literally means *free borough* but which implies nothing special in Liverpool's new status. He recognized the borough's right to have a merchant gild and a court, and gave its merchants the usual privilege of being free from tolls and similar charges throughout the kingdom. But he said nothing of the farm. The next day, for a further fee, he leased the burgesses the right to farm their taxes for a period of four years, and throughout the Middle Ages Liverpool never held its farm except on lease.

Some growing market towns were not on crown land.

Consequently if they wished to have a measure of self-government, the townspeople had to petition their lord, temporal or spiritual, to grant them the necessary charter. Such a charter is known as a seigniorial charter, and, during the last years of the twelfth century and most of the thirteenth, many such charters seemed to be almost as efficacious as if they had carried the king's seal. Some landowners, by licence of the crown, were able to give their boroughs all the attributes of a royal *liber burgus*, but others did not or could not grant their townspeople anything more than burghal instead of villein tenure, part of the market profits, and some minor judicial privileges. The *quo warranto* writs of Edward I, Edward II, and Edward III remorselessly revealed the legal weaknesses of many seigniorial charters. The lawyers of each succeeding generation seemed to take a stricter view of what constituted a *liber burgus*, and steadily the number of deprived boroughs increased. Manchester suffered this fate. In 1301 a charter from the local lord, Thomas Grelley, confirmed rights and privileges which the burgesses had enjoyed for many years, but in 1359 this document failed to satisfy judicial commissioners that it entitled the town to claim the status of a borough. They reclassified Manchester as a *villa mercatoria*, a market town, and so it remained, despite its size and importance, until the nineteenth century. Its first borough council met in December 1838. By right of its royal charter Liverpool sent members to the parliaments of 1295 and 1307 and, after a long period of poverty and indifference, to the parliament of 1547. It continued to be represented by two 'worthy burgesses' from that year until the Reform Act of 1867 increased the number of its members from two to three. But Manchester, a much bigger town than Liverpool for most of that period, had no separate representation in the commons. Because it did not rank as a borough, its inhabitants, if they were forty-shilling freeholders, could only vote for county members, and not until the Reform Act of 1832, when it still had not achieved the rank of borough, did Manchester send members of its own to Westminster.

*

The best study of municipal growth and of the borough constitutions is by James Tait, *The Medieval English Borough* (1936), but his treatment should be compared with those by F. W. Maitland, *Township and Borough* (1898) and Carl Stephenson, *Borough and Town* (1933). Two modern studies which deal with the internal affairs of the boroughs and also the part which they played in the national administration are by C. R. Young, *The English Borough and Royal Administration, 1130-1307* (1961) and E. F. Meyer, 'Boroughs', in *The English Government at Work, 1327-1336*, vol. I, ed. J. F. Willard and W. A. Morris (1940).

The part taken by the merchant gilds in the growth and administration of the boroughs is fully treated by C. Gross, *The Gild Merchant*, 2 vols. (1890). There are more recent studies of the London merchants and the growth of city government by Sylvia L. Thrupp, *The Merchant Class of Medieval London* (1948), and G. A. Williams, *Mediaeval London: from Commune to Capital* (1963).

Comparative collections of borough charters and custumals have been made by Mary Bateson, *Borough Customs*, 2 vols., Selden Society, XVIII and XXI, (1904-6); A. Ballard, *British Borough Charters, 1042-1216* (1913); A. Ballard and James Tait, *British Borough Charters, 1216-1307* (1923); and M. Weinbaum, *British Borough Charters, 1307-1660* (1943).

Miss Bateson contributed several pioneer articles to the *Eng. Hist. Rev.*, XV and XVI (1900-1901) on 'The laws of Breteuil' which were the prototype of many early British custumals; and articles to *Eng. Hist. Rev.*, XVII (1902), on the development of local government in London. Sir Frank

Stenton's Historical Association Essay on 'Norman London' is reprinted in a revised form and with a useful short bibliography in G. Barraclough (ed.), *Social Life in Early England* (1960). Helen Cam considers 'The Law Courts of Medieval London' in *Law-finders and Law-makers in Medieval England* (1962), 85–94.

## 5. CHARTER OF HENRY III TO LIVERPOOL, 1229

The original document is in the possession of the Corporation of Liverpool; the Latin text is printed in Ramsay Muir, *A History of Municipal Government in Liverpool* (1906), part I, 155, and in the appendix to the Municipal Commissioners' Report of 1833.

Henry, by the grace of God king of England, lord of Ireland, duke of Normandy and Aquitaine, and count of Anjou, sends greeting to the archbishops, bishops, abbots, priors, earls, barons, justices, sheriffs, reeves, officials, and bailiffs, and to all his faithful subjects.

Know that we have granted and confirmed by this our charter that our town of Liverpool shall be a free borough in perpetuity, and that the burgesses of the said borough shall have a gild merchant with a hanse and other privileges and trading rights by custom established as belonging to that gild; and no one who is not of that gild may trade in the said borough except with the consent of the same burgesses.

We have granted also to the said burgesses and their heirs that they shall have soke and sake, toll and theam, and infangenthief, and that they shall be exempt throughout our land and in all seaports from the payment of toll, lastage, passage, pontage, and stallage, and that they shall make no suit of counties or wapentakes [in the shire or hundred court] in respect of their holdings within the said borough.

We have granted also to the said burgesses and their heirs that any merchants bound for the said borough with their wares, from whatever place they come, whether they are foreigners or others, dwellers within our peace, or have come to our country by our licence, shall be brought safe and sound to the said borough with their wares, and shall stay there in safety, and in safety shall return, paying the proper and due customs on their trade.

We further forbid that anyone should cause trouble, loss, or injury to the said burgesses, on forfeiture to us of a fine of £10.

Wherefore, it is our wish and stern command that the said town of Liverpool shall be a free borough and that the said burgesses shall have the said gild merchant with a hanse and the other privileges and trading rights pertaining to that gild; and that they shall have all the other privileges and trading rights and exemptions as aforesaid.

In witness whereof, Hubert de Burgh earl of Kent and justiciar of England, Philip d'Aubigny, Ralph fitz Nicholas, Nicholas de Meols, John fitz Philip, Geoffrey Despenser and others.

Given by the hand of the reverend father, Ralph bishop of Chichester, our chancellor, at Marlborough on the 23rd of March in the thirteenth year of our reign.

## Charter of Thomas Grelley to the Burgesses of Manchester, 1301

The original Latin document is in the possession of the Corporation of Manchester; it is reproduced in facsimile and by transcript in John Harland, *Mamecestre*, Chetham Soc. Pubns., o.s., vol. LIII (1861) – the article itself continues in vols. LVI and LVIII; and by James Tait, *Medieval Manchester and the Beginnings of Lancashire* (1904), with commentary and rearrangement of clauses to facilitate comparison with the borough charters of Salford and Stockport. The conventional numbering of the clauses, which has no warrant in the original, has been adopted for the present translation.

Let all men of this and future generations know that I, Thomas Grelley, have granted and allowed the following concessions to all my burgesses of Manchester, and have confirmed them by this my present charter.

(1) All burgesses are to pay a standard rent of 12d. a year for each and every burgage, in lieu and discharge of all personal service.

(2) If the town reeve brings a charge against anyone in any form of action and the accused person fails to appear personally or by proxy at the lawmoot on the appointed day, he shall pay a fine of 12d. to the said lord, and the said lord shall bring his action against him in the portmoot. [The quarterly meetings of the borough court were known as the portmoot. When the court sat between these regular dates, it was known as the lawmoot.]

(3) If a burgess accuses any other burgess of any debt, and the accused admits the debt, the reeve shall set the term for repayment, namely the eighth day following. And if the debtor fails to appear on the appointed day, he shall pay a fine of 12d. to the lord and discharge the debt, and pay 8d. to the reeve.

(4) If anyone prefers a charge, but does not bind himself, by giving a pledge and naming sureties, to prosecute it, he shall not be fined if he later decides not to proceed.

(5) If a burgess wounds anyone in the borough on a Sunday or between noon on Saturday and daybreak on Monday, he shall be fined 20s.; and if he wounds anyone on Monday or other weekday he shall pay a fine of 12d. to the said lord.

(6) If a burgess quarrels with anyone and strikes him in anger, but not so as to draw blood and can regain his house without challenge of the reeve and his officers, he shall not be brought before the court by the reeve; but let him bear his victim's revenge if he can, or otherwise, and by the advice of his relatives, make his peace with him, without payment of any fine to the reeve.

(7) If anyone is accused in the borough in any form of action, whether by a burgess or a villein or even by a vavasour, he need not defend himself in any other court than the portmoot, pleas of the crown and theft excepted.

(8) If a burgess is accused of theft by anyone, the reeve shall obtain security from him that he will appear to answer the accusation in the lord's court and stand his trial there.

(9) If anyone is accused by his neighbour or by anyone else and puts in an appearance on three successive days when the court is in session, he shall not be required to make any further defence against the charge if the reeve and his fellows of the portmoot testify that the complainant failed to appear on these three occasions.

(10) The said burgesses shall do suit to the mill and oven of the said lord, paying the accustomed and due charges of the said mill and oven.

(11) The burgesses have and may exercise the right to elect anyone they please of their number to be reeve, and likewise to dismiss the reeve.

(12) No one may have his neighbour brought to trial on any complaint unless he can command sufficient supporting witnesses.

(13) No one may receive possession of any property within the town unless the reeve is present.

(14) If the need arises, a burgess may sell or give such part of his land as he has not inherited to anyone he pleases, except that his heir, if he wishes to purchase, shall have the right of pre-emption.

(15) A burgess may sell property which he has inherited either as a whole or in parcels of any size, provided that his heir consents. If the need arises, however, he may sell such land even without his heir's consent, of whatever age the heir may be.

(16) The reeves shall assign to any burgess and to the tensers [stall-holders] their stalls in the market, and receive from them 1d. for the need of the said lord.

(17) If a burgess or tenser wishes to stand in the merchants' stalls, he shall pay the said lord at the same rate as strangers; but if he stands in his own stall then he shall give nothing to the said lord.

(18) The burgesses may feed their swine which are nearly fattened in the lord's woods, except for the forests and parks of the said lord, until the time of pannage. When this time comes they may, if they so wish, leave without the lord's permission; but if they wish to stay for pannage they shall pay the said lord for it.

(19) If anyone is summoned to answer to a charge at the next meeting of the lawmoot and he attends that meeting, then he must answer to the charge and not proffer excuses to have the hearing deferred, on penalty of incurring a fine. But if he is then for the first time accused, he may have the hearing postponed until the next time the court meets.

(20) Burgesses may distrain upon their debtors, whether they be knights or priests or clerks, if they be found within the borough.

(21) If need arises for anyone to sell his burgage, he may buy another from his neighbour; such transfers of holdings between neighbours may be effected in the presence of fellow-burgesses.

(22) Burgesses may transfer their personal chattels to anyone they please within the said lord's fee, freely and without licence from the said lord.

(23) If a burgess has lent anything to a villein within the borough and the due date for repayment has passed, he may distrain upon the villein and by his distraint certify him. And he shall deliver the goods taken in distraint into the hands of sureties for the debtor for the space of eight days, and after that time the sureties are either to return the goods or the equivalent in money.

(24) A burgess, from whomsoever he buys or to whomsoever he sells within the fee of the said lord, shall be free from payment of toll. If anyone comes who is from another shire and ought therefore to pay dues, but leaves without paying his toll and is then detained by the reeve or other person, he shall pay a fine of 12s. to the need of the lord, and let him pay his toll.

(25) If anyone has lent anything to another without witness, the other shall not be answerable unless witness is produced;

and if there is witness, he may deny it by the sworn testimony of two men.

(26) Anyone who breaks the assize of bread or the assize of ale shall pay a fine of 12d. to the lord's need.

(27) If a man wounds another within the borough and is arrested by the reeve before gaining his house, the reeve shall obtain bail and sureties for his appearance in court.

(28) Every man has and may exercise the right to represent his wife and family in a suit, and any man's wife is competent to pay his rent to the reeve and to prosecute a suit on her husband's behalf if he happens to be away.

(29) If a villein accuses burgesses in any matter, they are under no obligation to make a defence against him unless he can produce as witnesses a sufficient number of burgesses or others who are legally competent.

(30) A burgess without heir may bequeath his burgage and chattels to whomsoever he pleases, so long as the service which is owed from the holding to the lord is safeguarded.

(31) When a burgess dies, his widow has the right to remain in his house and have necessary provision made for her there for so long as she chooses to remain without a husband, and the heir shall live with her. But if she decides to remarry, she shall leave the house and the heir shall remain there as master.

(32) On the death of a burgess, his heir shall not give the said lord any relief other than arms of some kind.

(33) If a burgess sells his burgage and wishes to leave the town, he shall be free to go wherever he pleases on payment of 4d. to the lord.

(34) All legal proceedings to which reference has been made are to be decided in the presence of the seneschal [lord's steward] and entered on a roll of record by the lord's clerk.

(35) All the above mentioned rights I, the said Thomas, and my heirs will preserve to the said burgesses and their heirs, for ever, saving for me and my heirs reasonable tallage when the lord king levies tallage on his own free boroughs throughout England.

To the intent that this grant of concessions be firm and lasting in its effects, I have strengthened it by affixing to it my seal. In witness whereof, Sir John Byron and Sir Richard Byron, knights; Henry de Trafford, Richard de Hulton, Adam de Prestwich, Roger de Pilkington, Geoffrey de Chadderton, Richard de Moston, John de Prestwich, and others.

Given at Manchester on the 14th day of May in the thirteen hundred and first year of Our Lord and in the twenty-ninth year of the reign of King Edward, son of King Henry.

# 6. *Magna Carta, 1215*

'THE ever-living fountain from which flow those liberties which the English world enjoys today' was one of the more sober pronouncements with which, in April 1939, the American press greeted the arrival of the Lincoln manuscript of the Great Charter at the World Fair in New York. Six months later, when the danger of bombing caused the British government to entrust the precious document to the wartime care of the Library of Congress, Lord Lothian, the British ambassador, handed it over with the words

The principles which underlay Magna Carta are the ultimate foundation of your liberties no less than ours. Samuel Adams [the Massachusetts politician who helped to lead the revolt of the American colonies] appealed to the rights of Magna Carta. . . . It was in their name that your ancestors threw the tea into Boston Harbour and rejected the claim of King George III to tax the colonies for defence.

The fact that in 1939 Nazi Germany was foremost in men's minds does not fully explain the fervour of these tributes to the importance of the Charter. Both journalist and ambassador were fully aware that, as they wrote and spoke, the independence of nations and the freedom of individuals were in acute danger, but it would hardly cross their minds that their words were echoing opinions and judgements voiced long before by nineteenth-century social reformers and seventeenth-century parliamentarians. For in their generation these too had attributed to Magna Carta the origin of the particular rights and privileges they were concerned to uphold and defend. Certainly from the days of James I, if not from Tudor times, Englishmen have looked on the Charter as a bulwark of democratic freedom. They have transformed a backward-looking medieval document into a declaration of constitutional rights. They have re-interpreted certain clauses, which originally were agreed solutions of feudal problems, and given them modern significance: they have claimed that the right of Englishmen to be free from arbitrary taxation and imprisonment goes back at least to the days of John, almost a century before the meeting of the Model Parliament.

This popular view of Magna Carta does not stand up to historical examination. But neither is it wholly false. At Runnymede the barons did not see themselves as curbing a tyrant or upholding the liberties of the humble. They felt impelled to put into writing the freedoms and responsibilities traditionally accepted in English feudal society, because in their opinion John had failed to observe them even more than his royal brother and father had done. This was the first time feudal rights had been written down in such detail, so that, for the next hundred years and more, while feudal issues still remained at all practical, it was natural that men should look back to this document to see what was 'legal'. From the moment it had been reissued a month or so after the death of John, Magna Carta began to acquire a special significance. Increasingly men regarded it not as an authoritative statement but as an unchangeable law. Neither assailants nor defenders of the government dared to ignore it. Simon de Montfort and Henry III both affirmed that the Great Charter 'shall be observed on our part and on the part of others of our realm in every particular'. In 1297 Edward I put his confirmation of it on to the statute roll, and at different times in the fourteenth century the leaders of the church, the citizens of London, and dissatisfied peasants each justified their agitation by claiming that they were upholding the Charter against those who would destroy it. Already Magna Carta was out of date, in the sense that after the Black Death England was facing problems unknown to

John and his barons. Yet in the Charter men still found clauses which seemed to fit the conditions of their own day. From the beginning of the Lancastrian–Yorkist struggle, however, the general desire for a strong monarchy tended to obscure the memory of the Charter until, as we have seen, the parliamentary lawyers of the early seventeenth century rediscovered it to use as a weapon in their struggle against the despotism of the Stuarts. Ever since, enthusiastic politicians have forgotten the feudal context of the document, and have highlighted principles which they have claimed to be timeless. It might be an exaggeration to hail the Charter as 'the most majestic instrument and sacrosanct anchor of English liberties', but at least it can be said that it upheld the supremacy of law and the sanctity of agreements, and asserted that privilege walked hand in hand with responsibility. Such principles are just as apposite today as they were in Victorian, Stuart, or Angevin England.

In 1199 John succeeded his brother, Richard I, and inherited a heavy task. The barons preferred John to his young nephew, Arthur of Brittany, but they were already full of sullen resentment against the crown. They were grumbling that the excessive charge of Richard's ransom had come on top of the cost of his campaigns, and they were resentful about the growing efficiency of the royal administration which seemed in a vague but sinister way to threaten their independence. They had no understanding of the effect which inflation was having upon the real value of the crown's fixed income, and they had little sympathy for John facing the difficult task of trying to hold together his father's possessions in France against Philip Augustus's obvious intention to destroy the Angevin empire. For John the future promised nothing but difficulties. He did not lack courage to face them, but he possessed neither patience nor sustained determination. He tended to rush at problems, and occasionally by acting foolishly or cruelly he destroyed all he had achieved. His marriage to Isabel of Angoulême, already betrothed to Hugh le Brun, broke one of the unwritten canons of feudalism, and gave Philip Augustus as good an opening as he could have hoped to have for making an attack upon the English king's continental estates. In the war that developed John showed neither the will to win nor the ability to defend those of his vassals who were prepared to support him. His murdering of Arthur provoked revolt in Brittany, and by the summer of 1204 he and his troops were forced to sail back to England and leave Henry II's empire at the disposal of the king of France. However convincingly it can be argued that the loss of these lands was both inevitable and, ultimately, beneficial to the English crown, the inept, spasmodic defence put up by John did not endear him to his war-loving barons.

A year after John had returned to England, he became embroiled in a serious prolonged struggle with the church. It was widely held that he was indifferent to religious practices and beliefs, and, when Archbishop Hubert Walter died in July 1205, this reputation, as well as their jealousy of each other, prompted the monks of Christ Church, Canterbury, and the bishops of the Canterbury province to by-pass the crown and send independent delegations to Rome to seek confirmation of their own 'elected' archbishops. John protested that he had not given either party permission to elect. The pope, Innocent III, ruled that election was rightly in the hands of the Canterbury monks, but that they should choose an archbishop acceptable to their king. The monks wanted Reginald, their prior, but John would hear of no one but John Grey, bishop of Norwich. In the end the pope settled the matter arbitrarily. He ignored John, 'persuaded' the monks to nominate Stephen Langton, an English scholar living in Italy, and in June 1207 consecrated the new archbishop at Viterbo.

John did not take this insult calmly. He refused to recognize Langton, seized the Canterbury estates for the crown, and forbade papal delegates to hear cases in England. Innocent countered first by placing England under interdict, which, theoretically at least, put an end to public worship, and secondly, in November 1209, by excommunicating John and thus calling on loyal bishops to desert him. John enjoyed confiscating church revenues, but within three years he found himself uncomfortably and dangerously isolated. His continued defiance of the church was disturbing more and more of his own subjects. The Scots and the Welsh were becoming restless, and, above all, Philip Augustus, backed by the pope, was preparing to invade England. John decided to capitulate. In May 1213 he accepted Langton's election to Canterbury, and, on 20 July at Winchester, the archbishop, newly arrived in England, absolved his king and readmitted him into the church. But in typical fashion John went further. He surrendered his two kingdoms of England and Ireland to Rome, and assumed the rank of a papal vassal. For a tribute of 1,000 marks a year, he believed that he had thus made sure of the support of the pope in any future struggle with the king of France.

Rising prices and the cost of the French war had aggravated John's inheritance of an empty treasury. Constantly, circumstances compelled him to raise fresh supplies of money to live and to rule. To get what he required he used every means he could – forest-law fines, scutage, feudal dues of all kinds, customs duties, and the new but difficult device of taxing movables. These exactions angered his barons as much as the measures later to be adopted by James I were going to anger the commons, and the barons were just as deaf as the parliamentarians to arguments about the declining value of money. All they could hear were frequent heavy demands made by a king who ignored time-honoured rules, won no military glory, quarrelled with the church, and sometimes behaved so abominably as to outrage even their jejune moral scruples.

Baronial unrest grew more obvious each year. By 1212 John had become so suspicious about what was being hatched against him that he began to take possession of castles and order barons to send him hostages as an earnest of their good intentions. The first major crisis occurred in the early summer of 1213, when a group of tenants in chief, mostly from the north, refused to muster the feudal host at Plymouth for a campaign in France. They argued that the host had already served its stint for that year, that their tenure did not require them to serve in Poitou, and that, therefore, the king's demands were excessive and unlawful. John set out to bring them to heel by force, and only Langton's prompt intervention prevented civil war. The archbishop reminded the king of his Winchester oath to punish only after lawful judgement, and when John eventually crossed the Channel in February 1214 he took with him not his feudal host but 'a handful of earls and a large collection of low-class mercenaries'. Nevertheless, this scratch army achieved such surprising initial success that by June it appeared to have recovered both Poitou and Angers. But the military situation suddenly changed. The approach of a French army under Louis, Philip Augustus's son, caused the Poitevins to withdraw their support from John, and Philip himself unexpectedly defeated John's ally, Otto of Brunswick, at Bouvines in Flanders. By the middle of October, a disconsolate John was again disembarking the remnants of a defeated army in England.

John considered that he was entitled to scutage from those barons who had not sent vassals to France, but his aggressive justiciar, Peter des Roches, met open opposition when he tried to collect it. The barons based their protest on Henry I's coronation charter, and called on the king formally to recognize this document as a definition of their rights and liberties. John played for time. He asked the pope for support, began to assemble mercenaries in Ireland, and took the vow of a crusader in order to claim three years' respite from his secular obligations. In April 1215 the more bellicose barons marched south, and rejected John's proposal that they should submit their grievances to a joint council of four from each side sitting under the presidency of the pope. At first John showed remarkable restraint, but when he felt sure that he had the support of the less extreme barons, he brought his mercenaries from Ireland to Winchester and prepared to crush the rebellion. Thereupon the leaders of the moderates intervened to prevent civil war. Their spokesman, Langton, argued that this was a matter for counsel and not for arms, and that it should be possible for both sides to agree on what was accepted custom. The peacemakers moved between John at Windsor and the rebel leaders, who were first at London and then at Staines. At length they succeeded in bringing the two parties together at Runnymede. There, apparently on 15 June, John agreed to accept the forty-nine clauses of the Articles of the Barons. The lawyers then took away this hastily drafted document, and by adding a few more clauses, including clause 1, and by rewriting the whole in more legal language, they produced the official text of the Charter of Liberties. The barons renewed their oath to the king, John authorized his seal to be attached to the Charter, and the protracted meeting broke up on 23 June.

It turned out to be a false and deceptive settlement. At first, during the weeks which followed the Runnymede meeting, John appeared to be a changed man. He issued several writs to put right particular baronial grievances, but once the rebel army had dispersed, it became clear that he did not regard himself bound by the Charter. Innocent III supported him: he condemned the Charter as 'shameful, debasing, illegal, and unjust', and forbade John, his new vassal, to observe it, and the barons to try and hold him to it. He summoned Langton to Rome. The rebellious Northerners, released from the archbishop's restraining hand, prepared for war against the king. Worse still they sought French help and offered the crown to Philip's son, Louis. John reacted with vigour. He harried rebel forces and strongholds from the Kent coast to the Scottish border, but he did not prevent the French from landing and giving new heart to the rebels. Only his own death in October 1216 prevented the struggle from developing into a major civil war.

William Marshal, regent for the child Henry III, restored peace within twelve months. The Charter was one of his main weapons; he reissued it as soon as he had been appointed regent, and again a year later. Eventually, in 1225, Henry III, then of age, published it under his own seal. Henry's version was the one to which Edward I gave the status of statute, for each of these reissues substantially modified the original text. They left out clauses, such as No. 50 and No. 58, which dealt with temporary grievances, and clauses, such as No. 25 and the revolutionary No. 61, which limited too severely the crown's freedom of action. The 1217 reissue took out clauses 44, 47, and 48 to enlarge them into a new Charter of the Forest, and, in order to distinguish one charter from the other, the lawyers designated the original one *Magna*. The name has stuck, although the adjective has long acquired a significance it never possessed in 1217.

A glance through the text which follows will show that Magna Carta was not a declaration of principles like the Petition of Right or the Atlantic Charter. It was chiefly concerned with comparatively petty domestic matters. The barons who insisted on the Charter and the lawyers who drafted it undoubtedly considered No. 61 the most important clause, but posterity has picked out No. 39 as the one of most enduring and fundamental value.

\*

Sealed copies of King John's charter of liberties were circulated to all the chief cities and ecclesiastical centres of the kingdom. Four of these copies survive: British Museum Cotton MS. Augustus II, 106, used for the present translation; the badly damaged British Museum Cotton Charter XIII, 31a; and two others in the archives of Lincoln and Salisbury Cathedrals. There are only technical variations between the texts of the four surviving copies.

The Latin text of the charter is printed in W. Stubbs, *Select Charters* (1913). W. S. McKechnie, *Magna Carta*, 2nd ed. (Glasgow, 1914; New York, 1958), has the text, with a translation, full commentary, and introduction; there is a useful appendix of related documents. J. C. Holt, *Magna Carta* (1965), gives the first analysis of the charter since McKechnie, and considers the significance of its provisions against the political background of the times. He also prints the Latin texts of the charter and supporting documents.

After the various revisions of Henry III's reign, the charter was first enrolled as a statute in 1297, by virtue of its confirmation by Edward I. The text of this confirmation, which is printed in *Statutes of the Realm*, Record Commissioners (1810–28), vol. I, 114–19, is virtually that of Henry III's reissue of 1225 (Stat. R., I, 22–5; also in McKechnie and Holt).

The present translation follows the modern convention of separating the contents of the charter into a preamble with sixty-three chapters. There is no warrant for this in the original, which reads continuously. Clauses which were not included in Henry III's reissue of 1225, the definitive form of the charter, are indicated by an asterisk.

## 6. Magna Carta, 1215

John, by the grace of God king of England, lord of Ireland, duke of Normandy and Aquitaine, and count of Anjou, sends greeting to the archbishops, bishops, abbots, earls, barons, justices, foresters, sheriffs, reeves, ministers, and all other officials and his loyal subjects.

Know that we have made the grants and concessions which follow, in the sight of God and for the salvation of our soul and the souls of all our ancestors and heirs, in honour of God and to enhance the prestige of Holy Church, and for the better ordering of our kingdom. We have been advised by our reverend fathers, Stephen archbishop of Canterbury, primate of all England and cardinal of the Holy Roman Church, Henry archbishop of Dublin, William bishop of London, Peter bishop of Winchester, Jocelin bishop of Bath and Glastonbury, Hugh bishop of Lincoln, Walter bishop of Worcester, William bishop of Coventry, and Benedict bishop of Rochester; master Pandulph subdeacon and member of the household of the lord Pope; brother Aylmer master of the Knights Templar in England; and the noblemen, William Marshal earl of Pembroke, William earl of Salisbury, William earl of Warenne, William earl of Arundel, Alan of Galloway constable of Scotland, Warin fitz Gerald, Peter fitz Herbert, Hubert de Burgh seneschal of Poitou, Hugh de Neville, Matthew fitz Herbert, Thomas Basset, Alan Basset, Philip d'Aubigny, Robert de Ropsley, John Marshal, John fitz Hugh; and others of our faithful subjects.

(1) In the first place, we have given to God, and by this our present charter have confirmed for ourselves and our heirs for ever, that the English Church shall have its freedom and shall enjoy full and undisturbed possession of all its rights and privileges. We desire that this grant be honoured; and that we are sincere in this is shown by our action before the outbreak of hostilities between us and our barons, when without prompting or hidden intent, we granted to the English Church that freedom of appointments which is counted as the greatest and most necessary of its privileges, confirming our grant by charter and

obtaining its further confirmation by the lord pope Innocent III. We will ourselves observe this freedom of the church, and we desire that it shall be similarly observed in all good faith by our heirs for ever.

To all free men of our kingdom we have granted for ourselves and our heirs for ever all the rights set down below, to have and hold for themselves and their heirs from us and our heirs.

(2) If any of our earls or barons, or any other of our tenants in chief, holding directly from the crown in return for knight service, dies and leaves an heir of full age from whom a relief is due, the heir shall succeed to his inheritance on payment of the accustomed relief, namely £100 from the heir or heirs of an earl for the whole estate of the earl; £100 from the heir or heirs of a baron for the whole baronial estate; 100s. at most from the heir or heirs of a knight for the whole knight's fee, with lesser amounts from those who owe less, according to the established custom of the individual fees.

(3) But if the heir of any such earl, baron, or other tenant in chief is under age and therefore a ward, he shall succeed to his inheritance when he comes of age without payment of any relief or fine.

(4) The guardian of the estate of an heir who is under age shall only take from it reasonable rents, customary dues, and labour services, without destruction or wastage of men or property. In cases where we ourself have entrusted the guardianship of any such estate to the sheriff or other person answerable to us for its revenues, and the guardian has made destruction or wastage of his trust, we will exact compensation from him and the estate shall be entrusted to two men of legal standing and discernment of that same fee, who shall be answerable to us or to our nominee for the estate revenues. Similarly, if we have given to anyone or sold him the guardianship of any such estate and he makes destruction or wastage of it, the guardianship shall be taken from him and transferred to two men of legal standing and discernment of that same fee, answerable to us as in the former case.

(5) But for so long as the guardian has the estate in his keep-

ing, he shall maintain the buildings, parks, game preserves, ponds, mills, and other appurtenances of the estate out of the estate revenues. And he shall restore to the heir upon his majority the whole of his estate stocked with ploughs and such other agricultural equipment as the time of year demands and the estate revenues can reasonably support.

(6) Heirs may be given in marriage by their guardians, but the marriage must be a suitable one socially, and before it is contracted notice shall be given to the near blood relations of the heir.

(7) Upon the death of her husband a widow shall receive her marriage portion and her inheritance forthwith and without difficulty; and she shall pay nothing to receive her dowry or marriage portion, or to succeed to the property which she and her husband owned on the day of his death.[1] She may remain in her husband's house for forty days after his death and within that time her dowry shall be assigned to her.

(8) No widow shall be forced to remarry for so long as she wishes to live without a husband, but she shall give security that she will not remarry without our consent if she is our tenant, or without the consent of the lord whose tenant she is, if she holds from another.

(9) Neither we nor our bailiffs will seize any land or distrain upon the rents for any debt so long as the chattels of the debtor are sufficient in value to satisfy the debt, nor shall distraint be made upon the debtor's sureties if he can satisfy the debt himself. But if the debtor has defaulted in payment and has not the means to discharge the debt, then the sureties shall answer for it. They may, if they so wish, take the debtor's lands and revenues into their possession until they have recovered the amount

1. This phrase, here translated literally, may relate to joint property of the husband and wife, or to property inherited by the wife and held for her by the husband; on another reading, however, it could refer to the widow's inheritance of the estate, where there were no other heirs, or to the widow's entitlement from her husband's estate, traditionally a third.

of the debt paid by them on his behalf, unless the debtor proves that he has discharged his obligations towards them.

*(10) If anyone has borrowed money from the Jews, whether the amount is great or small, and dies before the debt is repaid, no interest shall accrue on the outstanding capital of the debt during the minority of the heir, no matter whose tenant he is; and if such a debt passes into our hands we will take only the principal amount specified in the bond.

*(11) The widow of a man who dies owing a debt to the Jews shall receive her dowry in full and make no payment from it on account of the debt. Any children of the dead man who are under age shall have necessary provision made for them appropriate to the nature of their father's holding, and the balance of the estate shall then be applied in discharge of the debt, but the feudal incidents shall be reserved. Debts owing to others than Jews shall be treated in the same manner.

*(12) Scutage and aids shall only be levied in our kingdom by common counsel of our kingdom, unless occasioned by the need to ransom our own person, to make our eldest son a knight, or to give our eldest daughter once in marriage; the amounts of aid on these occasions shall be reasonable. Aids from the city of London shall be treated similarly.

(13) The city of London shall retain all its ancient privileges and traditional trading rights by land and water. We also desire and grant that all other cities, boroughs, towns, and ports shall retain all their privileges and traditional trading rights.

*(14) To obtain common counsel of the kingdom for the assessment of an aid – for other purposes than the three specified above – and scutage, we will send individual letters of summons to the archbishops, bishops, abbots, earls, and chief barons, and general summonses through our sheriffs and other officials to all our tenants in chief, calling them to meet together on a given date – which shall be not less than forty days after the issue of the summons – and in a given place; and in all the letters we will set down the business of the assembly. When summonses have been issued in this manner, items of business on the appointed

day shall be decided by the advice of those present, notwithstanding the absence of some of those who were summoned.

*(15) In future we will not allow anyone to levy an aid from his free tenants except for the purpose of ransoming his person, making his eldest son a knight, or giving his eldest daughter once in marriage; aids levied for such purposes shall be within reason.

(16) No one shall be compelled to render more service for a knight's fee or other free holding of land than is properly due from it.

(17) Common pleas shall not be heard in the various places where, from time to time, our royal court is established, but in some fixed place.

(18) Inquests of *Novel Disseisin*, *Mort d' Ancestor*, and *Darrein Presentment* shall be conducted only in the courts of the counties where the cases arise, and in the following manner. We, or our justiciar if we are out of the kingdom, will send two justices to each county four times a year, and they together with four knights of the county, elected by the county, shall conduct the said assizes in the county court on the same day and in the same place as the meeting of the county court.

*(19) But if the assizes cannot be taken on the day when the county court meets, then as many knights and freeholders as are needed for decisions to be given in proper form on the number of cases outstanding shall remain behind after the meeting of the county court.

(20) An offender who is liable for punishment at our hands shall be fined in proportion to the seriousness, or otherwise, of his offence; but fines shall not be imposed which are so heavy as to cause a freeholder to lose his holding, or a merchant to lose his stock-in-trade, or a villein to lose the means of earning his living. Fines shall only be imposed upon these categories of persons following the attestation of charges against them by sworn juries of local men of proved honesty.

(21) Earls and barons shall only be fined by judgment of their equals, according to the measure of their offence.

(22) Any fine imposed upon a clerk in holy orders in respect of his lay property shall be assessed on the foregoing principles, without taking the value of his ecclesiastical benefice into account.

(23) No town or individual shall be forced to build bridges at river-banks except those who are under a customary and legal obligation to do so.

(24) No sheriff, constable, coroner, or other of our officials shall hear cases which are the prerogative of the royal courts.

*(25) Each county, hundred, wapentake, and riding shall be assessed at the old farm without any increase, our own demesne manors excepted.

(26) If any one of our lay tenants dies, the sheriff or our bailiff, on production of the royal letters patent of summons for a debt which the dead man owed us, may make an attachment and inventory of such of the dead man's chattels found on the lay holding as are agreed by men of legal standing to represent the amount of the debt; and none of these goods shall then be removed until the debt which was clearly owing to us has been discharged. The rest of the dead man's property shall be left for the executors to dispose of in accordance with the terms of his will. But if the dead man owed us nothing, then all his chattels shall be disposed of according to his wishes, saving to his wife and children their reasonable shares.

*(27) If a freeman dies intestate his chattels shall be distributed by his near blood relations and friends under the supervision of the church, but the rights of anyone to whom the deceased owed a debt shall be safeguarded.

(28) No constable or any other of our officials shall take corn or other goods from anyone without immediate payment in money, unless the vendor is agreeable to a deferred payment.

(29) No constable shall force a knight to pay money in lieu of castle guard duty if the knight is prepared to discharge this duty in person or if, being unable to attend himself for some good reason, he is willing to send a suitable man in his place. A knight shall be exempt from guard duty for such periods as he is en-

gaged on military service, under our leadership or at our command.

(30) No sheriff, royal official, or any other person shall commandeer horses or carts for transport work from a freeman without his consent.

(31) Neither we nor our officials will take wood for castles or other of our works without the owner's consent.

(32) We will not retain possession of the estates of a convicted felon for longer than a year and a day, after which time the estates shall be returned to the man's overlords.

(33) For the future all fish-weirs shall be removed from the Thames and the Medway and throughout England, except along the sea-coast.

(34) The writ called *Praecipe* shall not in future be issued to anyone in respect of any disputed holding of land, where the effect might be to deprive a freeman of his right to the hearing of his case in a local court.

(35) There shall be standard measures of wine, beer, and corn – the London quarter – throughout the whole of our kingdom, and a standard width of dyed, russet, and halberject [better quality? worn under the hauberk?] cloth – two ells within the selvedges; and there shall be standard weights also.

(36) In future no payment shall be given or accepted for the issue of a writ of inquisition of life or limbs; the writ shall be granted free, and not denied.

(37) If anyone holds land from us in return for the payment of a fee-farm rent, socage, or a burgage rent, and at the same time holds land from someone else in return for knight service, we shall not be entitled to the guardianship of his heir or of the estate which he holds from another's fee merely by reason of the fee-farm rent, socage, or burgage rent which he pays us. Nor shall we have the guardianship of the estate from which the fee-farm rent, socage, or burgage rent issues unless, in the case of a fee-farm rent, the estate is also charged with providing us with knight service. Similarly, we shall not be entitled to the guardianship of a man's heir and of an estate which he holds

from someone else merely because he is also a tenant of ours in petty sergeanty in return for a payment of knives, arrows, and the like.

(38) In future no official shall bring anyone to trial on his own unsupported statement without producing trustworthy witnesses to the alleged offence.

(39) No freeman shall be arrested, imprisoned, dispossessed, outlawed, exiled, or in any way deprived of his standing, nor shall we proceed against him by force or send others against him, except by the lawful judgment of his equals and according to the law of the land.

(40) To no one will we sell, refuse, or delay the operation of right or justice.

(41) All merchants shall have free and undisturbed passage to and from England, and shall be safe and unmolested during their stay and in their travels by land and water throughout the country. No burdensome or extraordinary taxation shall be levied upon them, but they shall buy and sell freely on payment only of the proper and anciently established dues. These provisions, however, shall not apply in wartime to nationals of a country at war with us. All such foreign nationals found trading in our lands at the outbreak of war shall be interned, but without loss of life or property until we or our justiciar have ascertained the treatment accorded to such of our own merchants as the outbreak of war has surprised in enemy country; and if we find that our merchants are safe with the enemy, their merchants shall be safe with us.

*(42) In future anyone may leave our kingdom and return, safe and secure by land and water, saving his allegiance to us, except in wartime when temporary restrictions may be imposed for the common good of the realm. This provision does not apply to persons imprisoned or outlawed by due process of law; or to nationals of a country at war with us; or to foreign merchants, who shall be treated in accordance with the provisions of the last section.

(43) If a man dies holding land from an estate which has been

escheated to the crown as, for example, from the honours of Wallingford, Nottingham, Boulogne, Lancaster, or any other baronial estate escheated to us, his heir shall not pay us any other relief or perform any other service than he would have paid or performed for the baron, had the baron still held the estate. And we will hold the estate in exactly the same manner as the baron held it.

*(44) Men who are not resident in a royal forest shall not henceforth be brought before our justices of the forest by writs of general summons, unless they are to appear as defendants or as sureties for a person or persons bound over on bail for a forest offence.

*(45) We will only appoint as justices, constables, sheriffs, or other officials such men as are well versed in the law of the kingdom and intend to uphold it.

(46) All barons who have founders' rights in respect of abbeys, as evidenced by charters from kings of England or ancient title, shall have guardianship of them, as is their right, whenever there is a vacancy.

*(47) All forests created in our reign shall be immediately disafforested, and similarly river-banks which we have reserved for our sport during our reign shall be again thrown open.

*(48) All oppressive practices relating to forests, warrens, and river-banks, and the malpractices of foresters, warreners, the sheriffs, and their officers, and river-bank keepers shall, in every county, be the subject of immediate inquiry by twelve sworn knights of the same county, elected by the worthy men of the county; and within forty days of such inquiry, all abuses shall be stamped out, never more to be renewed, by the agency of the said knights; provided always that we, or our justiciar if we are out of England, have been previously informed.[1]

*(49) We will immediately return all hostages and bonds sur-

1. *by the agency of . . . informed.* This passage is not incorporated into the text of the charter in BM. Cotton MS. Augustus II, 106, but there appears as a footnote.

rendered to us by Englishmen as security for the peace and their faithful service.

*(50) We will utterly discharge from their offices – and they shall not hold office again in England – the relatives of Gerard de Athée, namely: Engelard de Cigogné, Peter, Guy and Andrew de Chanceaux, Guy de Cigogné, Geoffrey de Martigny and his brothers, and Philip Marc, his brothers and his nephew Geoffrey, and all their following.

*(51) As soon as peace is restored, we will expel from the kingdom all foreign knights, crossbowmen, sergeants, and mercenaries who have come with horses and weapons to the harm of the realm.

*(52) If anyone, without legal judgment of his equals, has been dispossessed or deprived by us of lands, castles, privileges, or rights, we will straightway restore these to him, and in the case of any dispute arising thereof, it shall be decided by the twenty-five barons mentioned below in the clause relating to the keeping of the peace. But with regard to anything of which a man was dispossessed or deprived without legal judgment of his equals by our father, King Henry, or our brother, King Richard, and which we now hold or others hold under our guarantee of title, we will be allowed the full period [three years] of immunity from legal proceedings which is customary for crusaders, except in cases where a suit had already been entered or an inquiry instituted at our command before we undertook to make our crusade. But as soon as we return from our pilgrimage or immediately if we abandon it, we will see that full justice is done.

*(53) We shall be allowed a similar period of immunity, and the same provisions for the implementation of justice shall apply[1] in respect of the disafforestation or retention[1] of forests made by our father, Henry, or our brother, Richard; in respect also of the guardianship of dead men's estates in other lords' fees, which we have hitherto held by reason of other land held from us by the deceased in return for knight service; and in respect of abbeys

1. *and the same provisions . . . apply*, and *or retention*, appear as footnotes in BM. Cotton MS. Augustus II, 106, and are not incorporated into the text.

founded on other lords' fees in which the lords of the fees claim to have rights. Immediately on our return from our pilgrimage or upon our abandonment of it, we will see that full justice is done on complaints arising about these matters.

(54) No one shall be arrested or imprisoned on the appeal of a woman for the death of anyone except her husband.

*(55) Any fines levied by us unjustly and against the law of the land, and any unjust and illegal amercements shall be remitted in their entirety, or judgment shall be delivered therein by the twenty-five barons mentioned below in the clause relating to the keeping of the peace, or by the majority of them and of the said Stephen, archbishop of Canterbury, if he can be present, and of such others as he may wish to bring with him for this purpose: but if the archbishop cannot be present, the business shall proceed without him. Provided always that if a case is set down for hearing, and any of these twenty-five barons have been involved in a similar dispute themselves, they shall be removed from the bench when the case is heard, and others shall be elected and sworn in their place by the rest of the twenty-five, to serve for this one occasion.

*(56) Any Welshman whom we may have dispossessed or deprived of lands, privileges, or anything else without legal judgment of his equals, in England or Wales, shall have immediate restitution made to him, and should a dispute arise it shall be decided in the March by the judgment of his equals; for English holdings, according to English law; for Welsh holdings, according to Welsh law; and for holdings in the March, according to the law of the March. The Welsh will do the same with us and ours.

*(57) But regarding anything of which a Welshman was dispossessed or deprived without legal judgment of his equals by our father, King Henry, or our brother, King Richard, and which we now hold or others hold under our guarantee of title, we will be allowed the full period of immunity customary for crusaders, except in cases where a suit had already been entered or an inquiry had been instituted at our command before we undertook to make our crusade. But as soon as we return from

our pilgrimage, or immediately if we abandon it, we will see that full justice is done according to the laws of the Welsh and of the said religions.

*(58) We will at once return the son of Llewelyn and all the Welsh hostages and bonds delivered to us as security for the peace.

*(59) We will act towards Alexander, King of the Scots, regarding the return of his sisters and other hostages, and the restoration of his privileges and rights, in the same way as towards our other English barons, except as is otherwise provided in the formal agreements which we hold from his father, William, formerly King of the Scots; this will be according to the judgment of his equals in our court.

(60) All the aforesaid customs and rights which we have granted to be maintained in our kingdom in the dealings between us and our people shall be similarly observed by all men of our kingdom, both clergy and laymen, in their dealings with their own people.

*(61) Whereas we have made all the aforesaid grants out of reverence for God, for the better ordering of our kingdom and for the more effective healing of the strife between us and our barons, and desire that our grant shall remain firm and unshaken in its entirety forever, we do therefore secure and safeguard it by the following provision, namely:

The barons shall elect any twenty-five barons of the kingdom whom they please, and they in their turn shall exert themselves to the full extent of their powers in preserving and upholding, and causing to be upheld, the peaceful settlement and grant of rights which we have made to them and have confirmed by this our present charter; and in the pursuance of these objects, they shall apply the following procedure. If we, the justiciar, our officials or any of our ministers offend against anyone in any respect, or break any of the provisions of the peace or of this guarantee, and the offence is made known to four of the said twenty-five barons, they shall come to us, or to the justiciar if we are out of the kingdom, and laying the cause of the complaint before us, require that we remedy it without delay. And if we, or the justiciar in our absence abroad, have not remedied the complaint within forty days after it was first presented to us, or to him, they shall refer the matter to the rest of the twenty-five barons, and these twenty-five with the commonalty of the whole kingdom shall then distrain and bring pressure to bear upon us in every way open to them, namely, by seizure of our castles, estates, and possessions and by any other means in their power until the complaint has been remedied to their satisfaction, saving only our own person and the persons of our queen and our children. And once satisfaction has been obtained they will stand towards us exactly as they did before.

Anyone in the land shall be free to swear his obedience to the commands of the said twenty-five barons in furtherance of all these aims, and to swear that he will join with them to the full extent of his power in bringing pressure to bear upon us. We publicly and freely give permission to take the oath to any-one who so wishes, and we will at no time prevent anyone from taking it: but rather will we compel those of our subjects who are unwilling of themselves to pledge their support to the barons by this oath of distraint and pressure against us to take the oath by our command.

If any one of the twenty-five barons dies or leaves the coun-try or is in any other way prevented from carrying out his aforesaid duties, the rest of the twenty-five shall choose another in his place, whomever they think best, and he will be sworn, in the same way as the others.

If all the twenty-five barons are present at a meeting and fail to agree on any of the matters which are entrusted to them for action, or if some of those summoned have refused or are unable to attend, any decision taken or instruction issued by the majority of those present shall be held to be as fixed and binding as if all twenty-five had agreed to it.

The twenty-five barons shall swear to observe all the afore-said provisions faithfully, and they shall use all means in their power to obtain a similar observance from others.

We will not, directly or indirectly, procure from anyone a release of any kind the effect of which would be to cancel or reduce any of the rights and privileges granted by this charter: and if, notwithstanding this provision, such a release is obtained, it shall be considered null and void, and we will never, directly or indirectly, make use of it.[1]

*(62) We have granted full and universal pardon and forgiveness for all feelings of ill-will, resentment, and rancour which have arisen between us and our clerical and lay subjects since the outbreak of hostilities. We have further granted our full forgiveness to all clerics and lay persons for all offences which they have committed in pursuance of the said hostilities between Easter in the sixteenth year of our reign and the restoration of peace, and we have pardoned them to the full extent of our personal concern. We have further caused them to be issued with letters patent under the seals of the lord Stephen archbishop of Canterbury, the lord Henry archbishop of Dublin, the other bishops who were previously mentioned, and master Pandulph, formally attesting the sanction contained in the last clause and the concessions granted by this charter.

*(63) It is accordingly our wish and stern command that the English Church shall have its freedom, and that men in our kingdom shall enjoy full and competent possession of all the aforesaid rights, grants, and privileges in their entirety, in peace and freedom and without disturbance for themselves and their heirs from ourself and our heirs, in every particular and in all places in perpetuity, exactly as is aforesaid.

Both we and the barons have sworn to observe all the foregoing provisions faithfully and without deceit, as witness the beforementioned persons and many others.

Given by our hand in the meadow called Runnymede between Windsor and Staines on the 15th day of June in the seventeenth year of our reign.

1. This clause is particularly directed against possible attempts to circumvent the charter by appeals to the papal authority.

# 7. *The Rule of St Francis*

In the twelfth century the monks taught the Western Church a deeper understanding of prayer and contemplation; in the thirteenth, the friars demonstrated throughout Europe their challenging concept of Christian discipleship.

At the beginning of the thirteenth century, most church leaders were well aware of the pressing need to preach the Gospel to the laity efficiently and attractively. The Lateran Decrees, issued by the general council which Innocent III had convened in 1215, spoke of the secular clergy's lack of discipline, poor standard of literacy, and widespread heretical beliefs. For the last four or five generations the more dedicated, capable young men had forsaken the world for the cloister, with the result that the second-rate and the misfits tended to be left to minister to laymen in the parishes. The Decrees proposed administrative reforms, and, though the thirteenth-century archbishops and bishops never implemented them all, they introduced some changes which tightened their hold on their dioceses and helped to improve the calibre of their clergy. They appointed suffragan bishops to share their spiritual duties, officers known as *officials* to take over most of their judicial work, and vicars general, chancellors, archdeacons, and staffs of household clerks to help them administer their dioceses. It was a further advantage that these officers usually lived in their bishop's household and enjoyed the stimulation of each other's society. Such households as that of Edmund of Abingdon at Canterbury or that of Richard Wych at Chichester were scholar-communities: they must be ranked as centres of higher learning and education alongside the few remaining colleges of secular canons and the schools which were attracting students to Oxford, Cambridge, and, at times, to Salisbury, Stamford, Northampton, and other towns. Yet however basic were these reforms and however soundly they were constructing new foundations for future development, they only had a limited influence on immediate problems. It was left to the friars, and not to a slowly improving body of secular clergy, to present to the people of thirteenth-century England a new vivid vision of Christian living.

Friars, like monks, took vows of obedience, poverty, and chastity, and lived under the rule of their order. They were *regular*, as opposed to *secular*, clergy, but the ideal which inspired their rule was very different from that which guided the lives of monks. In 1215, St Francis in Italy and, three years later, St Dominic in Spain established the first two orders of mendicant friars. Both enjoined absolute poverty on their followers. No friar could own any property beyond the rags he wore. He must beg his bread and be content with the most squalid accommodation. It was not only that Francis and Dominic required their followers to obey Christ's instruction to 'take nothing for their journey, save a staff only'. They both held poverty to be a virtue, and therefore expected members of their order to decline gifts of good clothing or weatherproof housing. For many years Franciscans and Dominicans also refused to own any property communally. Even their friaries they conveyed to such other bodies as the papacy or the local mayor and aldermen. This soon proved unacceptable in practice, but the Franciscan rule was not officially amended until John XXII gave the necessary papal permission in the first years of the fourteenth century. The Dominican prohibition was not revoked until 1465.

Thomas of Eccleston, himself one of the earliest Franciscans, has left us an account of the way the Franciscans — Grey Friars, or Friars Minor — rapidly carried their mission throughout England. In September 1224, four years after the first Dominicans had landed, a group of nine, led by the thirty-year-old Agnellus of Pisa, were 'charitably conveyed across the Channel by the monks of Fécamp'. These pioneers made Canterbury their first headquarters, but during the next two months they founded friaries in London and Oxford, and early the following year in Northampton and Cambridge. By 1225, according to Eccleston, forty-nine friaries were housing 1,242 friars. The Dominicans, or Black Friars, had made similar progress. Within a century of their first coming, the Franciscans had perfected their English organization. They had divided the *province* into seven *custodies* centred on London, Oxford, Cambridge, York, Worcester, Bristol, and Newcastle. Each custody controlled about eight or nine of the sixty-one Franciscan friaries which covered the country. By that time, the Minoresses or Poor Clares, the female counterpart of the Franciscans, had also arrived in England. They built their first house near Aldgate in London, and Edward I officially recognized its existence in 1293.

The mission of all friars was to preach the Gospel to the people. That was why they fixed their centres in strategically placed towns, so that they could radiate from them into neighbouring towns and villages. Their houses served as headquarters, but their chief work lay outside the walls. They sang the offices of the day wherever it was most convenient to do so. They observed fasts and kept vigils, but allowed nothing to limit their evangelism. Roger of Wendover, a chronicler in the abbey of St Albans, wrote that 'on Sundays and feast days they left their houses to preach the Gospel in the parish churches'. He was of the opinion that 'the less they were concerned with earthly affairs and bodily pleasures, the more remarkable was their devotion to heavenly matters', or, as Thomas of Eccleston put it, 'they served the Lord not so much by observing human constitutions as by freely pouring out their piety'. The first generation of English Franciscans disciplined itself most fiercely. Agnellus, who directed the English province until his death in 1236, was, in the words of Friar Thomas, 'outstanding for his virtue, his observance of the Rule, and his honesty of life'. He insisted that his friars should live in acute poverty, and that the first friaries should be built in mud and wattle on swampy sites. He forbade members of the order to eat and drink more than the necessary minimum, or to accept new clothing until their old robes were scarcely holding together. But from 1238, the date of the death of Albert of Pisa, who followed Agnellus as head of the English province, change crept in.

Haymo of Faversham, the next provincial, preferred that friars should labour rather than beg for their living. His successors, William of Nottingham and Peter of Tewkesbury, returned to the orthodox interpretation of the rule of poverty, but found themselves up against the legacy of Brother Elias, the go-ahead minister-general of the order, who had ignored the rule of poverty because it seemed to him a barrier unnecessarily hindering the success and influence of the whole movement. The pope had forced Elias to resign his office, but he had not killed his influence. Peter, following the Rule, might still be insisting that the Franciscans at Shrewsbury must replace the stone walls of their friary with mud walls, but the magnificent church at Assisi, which, ironically, Elias had begun to build in honour of Francis himself, was to prove to be the signpost which the order would follow.

From the first the Dominicans had recognized that if they were to fight heresy – perhaps in Dominic's mind the primary purpose of his order – they must be well read in the scriptures and the writings of the fathers of the Church. As far as each was able, Dominicans were bidden to study theology, so that they would be capable of confounding the heretic with counter-argument. On the other hand, St

Francis mistrusted learning. At best, he maintained, it could only enable man to see truth through a glass darkly, and it often weakened a friar's faith, or distracted him from his true purpose, which was to live as Christ had done. Even before their leader's death the Franciscans had begun to question this belief. In Oxford the outstanding theologian, Robert Grosseteste, tutored the first generation of English Franciscans. He argued that 'unless the friars studied hard and diligently learned the will of God, they would undoubtedly suffer the same fate as other religious whom we see walking in the darkness of ignorance'. Such arguments carried the day, and it was not long before both orders of friars were enjoying equal reputations as well-educated, fervent preachers.

Not surprisingly the coming of the friars roused jealousies. The laity welcomed Dominicans, Franciscans, and, later, Augustinians and Carmelites sincerely and enthusiastically, and the bishops considered them to be most valuable allies. But the monks quickly realized that most young clerics were preferring the mendicant orders to their own, and that gifts to friaries were probably being made at the expense of gifts to monasteries. Parish priests resented both the way people flocked to hear friars preach and the desire their parishioners were nourishing to have a friar baptize, marry, and bury members of their family. It was a blow to their pride, and, still more, a loss from their slender purse. Matthew Paris, another St Albans chronicler, noticed these changes with some disapproval: 'Some people declined to make their confession to their own priest either because he was a drunkard or because they had some other private reason, but they confessed confidently enough under the cover of consolation and counsel which passing Dominicans and Franciscans spread over them.' Fortunately the early friars never strove to be competitive. They preached whenever they found a group to listen, and they were just as prepared to hear the confession of a pauper as of a rich man. Indeed there were many hovels hidden away in the growing towns that no clergy but the friars were prepared to visit.

The very success and popularity of the mendicants soon created practical problems. Large, eager congregations could not be housed in mean, cramped churches, and adequate teaching required accommodation, manuscripts, and writing materials. The friars, in spite of their dedication to poverty, had rapidly become rich, for, out of admiration and thankfulness, scores of men and women, following the example of Henry III himself, had insisted upon giving them land and money. Therefore it was natural enough that the leaders of the orders in the middle decades of the thirteenth century should feel that they could rightly use their unsought wealth to build churches big enough for their congregations and schools adequate for the teaching they wished to do. From that decision it was a short, easy step to decide to replace the squalid wattle and daub friaries with stone and timber buildings.

The second generation of Franciscans rapidly turned their new enthusiasm for learning into action. Chosen friars continued to study theology at Oxford under other distinguished secular priests after Grosseteste had left to become bishop of Lincoln in 1235, and the provincial appointed Franciscan lecturers to teach members of the order throughout England. Young men who joined the mendicants in the comparatively distant counties of the south-west or the north enjoyed the advantage of studying theology under a competent tutor who had himself studied at Oxford, Paris, or some other university, and in 1247 the Franciscans took the further step of dispensing with the help of learned outsiders and appointing one of themselves, Adam of Morisco, as their Oxford lecturer. Henceforward they regarded themselves as educationally self-sufficient. During the next century Roger Bacon, the experimental scientist, Duns Scotus and William of Ockham, both outstanding theologians, were all Franciscans: Albertus Magnus and his pupil, St Thomas Aquinas, the most influential of medieval theologians, were both Dominicans. Learning, teaching, and preaching had become the outstanding characteristics of the friars. Poverty, not entirely forgotten, had been relegated to a secondary virtue.

The Black Death brought far more serious changes. The friars, unlike many seculars, considered it their business to tend the victims. Consequently they themselves suffered appalling losses. In the most disturbed years of the fifties and sixties, when people were trying to adjust themselves to vastly changed conditions and daily fearing a new outburst of plague, the mendicant orders found themselves incompetently led, very short of members, but richer than ever. They had to recruit, but, not surprisingly, for the most part they recruited men who looked on membership of an order primarily as a comfortable retreat from a bewildering world. Only in name were these new friars followers of Francis and Dominic. They brought contempt upon themselves, and upon their order. Langland and Chaucer were only speaking for their generation when they scornfully described friars 'preaching to the people for personal profit', and interesting themselves chiefly in food, dress, and carnal pleasures.

> For there he was not like a cloisterer,
>   With a threadbare cope, as is a poor scholar,
> But he was like a master or a pope.
>   Of double worsted was his semi-cope.

This backsliding from the original ideals was difficult to cure. The fifteenth century saw no general return to the strict interpretation of the Rule. But in the darkest days after the Black Death and in protest against the neglect of the Rule, a few Italian Franciscans broke away from their fellows to live their lives according to the precepts of their founder. These were the Observants. They first came to England in the mid-fifteenth century, and made their headquarters at Greenwich. Henry VII gave them remarkable support, and enabled them to found new houses at Richmond and Newark, and to convert to their use existing friaries at Canterbury, Newcastle, and Southampton. The young Henry VIII and Queen Catherine admired the Observants as much as Henry's father had done. They made their confessions to them and often invited them to preach in the chapel of Greenwich Palace. But later, when he separated the English church from Rome and forced the oath of succession upon his subjects, Henry VIII found that the very qualities he had admired in the Observants forced them to resist his will. They were only a comparative handful of men, but, alone of all the friars, they refused to accept the king's decisions. In their sermons they openly denounced them, and resignedly suffered imprisonment, exile, and execution to demonstrate to the world the sincerity of their vows and their loyalty to their Rule.

*

The First Rule of St Francis of 1221 itself replaced an earlier Primitive Rule which had been approved by Pope Innocent III in 1209. The First Rule was much longer and more full of quotations from the Scriptures, but less precise than the Second Rule of 1223, which here follows in translation. This is the definitive form of the Rule, which is still observed by the First Order of Franciscans.

The Second Rule was approved by Pope Honorius III in the Bull, *Solet annuere*, of 29 November 1223, and for this reason is often referred to as the *Regula Bullata*. The Bull and the Rule are preserved together in the *Sacro Convento* at Assisi.

The soundest edition of St Francis's works, *Opuscula Sancti Patris Francisci Assisiensis*, containing the Latin texts of both the First and Second Rules, was published in 1904, and republished in 1949, by the Fathers of St Bonaventura's College, Quaracchi. There are good English translations of the collected works by B. Flahy and P. Hermann, *The Writings of St. Francis of Assisi* (1964), and by Leo Sherley-Price, *St. Francis of Assisi* (1959).

For Thomas of Eccleston's account of the arrival and early history of the Franciscans in England, see A. G. Little (ed.), *Fratris Thomae . . . Tractatus de Adventu Fratrum Minorum in Angliam* (Manchester, 1951). There is an English translation by P. Hermann in *XIIIth Century Chronicles* (Chicago, 1961).

The standard modern survey of the activities of the friars in England is by Dom David Knowles, *The Religious Orders in England*, 3 vols. (1948–59); see especially vol. I, Part 2, 'The Friars, 1216–1340', 114–252. There are detailed local studies of the Franciscans by A. G. Little, *Grey Friars in Oxford* (1892), and J. R. H. Moorman, *The Grey Friars in Cambridge* (1952). See also the conveniently collected essays and studies by A. G. Little, *Franciscan Papers, Lists and Documents* (1943). Amongst the works that may be consulted for the Dominicans are R. F. Bennett, *The Early Dominicans* (1937); B. Jarrett, *The English Dominicans*, 2nd ed., revised by W. Gumbley (1937); and W. A. Hinnebusch, *The Early English Friars Preachers* (Rome, Istituto Storico Domenico: Santa Sabina, 1952). There is a useful study of the Austin friars by A. Gwynn, *The English Austin Friars in the time of Wyclif* (1940).

## 7. THE RULE OF ST FRANCIS

1. *This is the beginning, in the Lord's name, of the way of life of the brothers minor*

The Rule and way of life of the brothers minor is this: to regulate their conduct by the Holy Gospel of Our Lord Jesus

Christ, living in obedience, without personal possessions, and in chastity. Brother Francis promises obedience and reverence to the Lord Pope Honorius and his successors, canonically appointed, and to the Church of Rome. The other brothers shall be in duty bound to obey Brother Francis and his successors.

## 2. *Concerning those who wish to adopt this way of life; and of how they should be received*

If any come to our brothers and wish to adopt this way of life, the brothers shall send them to the provincial ministers, to whom alone, and to no others, shall the authority to receive new brothers be given. The ministers shall carefully examine them in the Catholic faith and in the sacraments of the Church; and if they believe all these things and will confess them with true faith and hold by them firmly to the end of their lives, and if they are not married, or their wives have already entered convents, or they have given them permission to do so under authority from the diocesan bishop, they themselves having taken a vow of continence and the wives being of such an age that no suspicion can arise attaching to them, the ministers shall instruct them, in the words of the Holy Gospel, to go and sell all that they have and study how best to give the proceeds to the poor. But if there are circumstances which prevent this, their good intention is sufficient. The brothers and their ministers shall not concern themselves about the temporal possessions of new members of the order, but shall leave them free to follow the inspiration of God concerning the disposal of their property. But if advice is needed, the ministers may send them to some God-fearing persons, by whose advice their goods shall be dispensed to the poor.

The ministers shall then allow them the garments of probation, namely, two tunics without hoods, a belt, breeches, and a cape down to the belt, unless, upon some occasion or another, a different form of habit should seem more appropriate to the ministers in the sight of God.

When the year of probation is over, they shall be received into obedience, promising to hold steadfast always by this rule and way of life. In accordance with the decree of the lord pope [*bulla Honorii III, 'cum secundum consilium'*, 22 September 1220], they will in no way thereafter be permitted to depart from the order, since we are told by the Holy Gospel that *no one who sets his hand to the plough and then looks back is worthy of the kingdom of God*.

Having promised their obedience, they shall have one tunic only with a hood and one other, for those who wish, without a hood. Any of them who must wear shoes shall be free to do so. All the brothers shall wear coarse habits, which they may repair with patches of sackcloth and other material, with God's blessing upon them. I warn and exhort them not to despise or pass judgement upon those whom they see in soft and coloured garments, or enjoying rich food and drink, but rather that each one of them shall despise and pass judgement on himself.

### 3. *Concerning the Divine Office; fasting; and of how the brothers should travel through the world*

Clerical brothers shall perform the Divine Office according to the rite of the Holy Roman Church, except for the psalter; and they shall have breviaries with which to perform the Office. Lay brothers shall say twenty-four *Our Fathers* for Matins; five for Lauds; seven each for Prime, Terce, Sext, and Nones; twelve for Vespers; and for Compline they shall say seven *Our Fathers* and offer up prayers for the dead.

The brothers shall fast from the feast of All Saints [1 November] until Christmas. Those fasting voluntarily for the holy period of forty days after Epiphany [6 January], which the Lord consecrated by his own holy fast, shall be blessed by the Lord, but there shall be no compulsion on those not wishing to fast at this time. All the brothers, however, shall observe the [Lenten] fast before Easter. Except for these times, and the Friday of each week, there shall be no other obligatory fasting; and on no occasion when they are clearly in need of sustenance shall the brothers be compelled to fast.

I advise, warn, and exhort my brothers in the Lord Jesus Christ, that when they travel through the world they shall not quarrel nor contend with words, nor shall they pass judgement on others: but they shall be gentle, peaceable and modest, courteous and humble, speaking to everyone politely, as is befitting. They should not ride, unless compelled to it by their infirmity or by some other obvious necessity. Whenever they enter a house, their first words shall be: *Peace be upon this house*, and, as it is written in the Holy Gospel, they may then eat of any dish that is set before them.

## 4. *Brothers not to receive money*

I strictly charge all brothers that in no circumstances shall they accept coin or money, either themselves or through third parties. The ministers and wardens, however, and they alone, shall direct their care and attention towards providing through spiritual friends for the needs of the sick and for the clothing of the other brothers, in such manner as they see that necessity requires, having regard to the place where they are, the time of year, and the severity of the climate; always provided, as was said before, that they accept no coin or money.

## 5. *Concerning their work*

Those brothers whom the Lord has graced by allowing them to labour shall work faithfully and devotedly, to the exclusion of idleness which is the enemy of the soul: but they shall not be so taken up in their work as to extinguish that spirit of prayer and devotion to which all temporal concerns should be subservient. As the wages of their labour, they shall receive bodily necessities for themselves and their brothers, but not coin or money; and they shall accept their wages with humility, as befits servants of God and followers of most holy poverty.

## 6. *The brothers to take nothing for their own; the seeking of alms; and concerning sick brothers*

The brothers shall take nothing for their own, neither a house, nor a place, nor anything at all. But like strangers and pilgrims in this life, serving God in poverty and humility, they shall go forth confidently to seek alms, nor be ashamed to do so, since Our Lord made himself poor for us in this world. This is that lofty height of the sublimest poverty which has raised you, my dearest brothers, to be heirs and kings of the kingdom of the heavens, poor in goods, but exalted in virtues. This shall be your portion, which leads you to the land of the living. Cling wholly to this, dearest brothers, and wish for nothing else, in the name of our Lord Jesus Christ, for the rest of your lives here on earth.

Wherever the brothers are, or may happen to meet, they shall show themselves servants to one another. And one shall declare his needs confidently to the other; for if a mother gives nourishment to the son of her body, and bestows on him her loving care, how much greater should be the love with which one nourishes and cares for his brother in the spirit? If any one of the brothers falls sick, the others have a duty to look after him, as they would wish to be looked after themselves.

### 7. *Concerning the penance to be imposed on brothers who sin*

If, at the prompting of the enemy, any of the brothers have mortally sinned, they shall resort as soon as possible and without delay to the provincial ministers, in the case of those sins for which it has been ordained amongst the brothers that resort should be had to the provincial ministers, and to them alone. These ministers, if they are priests, shall enjoin them, with mercy, to do such penance as seems to them most fitting in the sight of God: but if they are not themselves priests, they shall cause this penance to be enjoined upon them by others of the order who are priests. They should take care not to be angered or violently upset by the sin of any brother, since anger and disturbance within ourselves prevent us from showing charity to others.

## 8. Concerning the election of the minister general of the order; and of the chapter held at Pentecost[1]

The whole brotherhood shall be bound always to have one of their own number to be general minister and servant of them all, and to receive their unfailing obedience. Upon his death, the election of a successor shall be made by the provincial ministers and wardens at the Pentecostal Chapter. And if, at any time, it shall appear to the whole body of the provincial ministers and wardens that the minister general is incompetent to serve the brothers for their common profit, then these same brothers, to whom the election of a minister general is committed, shall be bound to elect another as their guardian, in the name of God.

The chapter at Pentecost shall be held once every three years, or at greater or less intervals of time, accordingly as the minister general shall ordain. The provincial ministers shall be bound, on each occasion when a chapter is held, to come together in chapter at the place appointed by the minister general. After the chapter, the provincial ministers and wardens may, if they so wish and think that it will serve a useful purpose, convene a chapter of their brothers, each one within his own district, once during that same year.

## 9. Concerning brothers who preach

Brothers shall not preach in the diocese of any bishop who has forbidden them to do so. And no brother shall dare to preach to the people at all, unless he has been examined and approved by the minister general of the order, and licensed by him to perform a preacher's duty. I also warn and exhort these brothers that when they preach, their words shall be pure and well-considered, and such as to profit and edify the people, by declaring to them the nature of vice and virtue, and the punishment and glory that respectively attend upon them; and that their discourse shall be short, since Our Lord spoke briefly in his life here on earth.

1. The contents of this chapter have been rearranged in translation to produce a more logical order and one which is easier to follow.

## 10. *Concerning the admonition and correction of brothers*

Those brothers who are ministers and servants of the other brothers shall visit and admonish them, and correct them with love and humility, laying no charge upon them which is against their conscience and contrary to our Rule. The brothers subject to their discipline shall, for their part, remember that they have surrendered their own wills in the service of God. I therefore strictly charge them to obey their ministers in all things which they have promised God to observe and which are not against their conscience or contrary to our Rule. And wherever there are brothers who are conscious of their own inability to follow out the Rule with a true spirituality, they may, and ought to resort to their ministers for advice. The ministers shall receive them kindly and with love, maintaining towards them so natural a manner that the brothers are able to speak and behave with them as masters with their servants; and this is just how it ought to be, the ministers serving all the brothers.

I admonish and exhort the brothers, in the Lord Jesus Christ, that they shall guard against all pride, vainglory, envy, and avarice; and not be concerned and anxious about the things of this world, nor engage in slander and murmurous complaints. Brothers who are illiterate should not be concerned to learn how to read and write, but should mark well that their duty above all things is to have the Holy Spirit of the Lord working within them, and to pray to the Lord unceasingly from a pure heart. They should know that they ought to be humble and patient in sickness and under persecution, loving those who persecute us and come against us with reproaches and contentious words, since the Lord tells us: *Love your enemies and pray for those who persecute and slander you. Blessed are they who suffer persecution for righteousness' sake; for theirs is the kingdom of the heavens. He who has persevered to the end, shall be saved.*

## 11. *The brothers not to enter monasteries of nuns*

I straitly charge all brothers not to associate or take counsel with women in such a manner as to arouse suspicion, and not to enter the monasteries of nuns; except for those who have been granted special permission to do so by the Apostolic See. Nor shall they act as godfathers for men or women, lest this be the occasion of scandal arising amongst the brothers or affecting them.

## 12. *Concerning those who go amongst the Saracens and other unbelievers*

Any of the brothers who are divinely inspired to go amongst the Saracens and other unbelievers shall apply for permission to their provincial ministers. The ministers, for their part, shall not give their permission for any to go, except those whom they see are fit to be sent.

## *Conclusion*

I further enjoin the ministers, upon their obedience, that they shall ask the lord pope for one of the cardinals of the Holy Roman Church to be the governor, protector, and corrector of our order, so that, by being ever subjects, submissive at the feet of the same Holy Church, we may remain steadfast in the Catholic faith, and hold fast by poverty and humility, and by the Holy Gospel of our Lord Jesus Christ, as we have firmly promised.

# 8. The Cosmography of John Holywood

JOHN HOLYWOOD — Sacrobosco to medieval Latinists — was born in Yorkshire, but earned his reputation as a scholar by teaching in Paris. He died in 1250. He wrote three books which were copiously copied in manuscripts and, later, printed in several editions. Two were concerned with arithmetic and the use of Arabic numerals; the third, *Tractatus de Sphaera*, described the cosmos and explained such phenomena as eclipses, zodiacal signs, and the diversity of climate in different parts of the earth. None of Holywood's writings added anything new to medieval knowledge, but all presented current views so clearly and understandably that they enjoyed wide circulation and lasting influence. They were the medieval equivalent of today's most successful scientific textbooks. For the remainder of the Middle Ages and during the sixteenth and part of the seventeenth century, most English students learned the basis of their astronomy, either directly or indirectly, from Holywood's *Sphaera*.

Holywood belonged to that generation of western European scholars which first had the advantage of studying Greek and Arabic texts in convenient Latin translations. During the middle and later decades of the twelfth century, pioneering scholars such as Adelard of Bath, Robert of Chester, and Gerard of Cremona had spent years in Spain or Sicily busily copying and translating Arabic manuscripts. By the end of that century most centres of learning in northwest Europe had begun collecting libraries of these texts, and before long enthusiastic scholars were learning Greek in order to study in the original language some of the 'new' Greek texts which had reached western Europe by way of the Arabic world. Albertus Magnus, Robert Grosseteste, and

Alexander of Hales, all contemporaries of Holywood, were conspicuous among those who set about the twin tasks of teaching the new knowledge to the rising generation and of assimilating it into existing Christian philosophy and belief.

Astronomy was part of the quadrivium, the four more advanced subjects which all university students had to read for their first degree. Three years spent in teaching and studying grammar bridged the gap between B.A. and M.A., and then the brightest and most ambitious scholars usually pressed on to study medicine, canon law, or theology, the last of which was generally acknowledged to be the crowning glory of all human learning. But these advanced scholars did not necessarily lose interest in astronomy and the other sciences; indeed for them astronomy and mathematics had as much in common with theology and medicine as they had with one another. Medieval academics were not specialists in the modern sense of that word. They believed knowledge to be indivisible, and they desired and attempted to create a *summa* or synthesis of all that God had revealed to human understanding.

The universe described by Holywood derived from the thought of Aristotle, but before Aristotle's theories had reached Holywood they had been revised by Ptolemy of Alexandria, the second-century astronomer, mathematician, and cartographer, and later interpreted in Christian terms by western scholars. Contrary to widely-held belief, educated people of the Middle Ages did not think the earth was flat; they knew it to be spherical. They accepted Aristotle's axiom that the sphere was the most perfect of shapes, and did not question his fundamental reasoning that the universe consisted of a number of concentric spheres wrapped round a fixed, spherical earth. Aristotle's work in the fourth century B.C. had been a contribution to the growing body of scientific knowledge which the Greeks were steadily accumulating. In his own view his description of the universe was an interim report, the best that could be put forward in the then present state of human knowledge. He admitted that it was not all his own work; like Newton in a much later age he saw himself as standing on other men's shoulders – the shoulders of Pythagoras, Eudoxus, and Plato in particular – and he expected that younger scholars would eventually stand on his. But the medievalists put Aristotle on so high a pedestal that it was impossible for any of their own scholars to surmount him. The few who questioned a particular fact here or a speculation there made no headway at all. Their criticism could be refuted by the mere mention of his name.

Ptolemy's contribution had been to refine the picture of the Aristotelian universe before it reached western Europe. He had added significant details here and there, and had used such ingenious mathematical explanations as eccentric circles and epicycles to make the revised picture accord with the observed, astronomical facts. His *Almagest* is a complicated work: the mathematical arguments in it go well beyond Greek arguments, but the basic concept remains Aristotelian. Round the static earth Ptolemy numbered nine concentric spheres. The one nearest to man was the orbit of the moon; then, in ever-increasing circles, there followed the orbits of Mercury, Venus, the Sun, Mars, Jupiter, and Saturn. Careful observation of the planets had determined the order of the orbits: of any two bodies traversing the sky, the one which appeared to move the faster was deemed to be nearer the earth. By the same reasoning, Ptolemy allotted the eighth sphere to the stars, but the ninth, the outside sphere of all, he considered the most mysterious and unknowable. He called it the first moved, *primum mobile*, and attributed to it the task of directing the rest of the universe. Christendom assumed *primum mobile* to be the realm of God, the creator of the heavens and the earth – '. . . Thy heavens, the work of Thy fingers, the moon and the stars which Thou hast ordained . . .' – and most medieval

Christians explained the movement of the stars and planets across the firmament by inventing bands of angels, first, second, and third class, to propel them.

The theory that greater spheres controlled lesser spheres applied to every section of the universe: the fixed stars directed the movement of the planets, and, in turn, the planets determined what happened on earth. From east to west the stars moved steadily, majestically, and predictably round their orbit. Men argued from this that they must have kept for themselves the control of such regular, unchanging cycles as night and day, the succession of the seasons, and the sequence of growth, maturity, and death. The planets, however, followed haphazard courses across the sky, and by similar reasoning men held that the stars must have entrusted to them the ordering of sudden death, plague, revolution, unexpected prosperity, and all the other uncertainties of human life. To study the movements of the planets, therefore, was tantamount to studying human destiny. The key to understanding seemed to lie partly in careful and regular observation of the sky – and this led to some accurate forecasting of eclipses and equally accurate sun, moon, and tide tables – and partly in the right interpretation of the signs of the zodiac.

The Babylonians of later Old Testament times were probably the first 'westerners' to study the apparent movements of the sun, moon, and planets against the background of the twelve zodiacal constellations of stars. The moon completed thirteen, and the sun one circuit each revolution of the firmament – that is, each year. Every one of their circuits took sun or moon through all twelve signs, and since they both moved at a steady rate and since each sign of the zodiac dominated exactly one twelfth of the heavens, sun and moon both spent the same number of hours each year in each sign. But the irregularly-moving planets did not. Not only did they take vastly different times to make their circuits, but also they moved at different speeds through different signs. They would linger in one and hasten through another. This erratic movement of the planets across the night sky, together with the numerous possible conjunctions of planets, moon, and sun in one or other of the twelve zodiacal signs, has remained the lore of astrologers and soothsayers from the streets of ancient Babylon to the columns of present-day Sunday newspapers. During the last three centuries of the Middle Ages and for many decades afterwards, intelligent men believed that, if only they had the wit to comprehend and interpret, they could foresee their destiny in the patterns which God created in 'this majestical roof fretted with golden fire'. Kings and noblemen consulted astrologers before venturing on expeditions. Doctors studied the stars so that they would know when best to physic or operate on their patients – Chaucer's 'very perfect practitioner' was 'grounded in astronomy' – and scientists as remarkable as the group at Merton College, Oxford, in the fourteenth century did not doubt that the movements of the heavenly bodies in the macrocosm of the firmament determined what would happen to mankind in the microcosm of the earth.

Medieval theories of the cosmos were further complicated by the belief that all 'elementary' or terrestrial matter was compounded of four elements, earth, water, air, and fire, each of which had its natural place in the universe and a compelling urge to gravitate or levitate there. Fire, 'pure and not turbid', could rise as far as the orbit of the moon, which marked the boundary between the 'elementary' and the 'ethereal' regions. Air's natural home lay between the sphere of fire and the surface of the earth, and water would have covered the face of the whole earth had not God empowered the dry land 'to stay the sea's tide to protect the life of animate beings'. Outside the moon's orbit everything was made of 'the fifth essence', lucid, invariable, and in no way subject to change, decay, or death. God made man in His own image, taught the Church, and He gave him a soul, a tiny spark of fifth essence, which after death and purgatory soared from the sublunary, mortal world to the ethereal regions above. But unexpiated sin could prevent this joyous release: the souls of the damned were condemned to sink to Hell in the bowels of the earth.

Only gradually over the years was this orthodox view of the universe modified. For all but a handful of scholars Holywood's *Sphaera* remained totally acceptable until the mid seventeenth century. Yet from the beginning there had been independent thinkers who had challenged its premises and arguments. Two generations after Aristotle, Aristarchus of Samos, developing the work of Philolaus of Tarentum, a scientist working in the fifth century B.C., was already arguing that the earth revolved on its own axis and travelled round the sun. The Arabs preserved, if they did not develop, such minority views, so that a few medieval scholars had the opportunity to study them sympathetically. In fourteenth-century Paris, Nicholas Oresme defended the theories of Aristarchus, in so much as he demonstrated that neither observation nor logic could prove them wrong. He revealed the falsity of the standard arguments by which the orthodox 'proved' that the world was a static sphere, but then went on to say that faith and faith alone impelled him to recognize the world as the unmoving centre of the universe. Twice the psalmist had declared that 'the world is stablished and it cannot be moved', and for Oresme no scientific argument however persuasive could overthrow so strong an authority. Jean Buridan, a contemporary of Oresme, rejected the generally accepted proposition that angels kept the stars and planets moving round their orbits. He put forward a theory of impetus to replace it. In the following century a German, Nicholas of Cusa, questioned the concept of a finite cosmos. If there were limits to the outer sphere, he asked, what lay beyond? There could not be a dividing line separating the universe from *nothing*, and yet, if the universe was limitless in extent, how could the earth or anything else be a centre?

During the first half of the sixteenth century, Copernicus, a Pole, approached still nearer to the truth by claiming that the sun was the centre of the universe and that the earth, with its orbital moon, moved round it. But he did not abandon the general notion of concentric spheres forming a finite universe. In Denmark later in the same century, Tycho Brahe's careful observations of a new star and of the movements of a comet led him to reject the belief that the ethereal region suffered no change, and Bruno, a Neapolitan philosopher who perished at the stake in 1600, put forward the revolutionary view that the universe was infinite both in space and time, that no planet or sun formed the hub, and that the stars were all at vast but greatly differing distances from the earth. In 1609, Kepler, a German and one of Tycho Brahe's pupils, published his *New Astronomy*, in which, among descriptions of observed phenomena concerned with the 'mutual attraction' of solid objects, he both asserted that the planets moved round the sun in ellipses, and offered a new mathematical explanation of their apparently irregular motion. In the very same year, the Italian, Galileo, began to study the heavens through his improved telescope. His many discoveries, including 'new' stars, Jupiter's satellites, and the rotation of the sun, enabled him to endorse both the Copernican view that the earth travelled round the sun, and Tycho Brahe's belief that no part of the universe was immune from change. He carried forward Bruno's propositions by arguing that space contained more universes than the earth-universe centred on the sun. At last, thanks to these and other efforts of many different thinkers and observers, the scientific revolution was under way. The new scientists of seventeenth-century Europe readily dismissed John Holywood's *Sphaera* as outdated legend, but the poets and romantics — to say nothing of the astrologers and Christian fundamentalists — still found its neat theories far more acceptable than the difficult mathematical concepts of the new astronomy.

\*

The *Tractatus de Sphaera*, or *Sphaera mundi*, exists in many early manuscripts, either singly or with Holywood's two textbooks in mathematics, the *Compotus* and the *Algorismus*; it also appears in collection with other astronomical works, such as the rival *Sphaera* of Robert Grosseteste, or with standard works in other fields, such as Roger Bacon's Greek and Hebrew grammars.

Lynn Thorndike, *The Sphere of Sacrobosco and its Commentators* (Chicago, 1949), prints a Latin text, based on the collation of eighteen manuscripts of the late thirteenth to the fifteenth centuries, together with a translation from which the following extracts are taken.

The *Sphaera* was first printed at Ferrara in 1472, and many editions from Italian presses appeared over the next few years. By 1501 there were at least thirty editions, and another 200 by 1600, in the original Latin or in translation. There is testimony to Holywood's influence from the thirteenth to the sixteenth century in Lynn Thorndike's *A History of Magic and Experimental Science*, 8 vols. (New York, 1923–58), vols. V and VI; and by F. R. Johnson, 'Astronomical Text-books in the Sixteenth Century', and Herbert Dingle, 'Astronomy in the Sixteenth and Seventeenth Centuries'. Both of these articles appear in *Science, Medicine and History: essays . . . in honour of Charles Singer*, ed. E. Ashworth Underwood, 2 vols. (1953), vol. I, 285–302 and 455–68 respectively.

There are useful accounts of medieval astronomy and of medieval scientific thought generally in Charles Singer, *A Short History of Scientific Ideas to 1900* (1959); A. C.

Crombie, *Augustine to Galileo*, 2 vols., 2nd ed. (1961); and S. Toulmin and J. Goodfield, *The Fabric of the Heavens* (1961).

# 8. THE COSMOGRAPHY OF JOHN HOLYWOOD

## Chapter 1

SPHERE DEFINED  A sphere is thus described by Euclid: a sphere is the transit of the circumference of a half-circle upon a fixed diameter until it revolves back to its original position. That is, a sphere is such a round and solid body as is described by the revolution of a semicircular arc.

By Theodosius a sphere is described thus: a sphere is a solid body contained within a single surface, in the middle of which there is a point from which all straight lines drawn to the circumference are equal, and that point is called the 'centre of the sphere'. Moreover, a straight line passing through the centre of the sphere, with its ends touching the circumference in opposite directions, is called the 'axis of the sphere'. And the two ends of the axis are called the 'poles of the world'.

SPHERE DIVIDED  The sphere is divided in two ways, by substance and by accident. By substance it is divided into the ninth sphere, which is called the 'first moved' or the *primum mobile*; and the sphere of the fixed stars, which is named the 'firmament'; and the seven spheres of the seven planets, of which some are larger, some smaller, according as they the more approach or recede from the firmament. Wherefore, among them the sphere of Saturn is the largest, the sphere of the moon the smallest.

By accident the sphere is divided into the *sphere right* and the *sphere oblique*. For those are said to have the sphere right who dwell at the equator, if anyone can live there. And it is called 'right' because neither pole is elevated more for them than the other [because they are equidistant from the two poles of the earth and from the two poles of the celestial sphere which is on the same axis and has the earth as its centre], or because their horizon intersects the equinoctial circle and is intersected by it at spherical right angles. Those are said to have the sphere oblique who live this side of the equator or beyond it. For to them one pole is always raised above the horizon, and the other is always depressed below it. Or it is because their artificial horizon intersects the equinoctial at oblique and unequal angles.

THE FOUR ELEMENTS   The machine of the universe is divided into two, the ethereal and the elementary region. The elementary region, existing subject to continual alteration, is divided into four. For there is earth, placed, as it were, as the centre, in the middle of all, about which is water, about water air, about air fire, which is pure and not turbid there and reaches to the sphere

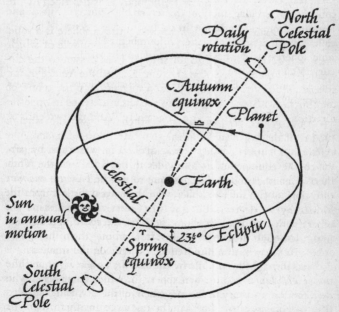

FIGURE I. *The Celestial Sphere.* The circle marked *Celestial* is the equator of the celestial sphere and is called by Holywood *equinoctial circle* (p. 145). Sun, moon, and planets move at different speeds round the ecliptic circle against the movement of the firmament (p. 140).

139

of the moon, as Aristotle says in his book of *Meteorology*. For so God, the glorious and sublime, disposed. And these are called the 'four elements' which are in turn by themselves altered, corrupted, and regenerated. The elements are also simple bodies which cannot be subdivided into parts of diverse forms and from whose commixture are produced various species of generated things. Three of them, in turn, surround the earth on all sides spherically, except in so far as the dry land stays the sea's tide to protect the life of animate beings. All, too, are mobile except earth which, as the centre of the world, by its weight in every direction equally avoiding the great motion of the extremes, as a round body occupies the middle of the sphere.

THE HEAVENS   Around the elementary region revolves with continuous circular motion the ethereal, which is lucid and immune from all variation in its immutable essence. And it is called 'Fifth Essence' by the philosophers. Of which there are nine spheres, as we have just said: namely, of the moon, Mercury, Venus, the sun, Mars, Jupiter, Saturn, the fixed stars, and the last heaven. Each of these spheres incloses its inferior spherically.

THEIR MOVEMENTS   And of these there are two movements. One is of the last heaven on the two extremities of its axis, the Arctic and Antarctic poles, from east through west to east again, which the equinoctial circle divides through the middle. Then there is another movement, oblique to this and in the opposite direction, of the inferior spheres on their axes, distant from the former by 23 degrees. But the first movement carries all the others with it in its rush about the earth once within a day and night, although they strive against it, as in the case of the eighth sphere one degree in a hundred years. This second movement is divided through the middle by the zodiac, under which each of the seven planets has its own sphere, in which it is borne by its own motion, contrary to the movement of the sky, and completes it in varying spaces of time – in the case of Saturn in thirty years, Jupiter in twelve years, Mars in two, the sun in 365 days and six hours, Venus and Mercury about the same, the moon in twenty-seven days and eight hours.

**REVOLUTION OF THE HEAVENS FROM EAST TO WEST** That the sky revolves from east to west is signified by the fact that the stars, which rise in the east, mount gradually and successively until they reach mid-sky and are always at the same distance apart, and, thus maintaining their relative positions, they move towards their setting continuously and uniformly. Another indication is that the stars near the North Pole, which never set for us, move continuously and uniformly, describing their circles about the pole, and are always equally near or far from one another. Wherefore, from these two continuous movements of the stars, both those that set and those which do not, it is clear that the firmament is moved from east to west.

**THE HEAVENS SPHERICAL** There are three reasons why the sky is round: likeness, because the sensible world is made in the likeness of the archetype, in which there is neither end nor beginning; wherefore, in likeness to it the sensible world has a round shape, in which beginning or end cannot be distinguished. Convenience, because of all isoperimetric bodies the sphere is the largest and of all shapes the round is most capacious. Since largest and round, therefore the most capacious. Wherefore, since the world is all-containing, this shape was useful and convenient for it. Necessity, because if the world were of other form than round – say, trilateral, quadrilateral, or many-sided – it would follow that some space would be vacant and some body without a place, both of which are false, as is clear in the case of angles projecting and revolved.

**A FURTHER PROOF** Also, as Alfraganius [an Arab scholar of the ninth century] says, if the sky were flat, one part of it would be nearer to us than another, namely, that which is directly overhead. So when a star was there, it would be closer to us than when rising or setting. But those things which are closer to us seem larger. So the sun when in mid-sky should look larger than when rising or setting, whereas the opposite is the case; for the sun or another star looks bigger in the east or west than in mid-sky. But, since this is not really so, the reason for its seeming so is that in winter and the rainy season vapours rise between us and the sun or another star. And, since those vapours are diaphanous, they scatter our visual rays so that they do not apprehend the object in its true size, just as is the case with a penny dropped into a depth of limpid water, which appears larger than it actually is because of a like diffusion of rays.

THE EARTH A SPHERE That the earth, too, is round is shown thus. The signs and stars do not rise and set the same for all men everywhere but rise and set sooner for those in the east than for those in the west; and of this there is no other cause than the bulge of the earth. Moreover, celestial phenomena evidence that they rise sooner for orientals than for westerners. For one and the same eclipse of the moon which appears to us in the first hour of the night appears to orientals about the third hour of the night, which proves that they had night and sunset before we did, of which setting the bulge of the earth is the cause.

FURTHER PROOFS OF THIS That the earth has a bulge from north to south and vice versa is shown thus: to those living toward the north, certain stars are always visible, namely, those near the North Pole, while others which are near the South Pole are always concealed from them. If, then, anyone should proceed from the north southward, he might go so far that the stars which formerly were always visible to him now would tend toward their setting. And the farther south he went, the more they would be moved toward their setting. Again, that same man now could see stars which formerly had always been hidden from him. And the reverse would happen to anyone going from the south northward. The cause of this is simply the bulge of the earth. Again, if the earth were flat from east to west, the stars would rise as soon for westerners as for orientals, which is false. Also, if the earth were flat from north to south and vice versa, the stars which were always visible to anyone would continue to be so wherever he went, which is false. But it seems flat to human sight because it is so extensive.

SURFACE OF THE SEA SPHERICAL That the water has a bulge and is approximately round is shown thus: let a signal be set up on the sea-coast and a ship leave port and sail away so far that the eye of a person standing at the foot of the mast can no longer discern the signal. Yet if the ship is stopped, the eye of the same person, if he has climbed to the top of the mast, will see the signal clearly. Yet the eye of a person at the bottom of the mast ought to see the signal better than he who is at the top, as is shown by drawing straight lines from both to the signal. And there is no other explanation of this thing than the bulge of the water. For all other impediments are excluded, such as clouds and rising vapours.

Also, since water is a homogeneous body, the whole will act the same as its parts. But parts of water, as happens in the case of little drops and dew on herbs, naturally seek a round shape. Therefore, the whole, of which they are parts, will do so.

THE EARTH CENTRAL  That the earth is in the middle of the firmament is shown thus. To persons on the earth's surface the stars appear of the same size whether they are in mid-sky or just rising or about to set, and this is because the earth is equally distant from them. For if the earth were nearer to the firmament in one direction than in another, a person at that point of the earth's surface which was nearer to the firmament would not see half of the heavens. But this is contrary to Ptolemy and all the philosophers, who say that, wherever man lives, six signs [of the Zodiac] rise and six signs set, and half of the heavens is always visible and half hid from him.

AND A MERE POINT IN THE UNIVERSE  That same consideration is a sign that the earth is as a centre and point with respect to the firmament, since, if the earth were of any size compared with the firmament, it would not be possible to see half the heavens. Also, suppose a plane passed through the centre of the earth, dividing it and the firmament into equal halves. An eye at the earth's centre would see half the sky, and one on the earth's surface would see the same half. From which it is inferred that the magnitude of the earth from surface to centre is inappreciable and consequently, that the magnitude of the entire earth is inappreciable compared to the firmament. Also Alfraganius says that the least of the fixed stars which we can see is larger than the whole earth. But that star, compared with the firmament, is a mere point. Much more so is the earth, which is smaller than it.

THE EARTH IMMOBILE   That the earth is held immobile in the midst of all, although it is the heaviest, seems explicable thus. Every heavy thing tends towards the centre. Now the centre is a point in the middle of the firmament. Therefore, the earth, since it is heaviest, naturally tends toward that point. Also, whatever is moved from the middle toward the circumference ascends. Therefore, if the earth were moved from the middle toward the circumference it would be ascending, which is impossible.

MEASURING THE EARTH'S CIRCUMFERENCE   The total girth of the earth by the authority of the philosophers Ambrose [St Ambrose *c*. 340–97], Theodosius [of Bithynia, first century B.C.], and Eratosthenes [a Greek mathematician of the third century B.C.] is defined as comprising 252,000 stades,[1] which is allowing 700 stades for each of the 360 parts of the zodiac. For let one take an astrolabe on a clear starry night and, sighting the pole through both apertures in the indicator, note the number of degrees where it is. Then let our measurer of the cosmos proceed directly north until on another clear night, observing the pole as before, the indicator stands a degree higher. After this let the extent of his travel be measured, and it will be found to be 700 stades. Then, allowing this number of stades for each of 360 degrees, the girth of the earth is found.

AND DIAMETER   From these data, the diameter of the earth can be found thus by the rule for the circle and diameter. Subtract the twenty-second part from the circuit of the whole earth, and a third of the remainder – that is, 80,181 stades and a half and third part of one stade – will be the diameter or thickness of the terrestrial ball.

1. Although there is some doubt as to the exact modern equivalent of a stade, one commonly accepted value is that forty stades equal 12,000 royal Egyptian cubits of 52.5 cm. On this basis, Eratosthenes' estimate of 250,000 stades gives 24,662 miles, as against the correct figure for the earth's circumference of 24,900 miles.

## Chapter 2

### Of the Circles and Their Names

CELESTIAL CIRCLES  Of these circles some are larger, some smaller, as sense shows. For a great circle in the sphere is one which, described on the surface of the sphere about its centre, divides the sphere into two equal parts, while a small circle is one which, described on the surface of the sphere, divides it not into two equal but into two unequal portions.

THE EQUINOCTIAL  Of the great circles we must first mention the equinoctial. The equinoctial is a circle dividing the sphere into two equal parts and equidistant at its every point from either pole. And it is called 'equinoctial' because, when the sun crosses it, which happens twice a year, namely, in the beginning of Aries and in the beginning of Libra, there is equinox the world over. Wherefore it is termed the 'equator of day and night', because it makes the artificial day equal to the night. And it is called the 'belt of the first movement'.

THE TWO MOVEMENTS AGAIN  Be it understood that the 'first movement' means the movement of the *primum mobile*, that is, of the ninth sphere or last heaven, which movement is from east through west back to east again, which also is called 'rational motion' from resemblance to the rational motion in the microcosm, that is, in man, when thought goes from the Creator through creatures to the Creator and there rests.

The second movement is of the firmament and planets contrary to this, from west through east back to west again, which movement is called 'irrational' or 'sensual' from resemblance to the movement of the microcosm from things corruptible to the Creator and back again to things corruptible.

THE NORTH AND SOUTH POLES  It is called the 'belt of the first movement' because it divides the *primum mobile* or ninth space into two equal parts and is itself equally distant from the poles of the world. It is to be noted that the pole which is always visible to us is called 'septentrional', 'arctic', or 'boreal'. 'Septentrional' is from *septentrio*, that is, from Ursa Minor, which is derived from *septem* and *trion*. . . . 'Arctic' is derived from *arthos*, which is Ursa Major, for it is near Ursa Major. It is called

FIGURE 2. *Plan of the Universe by Peter Apian, a sixteenth-century astronomer*. Note that outside the *primum mobile* he assumes there is a static heaven, the abode of God and the elect.

'boreal', because it is where the wind Boreas comes from. The opposite pole is called 'Antarctic' as opposed to 'Arctic'. It is also called 'meridional' because it is to the south, and it is called 'austral' because it is where the wind Auster comes from. The two fixed points in the firmament are called the 'poles of the world' because they terminate the axis of the sphere and the world revolves on them. One of these poles is always visible to us, the other always hidden. Whence Virgil:

This vertex is ever about us, but that
Dark Styx and deep Manes [Hades] hold beneath our feet.[1]

THE ZODIAC   There is another circle in the sphere which intersects the equinoctial and is intersected by it into two equal parts. One half of it tips toward the north, the other toward the south. That circle is called 'zodiac' from *zoe*, meaning 'life', because all life in inferior things depends on the movements of the planets beneath it. Or it is derived from *zodias*, which means 'animal', because, since it is divided into twelve equal parts, each part is called a sign and has its particular name from the name of some animal, because of some property characteristic of it and of the animal, or because of the arrangement of the fixed stars there in the outline of that kind of animal. That circle in Latin is called *signifer* because it bears the 'signs' or because it is divided into them. By Aristotle in *On Generation and Corruption* it is called the 'oblique circle', where he says that, according to the access and recess of the sun in the oblique circle, are produced generations and corruptions in things below.

THE TWELVE SIGNS   The names, order, and number of the signs are set forth in these lines:

There are Aries, Taurus, Gemini, Cancer, Leo, Virgo
Libra and Scorpio, Architenens [Sagittarius], Caper
[Capricornus], Amphora [Aquarius], Pisces.

Moreover, each sign is divided into 30 degrees, whence it is clear that in the entire zodiac there are 360 degrees. Also, according to astronomers, each degree is divided into 60 minutes, each minute into 60 seconds, each second into 60 thirds, and so on.

1. *Georgics* I, 242–3.

And as the zodiac is divided by astronomers, so each circle in the sphere, whether great or small, is divided into similar parts.

While every circle in the sphere except the zodiac is understood to be a line or circumference, the zodiac alone is understood to be a surface, 12 degrees wide of degrees such as we have just mentioned. Wherefore, it is clear that certain persons in astrology lie who say that the signs are squares, unless they misuse this term and consider square and quadrangle the same. For each sign is 30 degrees in longitude, 12 in latitude.

THE ECLIPTIC  The line dividing the zodiac in its circuit, so that on one side it leaves 6 degrees and on the other side another 6, is called the 'ecliptic', since when sun and moon are on that line there occurs an eclipse of sun or moon. The sun always moves beneath the ecliptic, but all the other planets decline toward north or south; sometimes, however, they are beneath the ecliptic. The part of the zodiac which slants away from the equinoctial to the north is called 'northern' or 'boreal' or 'Arctic', and those six signs which extend from the beginning of Aries to the end of Virgo are called 'northern'. The other part of the zodiac which tips from the equinoctial toward the south is called 'meridional' or 'austral', and the six signs from the beginning of Libra to the end of Pisces are called 'meridional' or 'austral'.

EXTENDED USES OF 'SIGN'  When it is said that the sun is in Aries or in another sign, it should be understood that *in* is taken for *beneath* according as we now accept *sign*. In another meaning a sign is called a 'pyramid', whose quadrilateral base is that surface which we call a 'sign', whilst its apex is at the centre of the earth. And in this sense we may properly say that the planets are *in* signs. *Sign* may be used in a third way as produced by six circles passing through the poles of the zodiac and through the beginnings of the twelve signs. Those six circles divide the entire surface of the sphere into twelve parts, wide in the middle but narrower toward the poles, and each such part is called a 'sign' and has a particular name from the name of that sign which is intercepted between its two lines. And according to this usage stars which are near the poles are said to be 'in signs'. Also think of a body whose base is a sign in this last sense which we have accepted but whose edge is on the axis of the zodiac. Such a body is called a 'sign' in a fourth sense, according to which usage the whole world is divided into twelve equal parts, which are called 'signs', and so whatever is in the world is in some sign.

[The rest of Chapter 2 describes the remaining four great circles, the four smaller circles, and the five zones of the world. Chapter 3 explains why the signs of the zodiac rise and set, and why the different parts of the earth have differing lengths of day and night and distinctive climates.]

## Chapter 4

MOVEMENT OF THE SUN  It should be noted that the sun has a single circle in which it is moved in the plane of the ecliptic, and it is eccentric. Any circle is called 'eccentric' which, like that of the sun, dividing the earth into equal parts, does not have the same centre as the earth but one outside it. Moreover, the point in the eccentric which approaches closest to the firmament is called *aux* or *augis*, meaning 'elevation'. The opposite point, which is farthest removed from the firmament, is called the 'opposition' of the *aux*.

Moreover, there are two movements of the sun from west to east, one of which is its own in its eccentric, by which it is moved every day and night about sixty minutes. The other is the slower movement of the sphere itself on the poles of the axis of the circle of the signs, and it is equal to the movement of the sphere of the fixed stars, namely, 1 degree in a hundred years. From these two movements, then, is reckoned the sun's course in the circle of the signs from west to east, by which it cleaves the circle of the signs in 365 days and a fourth of one day, except for a small fraction which is imperceptible.

OF THE OTHER PLANETS: EQUANT, DEFERENT, AND EPICYCLE  Every planet except the sun has three circles, namely, equant, deferent, and epicycle. The equant of the moon is a circle concentric with the earth and in the plane of the ecliptic. Its deferent is an eccentric circle not in the plane of the ecliptic –

nay, one half of it slants toward the north and the other toward the south – and the deferent intersects the equant in two places, and the figure of that intersection is called the 'dragon' because it is wide in the middle and narrow toward the ends. That intersection, then, through which the moon is moved from south to north is called the 'head of the dragon', while the other intersection through which it is moved from north to south is called the 'tail of the dragon'. Deferent and equant of each planet are equal, and know that both deferent and equant of Saturn, Jupiter, Mars, Venus, and Mercury are eccentric and outside the plane of the ecliptic, and yet those two are in the same plane. Also, every planet except the sun has an epicycle. An epicycle is a small circle on whose circumference is carried the body of the planet, and the centre of the epicycle is always carried along the circumference of the deferent.

STATIONARY, DIRECT, AND RETROGRADE  If, then, two lines are drawn from the centre of the earth to include an epicycle, one on the east and the other on the west, the point of contact on the east is called the 'first station', while the point of contact to the west is called the 'second station'. And when a planet is in either of these stations it is called 'stationary'. The upper arc of the epicycle intercepted between those two stations is called 'direction', and when the planet is there it is called 'direct'. But the lower arc of the epicycle between the two stations is called 'retrogradation', and a planet existing there is called 'retrograde'. But the moon is not stationary, direct, or retrograde because of the swiftness of its motion in its epicycle.

CAUSE OF LUNAR ECLIPSE  Since the sun is larger than the earth, it is necessary that half the sphere of earth be always illuminated by the sun and that the shadow of the earth, extended into the air like a cone, diminish in circumference until it ends in the plane of the circle of the signs inseparable from the nadir of the sun. The nadir is a point in the firmament directly opposite to the sun. Hence, when the moon at full is in the head of the dragon beneath the nadir of the sun, then the earth is interposed between sun and moon, and the cone of the earth's shadow falls on the body of the moon. Wherefore, since the moon has no light except from the sun, it actually is deprived of light and there is a general eclipse, if it is in the head or tail of the dragon directly, but partial if it is almost within the bounds determined for eclipse. And it always happens at full moon or thereabouts. But, since in every opposition – that is, at full moon – the moon is not in the head or tail of the dragon or beneath the nadir of the sun, it is not necessary that the moon suffer eclipse at every full moon.

CAUSE OF SOLAR ECLIPSE When the moon is in the head or tail of the dragon or nearly within the limits and in conjunction with the sun, then the body of the moon is interposed between our sight and the body of the sun. Hence it will obscure the brightness of the sun for us, and so the sun will suffer eclipse – not that it ceases to shine but that it fails us because of the interposition of the moon between our sight and the sun. From these it is clear that a solar eclipse should always occur at the time of conjunction or new moon. And it is to be noted that when there is an eclipse of the moon, it is visible everywhere on earth. But when there is an eclipse of the sun, that is by no means so. Nay, it may be visible in one clime and not in another, which happens because of the different points of view in different climes. Whence, Virgil most aptly and concisely expresses the nature of either eclipse:

Varied defects of the moon, and of the sun travails.[1]

ECLIPSE DURING THE PASSION MIRACULOUS From the aforesaid it is also evident that when the sun was eclipsed during the Passion and the same Passion occurred at full moon, that eclipse was not natural – nay, it was miraculous and contrary to nature, since a solar eclipse ought to occur at new moon or thereabouts. On which account Dionysius the Areopagite is reported to have said during the same Passion, 'Either the God of nature suffers, or the mechanism of the universe is dissolved.'

1. *Georgics* II, 478.

# 9. *The Statute of Winchester, 1285*

If a gesithcund man [a soldier under oath to serve his lord] owning land should neglect his service with the fyrd, let him pay 120 shillings and forfeit his land; let one not owning land pay sixty shillings, and a ceorl thirty shillings as his penalty.

KING INE of Wessex issued this law about 690. It is part of the evidence which enables historians to assert that the obligation of Englishmen to serve in the fyrd or people's army is older than our oldest records. Anglo-Saxon kings had their body-guards and their small armies of picked warriors. These constituted the military élite. But every free subject in the realm, whatever his primary function, was legally bound, whenever the need arose, to take arms to defend his king and his homeland. This obligation he fulfilled by serving in the fyrd.

As Anglo-Saxon England gradually coalesced into a single kingdom, tradition and practical convenience trimmed the fyrd into shire units, each under the command of an ealdorman. The rank and file were peasants, far more handy with a sickle and plough than with a sword or spear. But in war they were stiffened with more regular soldiers and led by experienced thegns. The fyrd's chief task was to safeguard the shire from invasion, to suppress riots, and arrest criminals. Alfred used fyrd troops in his 'national' army, with which he harassed the invading Danes, but normally the fyrd did not serve beyond the boundaries of the shire. In Anglo-Saxon England it played a part similar to that of the home guard in the wartime Britain of 1939–45.

Unlike the English invaders of the sixth and seventh centuries and the Danish and Norse invaders of the ninth and tenth, the Normans came in insufficient numbers to colonize England. They had to conquer the country in Roman style, and with military strength impose their rule on a defeated, native population. For almost three centuries the law distinguished between the Normans, the first-class citizens, and the English, the second-class citizens, and not until the end of the twelfth century did this distinction begin to lose practical significance. Consequently, the first Norman kings had reason to suppress rather than encourage the fyrd. Their military tenants — Normans almost to a man — regularly supplied troops for body-guard, castle-holding, and other routine military chores, and when the crown wanted a larger force, it normally raised the feudal levy through the same feudal agents, the military tenants. But the Norman kings did not amend the law. All men capable of carrying arms were still liable for military service, whether they were bound by tenure or not, and on rare occasions when necessity demanded, the Normans raised the shire levies. The Conqueror himself used the fyrd of Worcester against the rebellious earl of Hereford. In 1088 the fyrd of several southern shires helped Rufus to suppress the rebellion led by Odo of Bayeux, and that of Yorkshire enabled archbishop Thurstan to disperse the Scottish invaders at the battle of the Standard in 1139.

It was not, however, until Henry II's Assize of Arms, conventionally attributed to the year 1181, that the crown redefined the Englishman's obligation to fight in defence of his home. Henry II confined his instructions to free men:

Every holder of a knight's fee shall possess a hauberk [coat of mail], helmet, shield, and lance [i.e. the full fighting equipment of a knight]. And every knight shall have as many hauberks, helmets, shields, and lances as he has knight's fees in his demesne.

Also, every free layman who is worth 16 marks in goods or rents shall possess a hauberk, helmet, shield, and lance. Also, every free layman who is worth 10 marks in goods or rents shall possess a mail shirt, iron headpiece, and lance.

Also, all burgesses and all freemen shall possess a quilted tunic, iron headpiece, and lance.

Each one of them shall swear that he will be in possession of these arms by the feast of St Hilary [13 January] and that he will bear allegiance to the lord king Henry (that is to the son of the Empress Matilda) and that he will use these arms in his service, in accordance with his commands, and in loyalty to the lord king and his realm.

If anyone bearing these arms shall have died, his arms shall pass to his heir . . . .

Any burgess who possesses more arms than he ought to possess according to this assize shall sell, give, or otherwise transfer them to some man who will keep them for use in the service of the lord king of England. None of them shall retain more arms than he ought to have according to this assize.

No Jew shall possess a hauberk or mail shirt . . . .

Except by the lord king's orders, no one shall take arms out of England, nor sell arms to anyone who will take them out of England . . . .

The king charged his itinerant justices to see that the assize was read in each shire, and at the same time, lest any one should escape his responsibilities, that local juries of knights and freemen compiled lists of those men in their hundred or borough who had 16 marks' worth of property and of those who had 10 marks' worth. All who were liable under the assize had to swear before the itinerant justices that they would be in possession of their arms by the following January. Those who were absent from their shire when the justices held their court had to appear before them later in another shire; if anyone failed to do that, he had a third opportunity at Westminster at Michaelmas, but, 'as he valued his life and all his possessions', it behoved him to make sure that he took this last chance.

The shire levy was essentially a royal army, and during

the next hundred years the crown took occasional opportunities to extend its scope and increase its usefulness. Already it had found that the feudal levy, with its traditional restrictions on length of service, was both clumsy for full-scale warfare and unreliable in the suppression of baronial revolt. Therefore, in 1233, when faced with the threat of widespread unrest following the fall of Hubert de Burgh, Henry III issued a writ of watch and ward, which called for new duties from the same men who were liable to serve in the shire levies. Henry required every vill to mount a regular guard throughout the hours of darkness, and to arrest any strangers who could not give an acceptable reason for travelling. He reissued this writ ten years later, and later still, in 1252, coupled it with a more elaborate Assize of Arms. In the first part of this comprehensive new order he laid it down that, from sunset to sunrise between Ascension Day and Michaelmas, six armed men should be on guard-duty at each gate of every walled city, that twelve armed burgesses should keep watch in every borough, and that either six or four, according to the size of the settlement, should patrol every vill. They were to arrest strangers or any suspicious characters, and raise the hue and cry if anyone resisted arrest or escaped from custody. The second half of the writ divided into five categories all 'citizens, burgesses, free tenants, villeins and others from fifteen to sixty years of age'. Those who held land worth £15 a year or possessed goods worth 60 marks were regarded as equivalent to knights, for each had to possess a coat of mail, helmet, sword, dagger, and horse. Those with land worth £10 or goods worth 40 marks had to equip themselves with a shirt of mail, iron head-piece, sword, and dagger; those worth £5 in land or 20 marks in goods with a quilted tunic, iron head-piece, sword, lance, and dagger, and those worth £2 in land or 9 marks in goods with a sword, knife, and bow and arrows. Unlike Henry II's Assize of Arms, Henry III's writ included 'villeins and others', the unfree as well as the free, and ordained that those men not rich enough to qualify even for the fourth category should arm themselves with a scythe, halberd, knife, and 'other small weapons'. The third and last section of the writ outlined the administrative machinery by which the first two sections were to be put into operation.

Henry III's edict reads as a business-like instruction should read. It is precise in its requirements, and apparently logical in the way it proposed to supervise the enforcement of its provisions. But it failed lamentably to ensure law and order. The next twenty turbulent years included the major baronial revolt led by Simon de Montfort, and even after Edward I had re-established firm government at the centre, far too many bandits were terrorizing the countryside. The Welsh wars made matters no better; they turned more disbanded soldiers into potential criminals. By the Statute of Winchester the crown once again attempted to improve conditions by using the ordinary citizen as a policeman and as a soldier. Edward I's more immediate requirement was an efficient organization for the pursuit and arrest of criminals, but equally important were those sections of the statute which were concerned with the enlistment of men for military service.

The statute was based upon tradition and existing law. It broke new ground, but every one of its new provisions was a logical extension of what the law already required. It left unaltered the age range of men liable for service, and only slightly amended the 1252 equipment of the five classes of landholders. But in order to see that the law was fully observed, the new statute arranged for a view of arms twice a year, and held a hierarchy of constables responsible for presenting defaulters before the king's justices. It still regarded the shire levy as a local defence force, but it instructed the constables to prepare muster rolls for each township, hundred, and shire, so that commissioners of array could quickly pick out suitable men to serve the king outside the shire, and maybe overseas. In practice such troops were usually few in number. Edward I undertook to pay them as he paid indentured troops, but in the next century protracted disputes occurred about how far the shire should help to maintain them.

Against crime the statute organized a coordinated plan of campaign. Hitherto, the local watch and ward had been satisfied to see malefactors clear out of its area. It had shown no zeal to pursue them beyond its boundaries, with the obvious result that many felons escaped arrest and punishment all too easily. The Statute of Winchester hoped to counter this by widening every township's responsibility: for every criminal who escaped arrest, it proposed to levy a collective fine upon the hundred in which the crime was committed. Further, to deprive lurking or escaping criminals of ready cover, it ordered local landholders to cut back the brushwood along the royal highways to a distance of 200 feet.

From among local landholders the shire court appointed conservators or guardians of the peace to ensure that the statute was enforced. These unpaid officers were the forerunners of the justices of the peace, who, from the mid fourteenth century, as royal nominees, shouldered an ever-increasing responsibility for shire administration and the maintenance of local law and order. The parish constable, the high constable of the hundred, and the captain of the shire levy, whom Henry VIII later raised to the dignity of lord lieutenant, also had long and busy futures ahead. So had the statute itself, for though the governments of Henry IV, Mary Tudor, James I, and Charles II successively modified details, the essential provisions of the Statute of Winchester only began to become redundant after Charles II had established a regular army, after the Hanoverians had transformed selected militia men into reserve units, and after Victorian county and borough authorities had set up regular police forces.

*

The Norman-French text of the Statute of Winchester is printed in *Statutes of the Realm*, Record Commissioners (1810–28), vol. I, 96–8, from the original Statute Roll, but with damaged sections of the original supplied from other early copies, notably Close Roll 5 Richard II, which contains a writ from Richard II to the sheriffs of London, commanding the proclamation and observance of Edward I's statute.

This conflated text is reproduced by W. Stubbs, *Select Charters* (1913), 464–9, and has been followed in the present translation.

## 9. THE STATUTE OF WINCHESTER, 1285

(1) Robberies, murders, and acts of arson are now daily happenings and are occurring with greater frequency than ever before; and felonies cannot be brought home to those responsible for them upon the sworn testimony of jurors, who are more inclined to allow felonies committed against strangers to go unpunished than to indict offenders, since these, for the most part, are people of their own district, and even if the offenders are from another part of the country, those who harbour them are local men. They are encouraged to do this because jurors, and the districts where felonies are committed, are nowadays allowed to make their sworn statements of fact without concerning themselves about damages, since no penalty has so far been prescribed against them if they conceal anything or are lax in their duty. Our lord the king has therefore established a penalty in such cases to break down the power of felons, so that jurors who might not be afraid to perjure themselves will be deterred, by fear of the penalty which he prescribes, from sparing anyone in future or from concealing any felony.

The king commands that this penalty shall be solemnly proclaimed in every county, hundred, march [a border district between two or more jurisdictions], fair, and in every other place where people meet formally together, so that no one may excuse himself by a plea of ignorance, and so that the peace may be so well kept for the future in every part of the country that no sooner is a robbery or felony committed than an immediate pursuit is made after the criminals from vill to vill and from one district to the next.

(2) Inquests shall be held, as the need arises, to secure the indictment of offenders. They shall be first held in the vills, by the lords of the vills, and then in the hundreds and franchises [areas of independent jurisdiction], and in the counties. If felonies have been committed on the borders of two, three, or four counties, an inquest shall be held in each county.

The penalty which is prescribed is that, where a district fails by these methods to produce the criminals, its inhabitants shall answer for the robberies committed and for the damages sustained from other kinds of felony. A district shall be taken as the whole hundred within which the robbery was committed, together with the franchises which lie within it; and if the robbery was committed on the borders of two hundreds, both hundreds shall be answerable, together with the franchises which lie within them. They will only be allowed forty days after the commission of a robbery or felony within which either to make satisfaction for the robbery or other crime, or else to produce the criminals.

(3) The king does not wish that some should think him harsh because people are suddenly impoverished by the imposition of this penalty with immediate effect. He therefore allows that the penalty shall not begin to operate at once, but that its taking effect shall be deferred until next Easter. He will see how the country conducts itself for the intervening period and whether there is a reduction in the number of robberies and felonies committed. But once this time has elapsed, all men may be sure that the prescribed penalty will be generally enforced and that each district, which is to say its inhabitants, will be answerable for robberies and felonies committed within its area.

(4) To establish law and order more securely through the land, the king has commanded that the gates of towns which have walls shall be closed from sunset to sunrise; and that no one shall be given lodging in the suburbs or outlying parts of a town except during the day, and then only if the host is prepared to accept responsibility for his guest. By the king's further command, the town bailiffs shall make inquiries once a week, or at least once a fortnight, about persons given lodging in the suburbs or outlying parts; and if they find that anyone is providing lodging or giving any kind of hospitality to persons suspected of criminal acts or intent, the bailiffs shall enforce the law.

It is commanded for the future that watch shall be kept in the way that was long customary in the past, namely, from Ascension Day to Michaelmas Day, in a city by six men at each gate, and in each whole vill by six or four men, according to the number of the inhabitants. The watch shall be kept continuously throughout the night, from sunset to sunrise. If any stranger passes the watch, he shall be held until sunrise and then released if nothing suspicious is found against him: but if there are grounds for suspicion, he shall immediately be handed over to the sheriff, who shall receive him without question and keep him in safe custody until such time as he is properly released. If any stranger will not surrender to the watch, a hue and cry shall be raised against him and the watch shall pursue him with the whole vill and the vills adjoining; and a hue and cry shall be raised from vill to vill until he is taken and handed over to the sheriff, as was before provided. No one shall be punished because of arresting such a stranger.

(5) The highways leading from one market town to another shall be widened. Where there are trees, or hedges, or ditches within a distance of 200 feet on either side of the way, they shall be removed, so that no one may make use of their cover to lurk by the wayside with criminal intent. But oaks and large trees shall not be felled, provided there is clear space beneath them.

If a lord fails in his duty and wilfully refuses to fill in ditches or clear undergrowth and bushes, and robberies are then committed, he shall be liable for damages; and if it is a case of murder, he shall be fined at the king's pleasure. But if the lord has not the means to clear the undergrowth himself, the country around shall help him.

It is the king's will that ways through his own demesne lands and woods, whether within a forest or not, shall be similarly widened.

If a lord's park comes close to the highway, he shall take back the park boundary until it is clear from the highway by the required 200 feet, or else he shall build a wall, or make a hedge or ditch which is so substantial that evil-doers cannot escape across it or come back over it to commit an offence.

(6) Every man shall have weapons and equipment in his house to keep the peace, in accordance with the ancient assize [Assize of Arms]. Namely, each man between the ages of fifteen and sixty shall be assessed and sworn to arms on a scale according to the value of his lands or chattels. Those who have lands to the value of £15, or chattels to the value of 40 marks, shall provide themselves with a hauberk, a cap of iron [*chapel de fer*, or *chapawe*], a sword, a dagger, and a horse; those with lands to the value of £10, or chattels to the value of 20 marks, a hauberk of mail, cap, sword, and dagger; land to the value of £5, a parpoint [padded doublet, or *wambais*], cap of iron, sword, and dagger; lands to a value of between £2 and £5, a sword, bow, arrows, and a dagger. Anyone whose lands are of less value than £2 shall be sworn to provide gisarmes [long-handled weapons with curved blade and spike], daggers, and other cheap weapons; and similarly those with chattels of less value than 20 marks shall be sworn to provide swords, daggers, and other cheap weapons. Anyone else who can afford them shall keep bows and arrows, if resident outside a forest, and bows and bolts [blunt-headed arrows] if resident within one.

Arms shall be inspected twice a year. In each hundred and franchise two constables shall be chosen to make the inspection, and they shall report to the justices specially assigned for this purpose, when they visit the district, any failures to provide arms which they have discovered, and any remissness in the pursuit of criminals by the watch, or in the widening of highways. They shall make presentment also concerning those who give lodging to strangers in upland [outlying] communities, without being prepared to accept responsibility for them. The justices, in their turn, shall present these defaults to the king in each parliament, and the king will correct them.

Sheriffs, bailiffs of franchises and other bailiffs, great and small alike, who have bailiwicks and forests in their charge, in fee [hereditary] or otherwise, shall take good care for the future that they join with their districts in the hue and cry after criminals. They shall keep arms and horses for this purpose, on a scale of provision determined by their official status; and if any of them fails in his duty, his default shall be reported to the justices by the constables, and by the justices to the king, following the same procedure as before.

The king commands, for the honour of Holy Church, that no fair or market shall in future be held in a burial-ground.

Given at Winchester on the 8th day of October in the thirteenth year of the king's reign.

# 10. Modus Tenendi Parliamentum – *How to hold a Parliament*

To estimate the worth of a manuscript a historian must find out, if he can, who wrote it, in what circumstances, with what authority or special knowledge, and for what purpose. This is sometimes most difficult to do. Apart from administrative and judicial records, few original medieval manuscripts have survived. Their text remains alive in copies, and human fallibility being what it is, copies are rarely identical either with one another, or, it is fair to assume, with the missing original. Copies of a faulty copy perpetuate mistakes. Occasionally these mistakes are serious corruptions of the original; more often, fortunately, they consist of relatively minor omissions, additions, and changes of text.

The earliest surviving copy of *Modus Tenendi Parliamentum* appears to have been written in the last decade of the fourteenth century. Some twenty-five extant copies were written before the reign of Henry VIII. Most are in Latin, but four are in English and two in French. They fall into two groups, which Maude Clarke in her *Medieval Representation and Consent* labelled A and B. The chief difference between them is the order in which the sections or chapters of the manuscript are listed, and most, but not all, scholars believe that A, which is quoted in translation below, is nearer to the original text. When the *Modus* was first written is another debatable point. All that can be said with certainty is that it belongs to the fourteenth century, and that it is likely to have been written about 1320. No particular name is associated with the document. The author was obviously someone, or just possibly two or three men, actively concerned with parliamentary business: the interest he displays, in chapters 15, 16, and 25, in the status and work of the clerks, and the details he gives about procedure suggest the tidy mind and professional interest of an administrator. In a paper which he published in 1953 in the *Journal of the Warburg and Courtauld Institutes,* V. H. Galbraith suggested that the author might have been William Ayreminne, keeper of the rolls of chancery from 1316 to 1324 and, later, bishop of Norwich and treasurer to Edward III. He could well be right. Almost certainly the author was someone with Ayreminne's type of experience and interests.

The historical value of the *Modus* is a third matter for dispute. It is clear that it is not as detached or factual a description of existing practice as are the two twelfth-century guides for administrators, *The Establishment of the King's Household* and *The Dialogue of the Exchequer.* It is far less restricted in its intention: the enthusiasm of the author leads him in the first lines to make an absurd claim for the antiquity of parliament, and in the remainder of the document to describe fourteenth-century parliaments as, in his eyes, they ought to be rather than as they were. The first of these two faults, exaggeration coupled with a lack of historical accuracy and perspective, the author shares with almost all medieval chroniclers and historians; the second, excited partisanship and persuasive proposals, is itself of historical value in that it shows that, early in the life of the English parliament, one man at least realized the significance and potential importance of some of the changes that were gradually taking place. During the reigns of the three Edwards, representatives of counties and boroughs were steadily building the machinery and establishing the precedents of the form of government which was later to be hailed as the model for constitutional monarchies. The author of the *Modus* appears to have had a clearer view of what was happening – or of what he hoped was going to happen – than most of his contemporaries. His own purpose may well have been limited to bolstering the cause of Thomas of Lancaster and the Ordainers against Edward II or to bringing more power and prestige to parliamentary officials, but, later in the century, certain of his statements, especially those connected with the limitation of the royal prerogative and the commons' claim to be the sole voter of taxes, suited the aspirations of far more English people than a coterie of rebellious barons or a handful of ambitious clerks. That was why so many scribes troubled to copy out his manuscript during the next century. If he did not describe parliamentary government as it actually existed in the reign of Edward II, he produced a blue print of parliamentary government as it well could be.

The records of the activities of the early parliaments lack many details which historians would like to have, but there are sufficient established facts against which to measure the text of the *Modus*. Quite rightly the document stresses the supreme function of the crown – 'the king is the head, the beginning, and the end of parliament' – and just as historically correct is the difference in status which it draws between the archbishops, bishops, abbots, priors, earls, and barons, who claimed to be summoned to parliament 'in right of their tenure', and the proctors (who represented the lesser clergy), knights of the shire, citizens, and burgesses, all of whom were present as summoned representatives. But the graded list of fines for non-attendance (Chapter 9) and the complicated method of resolving difficult problems (Chapter 17) are the author's recommendations and not descriptions of existing practice, just as the roles played by the commons (Chapter 23) and the impressive staff of clerks (Chapters 15 and 16) were, in Edward II's reign, more hope and aspiration than sober fact. Chapter 23 is a mixture of falsehood and prophecy. 'The kings of those days' who held their parliaments before the advent of bishops, earls, or barons never existed, and the day had still to dawn when 'two knights representing a county in Parliament have a greater voice in Parliament in granting and refusing an aid than a lord earl of England'. Throughout the fourteenth century, the commons remained far and away the least important of the three estates. The knights and the burgesses recognized this, and there is no evidence to show that as a class they resented the aristocratic England in which they lived. It would be most misleading to endow them with the ideas and ambitions of a later age. Nevertheless, the *Modus* proves that at least one early-fourteenth-century man, a civil servant and not a politician, perceived the possibility of a shift of power, and there is no gainsaying that both the stature of parliament and the authority of the commons grew considerably during the politically stormy reign of Edward II.

The practice of the king summoning a meeting of representatives of the common people can be traced back to the early years of the thirteenth century. In 1213, for example, John instructed the sheriff of each shire to send four men to Oxford to attend a council meeting in order to discuss matters 'concerning our kingdom', and in 1254 Henry III called together a representative meeting of lesser clergy and knights of the shire to vote him an aid for military expenses in Gascony. To strengthen his new government, Simon de Montfort assembled his famous parliament of 1265, which contained knights from the shires and burgesses from a selected number of boroughs, and Edward I, as his reign advanced, more frequently summoned shire, borough, and lower clergy representatives to attend his councils. Edward followed no set pattern. He only sent writs to those groups which he thought would further the particular purpose he had in hand, but the parliament of 1295, to which he brought knights of the shire, burgesses, and clerical proctors, retrospectively earned the title *model*.

Edward I summoned clergy and barons 'to negotiate and

advise', and knights and burgesses 'to consent to and carry out what parliament decided'. The proctors soon began to decline invitations to sit in parliament, because it was a secular assembly. They preferred to think that any taxes they paid were gifts granted in charity, and therefore, despite continued summonses to attend parliament – and despite the personal opinion of our author – they absented themselves. Instead they voted their money to the king in convocation. But the archbishops, bishops, and a reduced number of abbots and priors, all summoned as tenants in chief by individual writs, continued to sit alongside the earls and barons and those court officials and law officers whom the king deemed it prudent to have present. In a separate place the shire knights, summoned through the sheriff and nominated by the shire court, sat with the burgesses, who were usually chosen by the influential men of their borough. The crown paid both of them wages: the knights four shillings and the burgesses two shillings for every day spent either in travelling or in attendance, which was far below the half mark a day which the *Modus* recommends for both knights and the citizen representatives of London and the bigger towns. The shires were punctilious in obeying the writs, although the shire courts often chose to represent them landholders who had not achieved the distinction of knighthood. Some small and distant boroughs saved themselves trouble and expense by not sending any representatives at all. Yet, despite the lack of popular enthusiasm, the lower house steadily established itself. Certainly from the middle of Edward II's reign, the likely date when the *Modus* was written, it would not have been considered practical for the king to summon parliament without instructing counties and boroughs to send representatives.

Except once or twice, as the prosecutor of unpopular ministers, the commons of the fourteenth century played no real part in the judicial work of parliament. Occasionally, the king asked for, but did not always accept, their advice on diplomatic, military, or commercial matters, but in law-making their authority grew as the century progressed. Several of their petitions became the substance of new statutes, and, although the king did not think twice about ignoring or repealing a statute when it suited him to do so, successive generations of judges were kept busy in the courts interpreting the increasing number of statutes and reconciling this new form of legal authority with the older common law. But the most significant advance made by the commons in the fourteenth century was to tighten their grip on taxation.

The twelfth clause of Magna Carta, which Henry III and Edward I pointedly left out of their reissues, had declared that the king was not to levy scutages or aids without 'the common counsel of our kingdom', except 'to ransom our own person, to make our eldest son a knight, or to give our eldest daughter once in marriage'. In the next reign, the council successfully countered some of the king's demands for money with demands for reform, and in 1297 the powerful Edward I felt it prudent to accept the maxim that he should impose no taxes, apart from the traditional 'aids, prises, and customs', except by 'common consent of the realm'. But it would be unhistorical to translate thirteenth-century *common counsel* and *common consent* into anything more democratic than the agreement of the leaders of the church and the tenants in chief. The commons began their slow advance to power in the next generation or two. By 1340 Edward III had accepted the principle that the crown would not levy direct taxes without the consent of 'the prelates, earls, barons, other great men, and the commons in parliament assembled', and his ever present need to refill his war-chest compelled him to follow the practice of seeking the consent of knights and burgesses before levying such taxes, especially on movable property. As early as 1334 the king's government had agreed that a fixed sum, £38,170, should represent a single subsidy, which theoretically consisted of one tenth of the value of the goods of those people living in boroughs or on the king's demesne, together with a fifteenth of the value of the goods of those living elsewhere. Each county and borough contributed its agreed share, so that if the commons voted the king two subsidies, the men of Norfolk, the most heavily assessed county, knew that they had to pay twice £3,485, and the citizens of London and York twice £733 and twice £162 respectively. In the same way, in 1350, the king accepted twenty shillings as the flat-rate contribution from each knight's fee whenever he levied the customary aids for knighting his son or marrying his eldest daughter. Fixed sums saved reassessment and, from the commons' point of view, placed a firm limit on the demands of the tax-gatherers, but as time brought its changes, these fixed, unrevised assessments bore less and less relation to the national distribution of wealth.

Edward III tried to prevent parliament from controlling the whole field of taxation by levying extra customs duties on his own authority. Parliament recognized his ancient right to charge half a mark for every sack of wool and for every 300 woolfells exported, but objected to him arbitrarily imposing *maltoltes* or additional duties. During the first twenty years of the Hundred Years War, the commons struggled continuously, but largely ineffectually, to reduce or cancel the unauthorized indirect taxes which Edward frequently imposed, but it was not until 1362, two years after the Black Prince and the Dauphin had sealed the truce of Bretigny, that they first won positive success. Edward III agreed not to levy further export charges on wool without first securing the consent of parliament. Not only did he keep his word, but nine years later extended this agreement to cover woolfells and leather. Richard II could not easily set aside this practice – indeed in the difficult days following the impeachment of Michael de la Pole, his chancellor and treasurer, he formally confirmed it – and a century later, Edward IV resorted to benevolences rather than 'illegal' customs duties in order to raise extra money.

The crown made none of these concessions either on principle or because it thought they would make for better government. It yielded ground only to expediency and necessity. The struggle for the control of the country's purse strings went on long after the end of the fourteenth century, although we can now see that the limited successes of the commons during that century pointed the way to their ultimate victory.

Only in the light of these and other sober facts is it possible to study this intriguing and perplexing *Modus* intelligently. Taken at its face value it can mislead and falsify, but placed alongside what is already known of parliament in the fourteenth century it can add to our knowledge and deepen our understanding.

*

The *Modus* is extant in twenty-five manuscripts from the period of the late fourteenth to the early sixteenth century; it these it usually appears in collection with statutes and other documents of an official and semi-official character. All the texts commence with the introduction and Chapters 1–7 in the same order, but there is considerable variation in the ordering of the remaining chapters. The manuscripts are examined in detail by D. K. Hodnett and W. P. White, 'Manuscripts of the Modus Tenendi Parliamentum', in *Eng. Hist. Rev.*, vol. XXXIV, 209–15, with the text of BM. MS. Harley 930, a fifteenth-century manuscript of the *Modus*, as an appendix.

The most comprehensive study of the *Modus*, with special relation to fourteenth-century political thought and institutions, is by M. V. Clarke, *Medieval Representation and*

*Consent* (1936). In the Appendix, pp 373–84, Miss Clarke prints a Latin text of the *Modus* which is based on a collation of seventeen of the early manuscripts, with preference to the oldest, BM. MS. Vespasian B, VII. This text has been adopted for the present translation.

The group of manuscripts which follows a different ordering of the clauses is represented by *Bibliothèque Nationale* MS. Lat. 6049, printed with an introduction and translation by T. D. Hardy, *Modus Tenendi Parliamentum*, Record Commissioners (1846). The extracts from the *Modus* in W. Stubbs, *Select Charters* (1913), 500–6, reproduce Hardy's text.

The *Modus* also exists in a version adapted to suit the conditions of Ireland; this Irish *Modus* was exemplified by the Deputy of Ireland in 1419 and the text survives in Huntington Library, California MS. EL. 1699, printed by Miss Clarke, op. cit., 384–92.

The translation below reproduces the strange mixture of moods and tenses which is a characteristic of the original, in which actual or purported descriptions of past procedure alternate with statements of present practice and expressions of the author's own political ideals, all presented within the same framework of apparent fact and as equally authoritative. Other passages in the text reveal inconsistencies and apparent contradictions of a kind to suggest that glosses on a lost original may have become incorporated into the text of the Modus, as we now have it, some time before the date of the earliest extant manuscript.

## 10. MODUS TENENDI PARLIAMENTUM

### Introduction

This is an account of the way in which the Parliament of the king of England and of his English people was customarily held in the time of King Edward, son of King Ethelred. It was related in the presence of Duke William of Normandy, conqueror and king of England, at his command, by the wiser men of the kingdom, and was approved by him and followed in his time and in the times of those who succeeded him as kings of England.

## 1. *The Summoning of Parliament*

Parliament should be summoned not less than forty days before the first day of Parliament.

## 2. *The Clergy*

The archbishops, bishops, abbots, priors, and other chief clergy who hold by an earldom or barony should be summoned and come to Parliament in right of their tenure. The lesser clergy ought not to attend in this right, but only if their presence and coming is required for some other reason, as for example because they are members of the king's council, or because their presence is otherwise thought necessary or useful to Parliament; the king ought then to pay the costs and expenses of their coming to Parliament, and of their stay. These minor clergy should not receive summonses to attend Parliament; instead, it was customary for the king to require their presence at his Parliament by issuing them with his mandatory writs.

The king would customarily command the archbishops, bishops, and others of independent authority within the church (such as abbots, priors, deans, and other clergy who are entitled by their privileges and the independence of their offices to exercise separate jurisdictions) that they should secure the election for each English deanery and archdeaconry of two experienced and suitable proctors from the said archdeaconry,[1] elected

1. The confusion of this passage is best resolved by reading it as a requirement for the election of two proctors for each archdeaconry, but with the deaneries having a voice in the election at some primary stage. Even on this reading, the extent to which the minor clergy were represented in Parliament may here be deliberately exaggerated by the author. cf. Miss Clarke, op. cit. pp. 326–9.

by the deaneries and archdeaconries themselves, to come and be present at Parliament, and there make such replies, submissions, and representations, and generally act in such manner as each and every cleric of the said deaneries and archdeaconries would have acted, if each and every one of them had been present in person. And that such proctors should bring with them sealed warrants in duplicate, issued to them by their superiors, to the effect that they have been sent as elected representatives to Parliament; they will deliver one of these letters to the clerks of Parliament to enrol, and they will keep the other one themselves.

In this way, under these two methods of summons, should the whole clergy be summoned to the king's Parliament.

## 3. *The Laity*

Each and every earl and baron, and their equals should be summoned and come to Parliament; an earl's equals being such as are in possession of lands and revenues to the value of a whole earldom, namely twenty fees, each supporting one knight and being reckoned at £20, which makes £400 in all; and a baron's equals being such as are in possession of lands and revenues to the value of one whole barony, namely thirteen and one third fees, each fee supporting one knight and being reckoned at £20, which makes 400 marks in all.

None of the lesser laity should be summoned or come to Parliament in right of their tenure. They should attend only if other considerations make their presence useful or necessary to Parliament; in which case, the same procedure should be followed as was previously specified for the minor clergy, who ought not under any circumstances to attend Parliament in right of their tenure.

## 4. *The Barons of the Cinque Ports*

It was the king's further custom to send his writs to the warden of the Cinque Ports, requiring him to secure the election for each port of two suitable and experienced barons elected by the port itself, to come and attend Parliament and there make such replies, submissions, and representations, and generally to act as their baronies would have acted if each and every individual from those baronies had been present there in person. And that such barons should bring with them warrants in duplicate, issued to them under the common seals of their ports, to the effect that they have been sent as the duly elected representatives and attorneys of the said baronies; they will deliver one warrant to the clerks of Parliament, and they will keep the other one themselves.

When such barons of the ports had been given permission to leave Parliament and took their departure, they would be provided with a writ under the great seal, addressed to the warden of the Cinque Ports, requiring him to see that they recovered their reasonable costs and expenses from the communities of their ports, from the first day of their journeying to Parliament up to the day on which they returned to their proper concerns. The writ would specify how long they had stayed at Parliament, from the day of their arrival to the day on which they were given permission to return home, and would sometimes stipulate the daily allowance to be paid by their communities to the said barons, these amounts varying according to the means and standing of the representatives. The daily allowance for the two barons together would not be more than 20s., and in arriving at an amount, regard would be paid to the length of time they stayed, the extent of their labours, and the nature of their expenses. The court does not reimburse the full amount of their expenses to those sent as elected representatives of the communities, unless they have acquitted themselves honourably and well in Parliament.

## 5. Knights of Counties

It was further customary for the king to send his writs to all the sheriffs of England, requiring them to secure the election, each sheriff for his own county, of two suitable knights of good standing and experience, elected by the county itself, to come to his Parliament, with the same powers of representation as were specified for the barons of the Cinque Ports, and with the same provisions regarding their warrants; but as to expenses, the daily allowance for a county's two knights together does not, by custom, exceed one mark.

## 6. *Citizens*

Writs would be issued in the same way to the mayor and sheriffs of London and to the mayors and bailiffs, or mayor and citizens, of York and other cities, instructing them on behalf of the communities of their cities to elect two suitable citizens of good standing and experience to come and be present at Parliament in the same way as was provided for the barons of the Cinque Ports and the knights of counties; citizens were always regarded as ranking on equal terms with knights of counties in the assessment of their expenses in coming to and from Parliament and over the period of their stay.

## 7. *Burgesses*

In the same way, writs ought to be, and customarily have been issued to the bailiffs and worthies of boroughs, instructing them to elect from their own number two suitable burgesses of good standing and experience, to come and represent them at the king's Parliament, in the same way as was provided for citizens. The daily allowance for the expenses of two burgesses together would not customarily exceed 10s., and there were times when it would not rise beyond half a mark. These expenses would be levied as tax by the borough councils, in amounts fixed in relation to the size and power of the borough and the standing of the persons sent as its representatives.

## 8. *The Composition of Parliament*

The manner in which attendance at Parliament is to be required, from whom, and how soon beforehand, has now been described, and a distinction has been drawn between those who attend by formal summons, and those who do not. An account must follow of those persons who are to come and be present throughout the Parliament because of the offices which they hold, without the need to require their attendance formally. It should be noted, accordingly, that the two principal clerks of Parliament, elected by the king and his council, together with other secondary clerks, about whom and their duties there will be more specific mention later, and also the chief crier of England and his deputy criers, and the chief doorkeeper of England (although in practice one man would combine both these offices, namely those of crier and doorkeeper) are all required to be present from the first day onwards. The chancellor of England, the treasurer, the chamberlains and the barons of the exchequer, the judges, and all the king's clerks and knights, as well as such serjeants-at-pleas who are members of the king's council, are required to attend from the second day onwards, unless there are telling reasons why they cannot be present, in which case they should send their good excuses.

## 9. *The Opening of Parliament*

The lord king will sit in the middle of the side of honour[1] and is required to be present for the first time on the sixth day of Parliament.

Non-attendances in Parliament were customarily recorded by the chancellor, treasurer, barons of the exchequer, and judges, in the following order. On the first day, there will be a roll-call of the burgesses and citizens of all England, and if the representatives of a borough or a city fail to appear on that day, the borough will be fined 100 marks and the city £100. On the second day, the knights of counties of all England will be called, and if any fail to appear on that day, their county of origin will be fined £100. On the third day of Parliament, the barons of the Cinque Ports will be called, and after them the barons and then the earls, and if any of the barons of the Cinque Ports do not attend, the barony from which they come will be fined 100

1. Literally, 'the middle of the greater bench'; the term is perhaps taken by analogy from the arrangements in the court of the exchequer, where the chancellor, or the king if present, sat at the middle of one end of the table on which accounts were rendered.

marks; in the same way, a baron will be personally fined 100 marks, and an earl £100 for his default, and so too with the equals of earls and barons, namely those who have lands and revenues to the value of an earldom or a barony, as was stated in the chapter concerning their summons to Parliament. On the fourth day, the proctors of the clergy will be called, and for each archdeaconry from which representatives do not come, the bishop of the diocese will be fined 100 marks. On the fifth day, the deans, priors, abbots, bishops, and finally the archbishops will be called, and in case of default an archbishop will be fined £100, a bishop who holds a full barony will be fined 100 marks, and so too with abbots, priors, and the rest.

On the first day, proclamation should be made, first in the hall, monastery, or other public place where Parliament is being held, and afterwards publicly in the city or town, that anyone who wishes to lodge a petition or complaint before Parliament should deliver it during the first day of Parliament and the five days next following.

## 10. *The Parliamentary Sermon*

One of the archbishops, or a bishop or one of the major clergy, chosen for his learning and eloquence by the archbishop in whose province Parliament is being held, should preach on one of those first five days of Parliament, in full Parliament and in the king's presence, at a time when Parliament is met and gathered together in greatest numbers; and in his sermon he should enjoin the whole body of Parliament with one accord to make prayer and supplication with him to God for the peace and tranquillity of the king and kingdom, as will be more specially related in the following chapter concerning the announcement to Parliament of the reasons for summons.

## 11. *The Announcement of Parliamentary Business*

After the sermon, the chancellor of England or the chief justice of England, namely the judge in charge of proceedings in the king's bench, or some other suitable judge of high standing and eloquence, or a clerk chosen by the chancellor and chief justice should announce the reasons for calling Parliament together, first of all in general terms and then afterwards in detail. He should make his announcement standing, and in this connexion it should be noted that all members of Parliament, no matter who they are, except the king, will stand whilst speaking, so that all members may hear them; and if anyone speaks so softly or indistinctly that he cannot be heard, he should repeat his words, or another should speak for him.

## 12. The King's Speech after the Announcement of Parliamentary Business

After the announcement of parliamentary business, the king should lay his charge upon the clergy and laity, specifying all their estates[1] – namely, archbishops, bishops, abbots, priors, arch-deacons, proctors, and other clergy; earls, barons, knights, citizens, burgesses, and other laity – that they should apply themselves diligently, with all their attention and from their hearts, to debate the business of Parliament and bring it to such a conclusion as they know or feel to be most in keeping with God's will, principally, and thereafter with the king's honour and interests and their own.

## 13. The King's Absence from Parliament

The king is required to be personally present without fail in Parliament, unless he is prevented by bodily illness; in which case he may keep to his room, provided that he is not lodged outside the manor, or at least outside the town, where Parliament is being held. He ought, under these circumstances, to send for twelve of the magnates and worthies who have been summoned

---

1. The Latin word here is *gradus*, and this is used throughout the document. For convenience we have translated the word as *estate*, except in Chapter 26 where we considered that *estates of parliament* might be misleading. *Gradus* has a more limited meaning than *estate*, so that, for example, the author of the *Modus* has two *gradus* within the *estate* of the church.

to Parliament, namely, two bishops, two earls, two barons, two knights of counties, two citizens, and two burgesses, to view his person and witness his state of health; and in their presence he should issue a commission to the archbishop of the province in which Parliament is meeting, the steward, and his chief justice, empowering them individually and collectively to open and continue Parliament in his name. The commission should make express mention of the reason for the king's absence, and this, taken together with the known witness of their twelve fellow-members, should be accepted as sufficient advice and notification to the other honourable gentlemen [*nobiles*] and magnates of Parliament.

The reason for this provision is that there used to be outcry and murmuring in Parliament about the absence of the king, because it is a harmful thing and dangerous to the whole community of Parliament and the kingdom when the king is absent from Parliament, nor should he, nor may he absent himself, except only in the aforesaid circumstances.


## 14. *Places and the Method of Seating in Parliament*

First, as was said before, the king will sit in the middle of the side of honour; the archbishop of Canterbury and the bishops of London and Winchester will sit on his right, with the other bishops, abbots, and priors in rows behind them, along the length of the hall; and the archbishop of York and the bishops of Durham and Carlisle will sit on the king's left, with the earls, barons, and lords behind them, in rows. The various estates and the places where they sit should be always so disposed that each man sits only with his peers; the steward of England has the responsibility of seeing that the proper order of seating is kept, unless the king wishes to assign someone else to perform this function. The chancellor of England and the chief justice of England, with their fellows and such of their clerks who attend Parliament, will sit by the king's right foot; and the treasurer, chamberlains, and barons of the exchequer, and the judges of the bench, with such of their clerks who attend Parliament, will sit by the king's left foot.

## 15. The Principal Clerks of Parliament

The two principal clerks of Parliament will sit amongst the judges, and they will enter all pleas and other parliamentary business on the rolls. It should be noted that these two clerks are not responsible to any of the judges, nor does any judge of England sit as a judge in Parliament; nor does he perform judicial functions in Parliament, except in so far as the king and the estates of Parliament may have endowed him with extra authority, as for example when he is deputed with others from whom attendance at Parliament is required, to hear and decide petitions and complaints of one sort and another, brought forward in Parliament. The two clerks, then, are directly responsible to the king and his Parliament, in common, unless it should happen that one or two of the judges are assigned to them, to examine and correct their enrolments.

Where members of Parliament are specially deputed to hear and examine petitions on their own, away from the main body, and have reached unanimity and full agreement in the judgments which they return thereon, they will read out the petitions and the proceedings held upon them, and deliver their judgment in full Parliament; this will enable the two principal clerks to enter all pleas and judgments on the principal roll of Parliament. They should deliver these rolls to the treasury before permission is granted for the dissolution of Parliament, so that the rolls are sure to be in the treasury before Parliament is dissolved; they may, however, if they so wish, have a transcript of the roll, or the counter-roll. If these two clerks do not hold other positions with the king and are not in receipt from him of salaries on which they can support themselves honourably, they should receive a daily allowance from the king, for their expenses, of one mark to be divided equally between them; unless they eat at the king's table, in which case they will receive, in addition to their board, a daily allowance of half a mark to be divided equally between them for as long as Parliament sits.

## 16. *The Five Clerks of Parliament*

The lord king will assign five clerks of experience and proved competence to the various estates of Parliament, of whom the first will be assigned to the bishops, in service and general attendance upon them, the second to the proctors of the clergy, the third to the earls and barons, the fourth to the knights of counties, and the fifth to the citizens and burgesses. Any of these clerks who is not in service with the king and in receipt from him of a salary or wages which provide him with a reasonable competence will receive a daily allowance from the king of 2s., unless he eats at the king's table, in which case he will receive 12d. a day. These clerks will write down the questions [*dubitationes*] and answers which the estates make to the king and Parliament, and if the estates desire their presence, they will attend their counsels. If they have any free time, they will help the principal clerks to enter up the rolls.

## 17. *Difficult Matters and Decisions*

When a contention, doubt, or difficulty arises in matters of internal and domestic policy, or in external relations and matters of war, the problem should be reduced to writing and referred to Parliament, and there it should be read out in a full assembly for debate and decision amongst the estates. If it becomes necessary, each estate should be instructed by the king, or on the king's behalf if he is absent, to withdraw by itself. Thereupon, a written statement of the matter under discussion should be issued to the clerk of each estate, and the members should cause this to be read out to them in some appointed place, to the end that they may consider and decide amongst themselves the best and most proper way for the matter to proceed, accordingly as they would be willing to answer before God, both for the king, for themselves, and for those whom they represent. They should bring back their replies and recommendations in written form, and when the replies, counsels, and recommendations of all the estates have been heard, the business should proceed in accordance with the best and most sensible counsel, and in any case in such a way as a majority of Parliament can agree together.[1]

Circumstances may arise in which the peace of the kingdom is being undermined by civil strife between the king and some of his magnates, or by strife amongst the magnates; or it may be that the people or the country is in some way troubled, so that it seems expedient to the king and his council that these troubles should be taken in hand and remedied through their being considered by all the estates of his kingdom. Or again, the king and his kingdom may be troubled by war; or a difficult problem may arise to confront the chancellor of England, or the judges may have had to return a difficult decision. All these and other similar problems may arise. And if it should happen, in their debates on suchlike concerns, that all members of Parliament, or at least a majority of them, cannot agree, then the earl steward, the earl constable, and the earl marshal, or two of them, will choose twenty-five members drawn from all the estates of the kingdom – namely, two bishops and three proctors to represent the whole clergy, two earls and three barons, five knights of counties, and five citizens and five burgesses, making twenty-five altogether. These twenty-five can, if they so wish, choose, and reduce themselves to twelve of their own number; and these twelve in turn can choose, and reduce themselves to six; and these six again can choose, and reduce themselves to three. But these three cannot reduce themselves to a smaller number without first obtaining the lord king's permission. If the king consents, these three can reduce to two, and of these one can withdraw in favour of the other; whose decision, finally, will be binding on the whole of Parliament. In this way, by a reduction in numbers from twenty-five to one man only (except where a greater number has been able to agree together and reach a decision) one man finally, as was said before, will make the

1. The language and thought of the original is extremely compressed at this point, but the suggestion seems clear that the majority decision will be binding, whether or not it accords with the *melius consilium*. But cf. Miss Clarke, op. cit., p. 335 ff. for the opposing view that in the event of conflict decisions would be referred to the committee of twenty-five, described later in this section of the *Modus*.

decision on behalf of all, since one man cannot disagree with himself. When decisions reached in this way have been reduced to writing, the king and his council may examine and amend them, if this is their wish and they know how, always provided that they do so there and then, in full Parliament and with Parliament's consent, and not afterwards.

## 18. *The Order of Parliamentary Business*

The business for which Parliament has been summoned should be taken in the order of the parliamentary calendar, following the order in which petitions have been lodged and filed; there shall be no regard paid to persons whatsoever, but the first case entered shall be the first case heard. The parliamentary calendar should list all parliamentary business in the following order: first, war matters if there should be a war, and other business touching the persons of the king, the queen, and their children; secondly, matters of public concern to the kingdom, as for example the statutory amendment of defects in the law, whether customary law or law established by the executive or by the practice of the courts, after judgments have been returned to establish which matters are of the highest public concern; and thirdly, private business should be taken according to the order in which petitions have been filed, as was said before.

## 19. *The Days and Times of Parliamentary Meetings*

Parliament ought not to be held on Sunday, but may meet on every other day, Sundays always excepted and three other days besides, namely, the feasts of All Saints, All Souls, and the Birth of St John the Baptist.[1] Each day's meeting should begin at mid-prime,[2] at which hour the king and all the estates of the kingdom are required to be present. Parliament should be held in a public

---

1. 1 and 2 November and 24 June. The other great festivals of the Christian year fell outside the normal terms of Parliament.
2. Mid-prime was the middle of the first hour of the day, which began at 6 a.m. or, in summer, at sunrise.

place, and not in a private or a secret place. On feast days, meetings should begin at prime because of divine service.

## 20. *The Doorkeepers of Parliament*

The principal doorkeeper of Parliament will stand on the inside of the main door of the monastery, hall, or other place where Parliament is being held, and will guard the door against entry by anyone but those who have a duty to come and attend Parliament, and such others as may have been called because of particular parliamentary business. This doorkeeper should know everyone who has the right to enter, so that no one whose presence in Parliament is required shall ever, under any circumstances, be refused admission. He may and, if it is necessary, ought to have deputy doorkeepers under him.

## 21. *The Crier of Parliament*

The crier of Parliament will stand on the outside of the door into Parliament, and the doorkeeper will tell him what to announce. The king would customarily assign his body-guard to stand in the open space before the entrance to Parliament, to guard the entrance and prevent obstruction of Parliament by crowds gathering or disturbances arising round the doors, and to arrest offenders. This is because the door to Parliament should not properly be closed, but should instead be guarded by the doorkeepers and the king's body-guard.

## 22. *Speakers in Parliament to stand*

All members of Parliament will sit and no one will stand except to speak. Members should speak so as to be heard by everyone in Parliament. No one will enter or leave Parliament, except by the one door. A member will stand to say anything which should be debated by Parliament. The reason for this is that he may be heard by his fellow-members, since all members are arbiters and judges.

## 23. *Aids to the King*

It was not customary for the king to seek an aid from his kingdom for any other reason than for an impending war, or to knight his sons or to give his daughters in marriage. Aids on these occasions should be sought in full Parliament; the requests should be made in writing and delivered to each of the estates of Parliament, and they should make written replies. It is to be noted as fitting that aids of this kind should be granted by the common consent of all members of Parliament; and it should be clearly understood that two knights representing a county in Parliament have a greater voice in Parliament in granting and refusing [an aid] than a lord earl of England, and likewise the proctors of the clergy of a diocese have a greater voice in Parliament, if they all agree, than the bishop himself; and this applies to everything that can be granted, refused, or otherwise done by Parliament. This is clear from the fact that the king can hold Parliament with the commons of his kingdom, without bishops, earls, and barons, provided that these have been summoned to Parliament, albeit none of them have come in answer to their summonses; because once there were no bishops, earls, or barons, and yet the kings of those days still held their Parliaments. But it is different in the contrary case; for if the commons, both clergy and lay, were summoned to Parliament, as they ought by rights to be summoned, but refused to come for some definite reasons, as for example if they held that the king was not ruling them as he should, and adduced particular instances of how he had failed in his kingly duty towards them, then there would be no Parliament at all, notwithstanding that all the archbishops, bishops, earls, barons, and their equals were present with the king. For this reason, therefore, everything that has to be affirmed, annulled, granted, or denied, or otherwise done by Parliament, should be granted by the commons of Parliament, which is composed of three estates or degrees of Parliament, namely the proctors of the clergy, the knights of counties, and the citizens and burgesses, who together represent the whole commons of England. This is not true of the magnates, each one of whom attends Parliament only in his own right as an individual, and not as the representative of anyone else.

## 24. *The Dissolution of Parliament*

Parliament ought not to be dissolved as long as any petition remains undiscussed or rather until the answer to be made upon it has been decided; and if the king allows otherwise, he is forsworn. No member can, or should, leave Parliament on his own, before the rest leave, unless he obtains permission from the king and from all the fellow members of his estate, in a full meeting of Parliament. Any such permission which is granted should be recorded on the roll of Parliament. If, during the life of Parliament, any member is prevented from attending Parliament through illness, he should send people to make his excuses to Parliament over a period of three days. If, after this time, he still does not come, two fellow-members of his estate should be sent to him, to see and be witnesses of such illness; and if a suspicion arises that he is malingering, they should be sworn under oath to tell the truth of the matter. If the suspicion is then confirmed, he should be fined on the same scale of penalties as for non-attendance; but if he is cleared of the suspicion, he should appoint some sufficient person in the presence of his two fellow-members to act as his attorney and represent him in Parliament. He cannot be excused from attendance whilst in good health, unless his memory fails.

Parliament should be dissolved as follows. First, it should be asked by public proclamation in Parliament and outside the place of Parliament, whether any petitioner to Parliament has not yet received a reply. If no one comes forward upon this proclamation, it is to be supposed that all grievances have been righted or, at least, that every petitioner has been answered to the extent that right allows. Only then, namely when no petitioner to that Parliament comes forward upon the proclamation, will 'we license our Parliament to depart'.[1]

1. This device of direct speech has been adopted from Hardy's translation, op. cit.; the passage only makes sense if thus read as a quotation of the king's words in dissolving Parliament.

## 25. Transcripts of Parliamentary Records and Proceedings

The clerks of Parliament will not refuse anyone a transcript of his own case, but will supply one on request. There will be a standard charge of one penny for each ten lines, but if a man shows in good faith that he cannot afford to pay, no charge will be made. The rolls of Parliament will be ten inches wide. Parliament will be held wherever the king pleases.

## 26. The Ranks of Parliament

The king is the head, the beginning, and the end of Parliament, and so he has no equal with him in his rank; for this reason, the king alone comprises the first rank. The bishops, abbots, and priors, who hold by baronies, make up the second rank. The third rank comprises the proctors of the clergy. The fourth rank comprises the earls, barons, and other magnates and chiefs who hold to the value of an earldom or barony, as was previously stated in the chapter on the laity. The fifth rank comprises the knights of counties. The sixth rank comprises the citizens and burgesses. Parliament is, in this way, composed of six ranks, but it should be clearly understood that, even if one of the five ranks after the king is absent, provided that they have all been notified in advance by summonses in due form to attend Parliament, nevertheless Parliament shall be considered to be complete.

## 11. *The Statutes of Provisors, 1351, and Praemunire, 1353*

ONE of the continuous themes of medieval European history is the struggle between ecclesiastical and temporal authority. It existed at parish and diocesan level, but in England as elsewhere it is most obvious, and occasionally dramatic, in the relationship between the papacy and the crown. Theoretically, pope and emperor were set above more local rulers – kings, dukes, margraves, and the rest – to control and guide them, the one in spiritual and the other in secular matters, but only rarely did a pope or emperor content himself with acting as an arbiter and judge. He usually fell to the temptation of trying to snatch some political or economic advantage from the situation, and so demeaned his status by becoming just another contestant in the arena. Consequently, issues fought between Rome and secular governments were never free of material interests.

From 1066 onwards England was drawn closely into the organization of the western church. Inevitably there were periodic trials of strength between king and pope. One claimed and the other contested particular rights to appoint, to judge, or to receive fees. To try and get his way the pope stimulated internal and external opposition to the king and paraded his ultimate deterrents of interdict and excommunication; the king fought back with financial sanctions, local demonstrations of force, and anti-papal political alliances. But eventually the king realized that he could not rule indefinitely without the pope's connivance, and the pope found a long struggle so exhausting and distracting that in the end both were usually ready to patch up their quarrel with a working compromise.

On balance the papacy was more successful than the crown during the first two centuries after the Conquest. William I disputed with Gregory VII about papal legates and letters entering England and about English bishops visiting the papal curia without royal permission. He was strong enough to insist that, unless he authorized it, no litigant should appeal to Rome from the court of the archbishop of Canterbury, but William II's claim to similar independence led, in 1097, to the exile of Archbishop Anselm. Henry I brought Anselm back to England but, after much dispute, had to make concessions about the crown's right to demand homage from bishops and abbots. Stephen could not afford to strike independent attitudes, and Becket's martyrdom forced Henry II to acknowledge the right of clerics to have their own courts and to appeal to Rome. The climax came in John's reign. Innocent III refused to consecrate the king's nominee as archbishop of Canterbury, and demanded that John should accept Stephen Langton instead. For four years John held out against interdict and excommunication, but in 1213 mounting opposition at home and abroad left him no alternative but to give way. His submission appeared to be as thorough as his opposition had been resolute, for by a charter sealed at Dover in May 1213, he went so far as to surrender his kingdoms of England and Ireland to the papacy.

. . . we, ready to humble ourselves for Him who humbled Himself for us . . . under compulsion neither of force nor fear but of our good and free will, and by our barons' unanimous advice, present and freely give to God and His holy apostles Peter and Paul, and the holy church of Rome, our mother, and to our Lord Pope Innocent and his successors, the whole realm of England and the whole realm of Ireland with all their rights and belongings . . . .

John looked on this surrender as a sound business deal. For a small annual rent of 1,000 marks, recognition of the pope as his titular feudal overlord, and the acceptance of a handful of nominees as English bishops, he had transformed an implacable and dangerous opponent into a benevolent ally, and was free to pursue his war against France. For his part Innocent did not seek vengeance. He was glad to have the matter settled so that he could concentrate on his preparations for the Fourth Lateran Council and another crusade. But by his submission John tacitly acknowledged and upheld the pope's right of *provision*, by which he could appoint an incumbent to a benefice over the head of the acknowledged patron.

During the remainder of the Middle Ages, papal provisions to English benefices constantly provoked anti-papal outbursts. The complaints were of two kinds. Cathedral deans and chapters frequently protested against being denied their common-law right to elect their bishop, and bishops objected when papal pressure forced them to fill benefices in their diocese not with men of their own choice, but with clerics who brought from Rome papal letters of grace. Many laymen too resented papal provision. The king himself had to be constantly on the alert that none of his rights or interests were infringed, lay patrons of benefices were ever apprehensive, and neither nobles nor merchants liked to see stipends, fees, and annates needlessly leaving the country. Especially after the outbreak of the Hundred Years War, they feared that this alienated wealth might eventually be used to support the king's enemies, and as national feeling grew stronger, popular resentment against foreign clerics holding English benefices increased.

During the thirteenth century the papal curia became more and more bureaucratic. Mounting administrative expenses forced the pope to find new ways of raising money, and, whenever he could, he preferred to pay his officials by appointing them to 'foreign' sinecures rather than out of papal funds raised by unpopular taxes on clerical incomes.

In 1265 Clement IV claimed that no one but he had the right to fill benefices which had been vacated when their holders were within the precincts of the papal curia. Successive popes interpreted this claim ever more widely, so that during the fourteenth century papal provision to minor benefices became the rule rather than the exception. The colleges of Oxford and Cambridge, and even the king occasionally, recognized this by petitioning the pope to grant their protégés letters of grace to particular benefices, and every fourteenth-century bishop experienced the difficulty of having more accredited candidates than vacant offices and livings. But papal provision had merit as well as disadvantages. Had they had a free hand, many bishops would have given benefices to relatives, influential friends, and loyal supporters, whereas the pope, not concerned with English family and factional rivalries, was more likely to look with favour on petitions from good churchmen, although they might only be deserving scholars and humble clerks. Papal provision did not end the scandal of pluralities, but neither did it encourage it. Pluralities would have continued whoever had had the giving.

Under the three Edwards it became usual practice for the king to place his senior officers in bishoprics. Edward I rewarded his favourite chancellor, Robert Burnell, with the bishopric of Bath and Wells and would have made him archbishop of Canterbury had Pope Nicholas III not refused to agree. Walter Reynolds and John Sandale both served Edward II first as treasurer and then as chancellor. After five years as bishop of Worcester, Reynolds moved to Canterbury. Sandale's reward was Winchester, but unfortunately for him he did not live long to enjoy it. Two of his distinguished successors, both chancellors, did far better. John Stratford held Winchester for ten years before moving to richer Canterbury for another fifteen, and William of Wykeham supplemented the considerable revenues of the see of Winchester, which he enjoyed for thirty-seven years, with a host of pluralities. To finance much of its administration out of church revenues in this way obviously meant that the crown needed to have firm control over the appointment of bishops. Magna Carta had declared that freedom of elections was most important and essential to the well-being of the English Church, but late thirteenth- and fourteenth-century kings usually had little difficulty in forcing their nominees upon deans and chapters. By the beginning of Edward III's reign, they had firmly established the electoral routine. Some time after the death or translation of the previous bishop (during which interval the crown appropriated the revenue of the see) the king issued a *congé d'élire*, which permitted and instructed the dean and chapter to elect a successor. Unofficially he let them know whom he wished them to choose, and then submitted their, or rather his, nomination to the pope. Occasionally, the pope would question and even reject a nomination, but increasingly in the late fourteenth and fifteenth centuries it became customary for him to accept the royal candidate without question. The popes of the period of the Great Schism, 1378–1417, had particular reason to be circumspect, but every pope of the later Middle Ages knew how impractical it would be to consecrate a bishop whom the king could not tolerate.

Politically, therefore, the English crown had little need for the Statute of Provisors. It found it useful to hold in reserve, but the practical understanding existing between crown and papacy usually worked so well that it would have been foolish to imperil it with needless threats. The initiative which produced the statute came from parliament, which, except for its Lollard members in Richard II's and Henry IV's reigns, did not deny the spiritual leadership of Rome, but persistently resented both the diminishing of the authority of lay patrons in the church and the sight of

English wealth unnecessarily crossing the Channel. At Carlisle in 1307, Edward I's last parliament passed a statute forbidding ecclesiastical 'rents, tallages, tributes, or any kind of impositions' to leave the country. It aimed this prohibition particularly against alien priories which sent regular payments to their mother houses abroad, but many members of the commons were also convinced that giving English benefices to foreign clerics was an abuse of the original endowments. After the outbreak of war in 1340, lords and commons could not help but associate the pope of Avignon with the enemy king in Paris, and the commons' petitions of 1343 and 1344 against papal provisions, together with the statute of 1351, express their intensified resentment. From time to time they renewed their protests, because, in their eyes, the crown strangely neglected and often flew in the face of the powers which common law and the statutes of 1307 and 1351 had given it. In 1365 parliament persuaded Edward III to reaffirm the 1351 statute, and for two or three years was gratified to see his government implementing it. But a new understanding reached between Edward and Pope Gregory XI, compelled the Good Parliament of 1376 again to call for the enforcement of the law. This particular endeavour was ineffective, for during the following year king and pope, the latter lately re-established in Rome, renewed and deepened their understanding and resolved to divide between them all the appointments to English benefices. Once again, in 1388, the parliament which met in Cambridge protested against the continuance of papal provision, and Wycliffe owed part of his popularity to the way he preached that the king should seize the money which was leaving England for Rome. In 1390 parliament passed the Second Statute of Provisors. This recited and reaffirmed the text of the 1351 statute, and then imposed heavy penalties on any cleric who henceforward accepted a benefice 'contrary to this statute':

. . . if he should be out of the country, he shall remain exiled and banished from the realm for ever, and his lands, goods, and chattels shall be forfeit to the king; if he should be within the realm, he shall be exiled and banished and, in the same way, forfeit his possessions, and within six weeks of accepting the benefice he must be out of the kingdom. And if anyone should knowingly shelter any such banished person, either returning from overseas or remaining in England after the six weeks, he also shall be exiled and banished and forfeit his possessions . . . .

To fortify itself against papal counter-attack, the statute ended by prohibiting, under penalty of confiscation, imprisonment, and possible execution, anyone from bringing into the king's realm 'any summonses, sentences, or excommunications against any person, of whatever degree he be, because of the moving, passing, acceptance, or execution of the said Statute of Provisors'.

The Statute of Praemunire (so called because writs under it began with the words *praemunire facias*) already gave general protection against the danger which parliament anticipated in the last clause of the statute of 1390. It was collateral with the Statute of Provisors in that it upheld the traditional claim of the king's court to be the only court entitled to hear suits concerning 'presentations to churches, prebends, and other benefices of Holy Church', and, in support of previous legal practice, it strictly forbade any litigant either to ignore this claim or to appeal over the head of the king to a foreign court. When the statute was reissued in 1365, the revised text made it clear that by *foreign court* parliament meant the papal court, and the Third Statute of Praemunire in 1393 added to the substance of the previous acts a more comprehensive version of the last clause of the 1390 Statute of Provisors:

. . . Wherefore, our said sovereign lord the king, with the aforesaid consents and on the entreaty of his said commons, has ordered and proclaimed that if any person purchases or petitions for such translations, audiences, excommunications, bulls, instruments, or any other thing whatsoever that is detrimental to our sovereign lord the king, his crown and sovereign power, or to the realm, as said, and anyone who instigates such purchases or proceedings, or brings papal mandates to England or receives them, or has them proclaimed or carried out in any way whatsoever within or without the realm, such persons, their legal representatives, agents, patrons, accomplices, supporters, and advisers shall lose the protection of our sovereign lord the king. Their lands, holdings, goods, and chattels shall be forfeited to the king our sovereign lord, and they shall be arrested wherever they can be found and brought before the king and his council to answer for their offences . . . .

Strong anti-papalism, considerable embryonic nationalism, and not a little anti-clericalism inspired lords and commons to present these praemunire petitions to the king. Edward III and Richard II sealed them as statutes, but neither monarch, Richard especially, intended to make drastic use of them. Five years after Richard had accepted the 1393 statute, he signed a comprehensive concordat with Pope Boniface IX, by which he agreed to share with the pope nominations to English bishoprics, and allow papal provision for almost all minor benefices during the next two years. The concordat, dictated by cold political considerations, seemed to have killed the statute, which had sprung from the heated prejudices and feelings of the representatives of the laity.

But the statute was not dead. For most of the fifteenth century, English royal governments could afford to leave it inert and undisturbed, but they took care to keep it alive. In 1426 the regency council of Henry VI resisted Martin V's strenuous attempt to persuade it to repeal the two Statutes of Provisors and Praemunire, and Humphrey, duke of Gloucester, the regent, threatened to issue a writ of praemunire against Henry Beaufort when he accepted a cardinal's hat without permission from the king's council. But the monarch who found the Statute of Praemunire of most use was Henry VIII. During the first dozen years of his reign, when he posed as a secular champion of the papacy, he ignored it, but later, when he was trying to coerce the pope into declaring his marriage null and void, he resurrected it and widened its interpretation considerably. In October 1529 he indicted Wolsey for having broken the statute, when, at Henry's own orders, he had sat with Campeggio at Blackfriars to hear 'the king's great matter'. A year later he publicly proclaimed the terms of the statute of 1393, and then accused the whole church in England of breaking the statute by having accepted and recognized Wolsey's legatine authority. The convocations of Canterbury and York paid fines of £100,000 and £19,000 respectively, but, more significantly, they agreed to recognize Henry as 'singular protector, only and supreme lord, and, as far as the law of Christ allows, even supreme head' of the English church. On his interpretation of the Statute of Praemunire Henry VIII based his political campaign to separate the English church from Rome.

\*

Classic treatments of the relationship between church and state, and with the papacy, are by F. W. Maitland, *Roman Canon Law in the Church of England* (1898), and by F. Makower, *Constitutional History and Constitution of the Church of England* (1895). An excellent modern study is by W. A. Pantin, *The English Church in the Fourteenth Century* (1955); pp. 30–102 are particularly relevant for the Statutes of Provisors and Praemunire. B. Wilkinson, *Constitutional History of Medieval England, 1216–1399* (1958), vol. III, 376–404, gives an account of relations between church and state during the thirteenth and fourteenth centuries, and prints supporting documents in translation. For relations with the papacy over a wider period, see the essays, ed. C. H. Lawrence, *The English Church and the Papacy in the Middle Ages* (1965).

The Norman-French text of the First Statute of Provisors is printed in *Statutes of the Realm*, Record Commissioners (1810–28), vol. I, 316–18, and more conveniently in S. B. Chrimes and A. L. Brown, *Select Documents of English Constitutional History, 1307–1485* (1961), 72–6.

The original document reads continuously without a break, but the translation which follows has been paragraphed, and the provisions of the statute have been numbered. For greater clarity, the recital of the petition presented to Edward I in 1307, which constitutes a large part of the preamble, has been translated in direct speech, and not in the reported speech of the original. Between this translated version and the text of the petition, as printed in *Rotuli Parliamentorum*, ed. J. Strachey and others (1767), vol. I, 219, there are variations due to free reporting in the statute, but these differences are not significant.

The text of the Second Statute of Provisors of Richard II's reign is in *Statutes of the Realm* (op. cit.), vol. II, 69–74, and in Chrimes and Brown (op. cit.), 155–7. There is a translation in Henry Bettenson, *Documents of the Christian Church*, 2nd ed. (1963).

Special articles are by Anne Deeley, 'Papal Provision and Royal Rights of Patronage in the early Fourteenth Century', in *Eng. Hist. Rev.*, vol. XLIII (1928), 497–527, and by C. Davis, 'The Statute of Provisors of 1351', in *History*, vol. XXXVIII (1953), 116–33.

The decree which has come to be known as the First Statute of Praemunire, but which was originally entitled *A Statute against Annullers of the Judgments of the King's Court*, is the first of several miscellaneous provisions of 27 Edward III, statute 1; the preamble which appears as the first paragraph of the following translation is common to all the provisions.

The Norman-French text of the statute is printed in *Statutes of the Realm*, Record Commissioners (1810–28), vol. I, 329, and the petition of the commons which gave rise to it is in *Rotuli Parliamentorum*, ed. J. Strachey and others (1767), vol. II, 252. S. B. Chrimes and A. L. Brown (eds.), *Select Documents of English Constitutional History, 1307–1485* (1961), 80–81, print the original text except for the penalty clauses at the end.

For a discussion of the statute and an account of some cases brought under its provisions, see Edgar B. Graves, 'The Legal Significance of the Statute of Praemunire of 1353', in *Anniversary Essays in Mediaeval History by Students of C. H. Haskins* (Boston and New York, 1929), 57–80. Another article, dealing specifically with the statute of Richard II, but with much that is useful on the earlier statute and on the nature of the conflict with the papacy, is by W. T. Waugh, 'The Great Statute of Praemunire 1393', *Eng. Hist. Rev.*, vol. XXXVII (1922), 173–205.

## 11. THE FIRST STATUTE OF PROVISORS, 1351
### 25 Edward III, st. 4

Formerly, in the parliament of the lord Edward of good memory, king of England, the grandfather of our present lord the king, held at Carlisle in the thirty-fifth year of his reign [1307] a petition was heard by the king's grandfather aforesaid and his council in the said parliament, brought before them by the commonalty of the realm, and worded to this effect:

The Holy Church of England was founded upon an establishment of prelates within the realm of England, by the king and his progenitors, and by the earls, barons, and other nobles of his realm and their ancestors, to teach God's law to them and to the people, and to supply hospitality, alms, and other works of charity in the places where the churches were established, for the good of the souls of the founders and their heirs, and of all Christian people.

For the support of this work, certain possessions in fees, lands, rents, and advowsons [rights of presentation to benefices], whose total value is considerable, were assigned by the said founders to the prelates and other people of Holy Church of the realm. In particular, possessions were assigned to archbishops, abbots, priors, religious [members of religious orders], and other people of Holy Church, by the kings, earls, barons, and other nobles of the realm, who therefore have, and ought to have, in their right as lords and holders of the advowsons, the custody of these prelacies when they fall vacant, and the right at such times to present [nominate] and collate [directly appoint] to the benefices which attach to them. The said kings in time past would draw for the most part upon prelates and clerics so appointed to advise them concerning the safety of the realm, whenever there was need.

But now the pope of Rome appropriates the lordship of these possessions and benefices to himself, and gives and makes grants of them to aliens, who are never at any time resident within the realm of England, and to cardinals, who are precluded by their office from residing here, and to other aliens [foreigners residing abroad] or denizens [foreigners residing in England], as though he were patron or were possessed of the advowsons of the said dignities and benefices, which he cannot rightfully be, according to the law of England.

If these proceedings are allowed to go unchecked, there will, within a very short space of time, be hardly a benefice within the realm which is not in the hands of an alien or of a denizen because of these provisions, to the frustration of the desires and good intentions of the founders of the said benefices. There will be no more free elections of archbishops, bishops, or of other religious heads. Alms, hospitality, and other works of charity will be withdrawn from the places where they should be administered. The king and other lay patrons will lose their rights of presentation to these benefices, when vacancies occur; the king's council will founder; and goods without number will be taken out of his realm.

And so it will come about, if no action is taken, that the estate of the Holy Church of England is annulled, and that the king, and his earls, barons, and nobles are deprived of their hereditary rights; the laws and established rights of the king's realm will be broken and destroyed, and great harm will be brought to his people; the estate of his realm will be overthrown; and the desires and good intentions of the first founders of benefices will be set aside.

This statement of wrongs and injuries was considered, and it was provided, ordained, and established in the said full parliament, with the consent and at the urgent request of the earls, barons, and nobles and of all the commonalty, that these injuries, oppressions, and wrongs would not be suffered in any manner for the future within the realm.

But now again it has been shown to our lord the king in this parliament held at Westminster on the octave of the Purification of Our Lady [9 February] in the twenty-fifth year of his reign over England, and in the twelfth year of his reign over France, by the grievous complaint of the whole commonalty of his realm, that these same wrongs and mischiefs abound from day to day, to the greater damage and destruction of the whole realm than ever before: because now our holy father the pope, by bringing his influence to bear upon clerics, and by other means, has again reserved to his own collation, and goes on reserving to it day by day, as a general rule and in particular cases, both archbishoprics, bishoprics, abbeys, priories, and all other dignities and benefices of England which are in the advowson of people of Holy Church, and gives them to aliens and denizens alike, and takes the first fruits [the first year's income of a new incumbent] and many other profits besides from all these benefices, so that a great part of the treasure of the realm is carried away and spent out of the realm by those who have bought these favours from the pope; and it further follows, as a result of his taking such rights from others and reserving them to himself, that many clerics who have been advanced in this realm by their true patrons, and have enjoyed their preferments undisturbed over long periods of time are now suddenly dispossessed.

The commonalty of his realm has therefore brought these wrongs and mischiefs to the notice of our lord the king, beseeching him to ordain a remedy; since the right of the crown of England and the law of the realm is such that, when mischiefs and wrongs beset his realm, he ought, and is bound by his oath, to remedy them, with the accord of his people in his parliament.

Our lord the king, perceiving the mischiefs and wrongs set out above, and having regard to the statute made in the time of his grandfather and the reasoning therein contained, which statute is still in force and has never been revoked or annulled in any of its provisions, and in as much as he is bound by his oath to uphold it as the law of his realm, notwithstanding that later attempts to contravene it have been suffered and carelessly allowed, and having regard also to the grievous complaints made to him by his people in his several parliaments held to discuss the matter, and wishing to provide a statutory remedy for these very great wrongs and mischiefs which have arisen and are daily arising to the hurt of the church of England, [the king] with the assent of all the magnates and commonalty of the realm, to the honour of God and to the profit of the church of England and of all his realm, has ordained and established the following provisions:

(1) Elections of archbishops and bishops, and elections to all other dignities and benefices elective in England shall in future be held freely and in the manner granted by our lord the king's progenitors and by the ancestors of other lords, who were the founders of such dignities and benefices.

(2) All prelates and other people of Holy Church who have the advowsons of any benefices by gift from our lord the king or his progenitors, or from other lords and donors, to provide divine service and other specified charges in them, shall freely exercise their rights of collation and presentation to these benefices, exactly as they were placed in possession of them by their donors.

(3) And if the court of Rome, in disregard of these rights of free election, collation, or presentation, has made reservation, collation, or provision to any archbishopric, bishopric, dignity, or any other benefice, the king and his heirs, at the times when these dignities and benefices fall vacant and the reservations, collations, and provisions [made by the court of Rome] are due to take effect, shall have and enjoy, on these single occasions, that same right of collation to archbishoprics, bishoprics, and other dignities elective in his advowson which his progenitors had, before the Church was granted the right to make its own elections freely. [It is proper that these rights should revert to the king] because free elections were first granted to the Church by his progenitors on certain forms and conditions, as that the king's *congé d'élire* [leave for an election to be held] should be sought before an election, and that his royal assent should be obtained to the election once made; and that no other procedure whatever should be adopted. If these conditions are not observed, it naturally follows that matters should stand as they were before the concession was made.

(4) Similarly, if reservation, collation, or provision is made [by the court of Rome] to any house of religion which is in the king's advowson, in disregard of the right of free election, our lord the king and his heirs shall have the collation on this occasion and confer the dignity upon a suitable person.

(5) Similarly, if reservation, collation, or provision is made at the court of Rome to any church, prebend [church living], or other benefice which is in the advowson of people of Holy Church, and of which the king is the immediate advowee [holder of the advowson] in chief, then as soon as such benefices fall vacant and the reservations, collations, or provisions made by the court of Rome are due to take effect, the king and his heirs shall have the presentation or collation on these occasions, and on every subsequent occasion when the people of Holy Church are denied their presentations and collations, because reservation, collation, or provision has been made by the court of Rome. But they shall exercise the rights of their advowsons and of presenting to these benefices when

no collation or provision is made by the court of Rome, or where they have the courage and inclination to present or collate to these benefices on their own initiative; and if they do this, the persons whom they present shall enjoy the full effect of their collations or presentations.

(6) Every other lord, similarly, whatever his condition, shall have the right of collation or presentation to the houses of religion which are in his advowson, and to the other benefices of Holy Church which belong to these houses. If the owners of such advowsons fail to present to their benefices within six months after vacancies occur, and the bishop of the place, to whom the rights of presentation then lapse, does not bestow them within a further period of one month, the king shall then have the same right of presentation and collation to these houses of religion and their attached benefices as he has to those others of his own demesne advowson.

(7) If any persons are presented by the king, or by patrons of Holy Church, or by their advowees, or by those to whom the king or other patrons and advowees above mentioned have given benefices belonging to their presentments or collations, and are then prevented by provisors [appointed by the court of Rome] from entering into possession of the benefices to which they have been so presented or collated; or if those who are already in possession of such benefices are challenged upon their possession by provisors, then these said provisors, their agents, executors, and attorneys shall be arrested and brought to trial; and if they are convicted, they shall be kept in prison and not be allowed mainprize [release into the hands of sureties] or bail, or be in any way released, until they have paid a fine and ransom to the king at his pleasure and made satisfaction to the party who feels himself aggrieved. And notwithstanding [that they have paid these other penalties] they shall, nevertheless, before they are released, fully renounce their claims and find sufficient surety that they will not make any such attempts in future, nor bring any suit themselves or through others, against anyone, in the court of Rome or elsewhere, in respect of their imprisonment, renunciation of claim, or any other related matter. If the provisors and their agents,

executors, and attorneys are not found, the exigent shall run against them by due process of law [they shall be commanded to appear, on pain of outlawry], and writs shall be issued, in the king's name as well as in that of the aggrieved party, commanding their arrest, wherever they are found. In the meantime, the king shall have the profits of such benefices as the provisors occupied, except for abbeys, priories, and other houses where there are convents or colleges; in such cases, the convent or college shall have the profits, saving always to the king and to the other lords their ancient rights.

(8) This statute shall operate equally with regard to reservations, collations, and provisions made and granted in the past, as with regard to those to be made and granted in future; in favour alike of all those who have never yet, because of the workings of these same reservations, collations, and provisions, gained corporeal possession of the benefices granted to them, as in favour of all those who shall be similarly placed in the future.

This statute shall take effect from the octave of the Purification of Our Lady aforesaid.

## The First Statute of Praemunire, 1353
### 27 Edward III, st. 1, c. 1

Our lord the king, with the consent and at the request of the magnates and commonalty of his realm of England, at his great council held at Westminster on the Monday after the feast of St Matthew the Apostle [23 September], in the twenty-seventh year of his reign over England and the fourteenth year of his reign over France, has made the following ordinance and statute for the better ordering of his kingdom and to uphold its laws and traditions.

In the first place, the magnates and commons have made strong and loud representation and complaint to our lord the king that many defendants in actions of which the court of our lord the king has cognizance [sole right of hearing] have been, and are being compelled to present their defence abroad; and that judgments given in the king's court are challenged in a foreign court to the prejudice and disenfranchisement of our lord the king and his crown and of all the people of his realm, contrary to the common law of the kingdom, as immemorially established, and in a manner calculated to destroy it.

Our lord the king has considered the matter fully with the magnates and others of his council, and has agreed and granted, with the magnates and commons, that if any of his subjects, of any estate or degree, shall cause anyone to appear abroad to defend an action which is within the cognizance of the king's own court, or one upon which the king's court has already pronounced judgment, or if, as suitors in a foreign court, they shall call in question or seek to have reversed decisions which the royal court has made, they shall be summoned, by two months' prior notice served on them by the sheriff or other royal official in the place where the property in dispute lies, or where they have lands or other property of their own, to appear before the king and his council, or in the court of chancery, or before the royal justices in their courts of the king's bench or of common pleas, or before other justices specially appointed by the king, to answer personally to the king for the contempt constituted by their actions.

If they fail to present themselves for trial on the appointed day, they, their agents and representatives, legal advisers and supporters, shall from that day forward be set outside the king's protection. They shall be arrested, wherever they are found, and shall suffer imprisonment, and their ransom shall be at the king's pleasure. Writs shall be issued for their arrest and for the seizure of their lands, goods, and possessions into the king's hands. If answer is returned that they could not be found, they shall be placed in exigent[1] and then be outlawed. Provided always that if they present themselves at any time before they are made outlaws, and are prepared to deliver themselves up at the king's

1. i.e. writs of *exigi facias* shall be issued to the sheriffs, commanding them to summon the defendants to appear and surrender themselves to judgment, on pain of outlawry.

prison, to be judged by the law and to abide by the adjudication of their case by the king's court, their surrender to justice shall be accepted. But the forfeiture of their lands, goods, and chattels shall remain in force unless they have surrendered themselves within the specified period of two months.

## 12. *The Statute of Cambridge, 1388: Labourers and Servants, Beggars and Vagrants*

DURING the whole of the Middle Ages and for many years afterwards, no part of Europe was long free from plague or pestilence. But outbreaks of plague varied considerably in killing power and in the speed with which they spread through the community, chiefly because medieval doctors used the one word, *plague*, to describe epidemics of typhoid, typhus, virulent influenza, and a variety of fevers, as well as the infections known today as bubonic and pneumonic plague. Easily the most lethal attack of plague to strike medieval England was the Black Death of 1348–51, which medical historians believe was either bubonic or pneumonic plague or a mixture of both. It swept north-westwards across Europe: we can trace its devastating progress over the Alps, through France and England into Scotland. The death roll was enormous. The first, long visitation killed more than a million people in England and Wales. This was roughly one third of the population, and further outbreaks in 1356, 1361–2, and 1368–9 raised the fraction to something nearer one half.

Naturally, such a calamity had a profound and lasting effect upon society. Economically, it turned a surplus of labour into a shortage, land hunger into land plenty, and it accelerated changes which had already begun to transform the social pattern of medieval England. The Black Death did not strike evenly all over the country. Some communities were virtually wiped out, and a few escaped with relatively little loss, so that in different areas men took different measures to adapt themselves to the dramatically changed conditions. Some landholders simply reduced the area of their arable fields to match their shrunken labour force; others tried to buy additional labour with tempting offers of wages. Some, especially the monasteries, eagerly leased surplus demesne lands and buildings to peasant families willing to pay a rent; others, clinging desperately to their controllable labour, attempted to reverse the trend of the previous hundred years, and refused to free any more of their villeins from bondage. In these strange economic circumstances of rising wages, cheap rents, falling prices for grain and wool, easily acquired tenancies of land, and the slow growth of crafts and infant industries, many families prospered while others frustratedly struggled against restrictions, which they felt were arbitrary and unjust and the only factors which were preventing them from improving their lot. Bad harvests, cattle plague, military defeats in France, and the scourge of discharged soldiers menacing the safety of roads and villages, all helped to create the chronic despair and unrest which bedevilled so many Englishmen during the second half of the fourteenth century.

Edward III's government looked on this changing England with trepidation. The Statutes of Merchants and of Winchester, 1283 and 1285, had improved conditions of travelling, but had been far from putting an end to disorder and danger. The slow disintegration of feudalism periodically added new recruits to the squads of ambitious freemen and ex-villeins tramping the roads in search of more lucrative employment, and both the Scottish wars and the prolonged civil strife of Edward II's reign had increased the number of thieves and cut-throats who kept themselves alive by raiding villages and robbing travellers. Edward III's government had attempted to reduce this disorder. As early as 1328 the Statute of Northampton had denounced those who used parties of armed retainers to coerce judges or destroy the safety and freedom of markets, and later acts, in 1331 and 1335, had increased the sheriff's powers to arrest suspected persons and had given the merchants, especially foreign merchants, greater protection. But the economic consequences of the Black Death threatened to undo all that had been achieved. A labour shortage with its consequent increase in wages would certainly swell the ranks of vagrants seeking new work, and rising wages coupled with falling prices would imperil the standard of living of all employers, especially those who employed no more than a handful of agricultural labourers or journeyman tradesmen. Accordingly in 1349, the first full year of the plague, the king issued an ordinance imposing a wage freeze.

Because a large number of people, especially labourers and servants, have lately died of plague, many, perceiving the plight of employers and the great shortage of servants, refuse to work unless they are paid excessive wages, and some would rather beg in idleness than work for their living . . . [therefore] . . . every man and woman, of whatever condition, free or bond, able in body and less than sixty years of age, not making a living by trading or plying a craft, nor living on their own resources or by tilling their own land, nor already serving another, shall be bound to serve him who shall require their labour, and receive only the wages, livery, reward, or salary traditionally paid for such service. And if any such man or woman refuses to work for such wages, and if two responsible men testify to this before the sheriff or the bailiffs or constables of the town, he or she shall be arrested and kept in jail until he find surety to ensure that he will serve . . . and if any reaper, mower, or other workman or servant, retained in any man's service, leaves the service without permission or reasonable cause before the agreed time, he shall be imprisoned. . . . No man shall pay, or promise to pay, any servant more wages, livery, reward, or salary than is customary, nor in any other way demand or receive the same, upon pain of paying double that which shall be so paid or promised, required or received, to the aggrieved party who was competing for the same labour. . . .

The ordinance went on to prohibit 'sellers of all manner of

victuals' from increasing their prices, and to forbid crafts-men – 'saddlers, skinners, towers, shoemakers, tailors, smiths, carpenters, masons, tilers, shipwrights, carters, and all other artificers' – to ask for or accept wages and rewards in excess of those they had been receiving during the last five or six years.

During the next few months the plague continued to reduce the labour force still further, so that when parliament met in February 1351, the commons, which for the most part represented the middle landholders, successfully petitioned the crown to issue the Statute of Labourers. They complained that, despite the 1349 ordinance, their servants were leaving them 'to serve great men and others, unless they are offered livery and wages double or treble that which they received before'. The statute could do little more than reiterate the terms of the ordinance, but as a guide it stipu-lated a number of acceptable wages and conditions. Agri-cultural labourers were to be hired not by the day but by the year or by the period of time traditional in their district. Usually they were to work in the same place winter and summer, but men from beyond the Trent could continue their practice of moving into more southern counties to help with the harvest. Corn reapers were to receive 2d. or 3d. a day, threshers 2d. for threshing a quarter ton of wheat and mowers 5d. for mowing an acre of hay. Masons, tilers, thatchers, and master carpenters were all to be paid a maximum of 3d. a day – just half the daily wage paid to the private soldiers and archers who fought for Edward III at Crécy and Poitiers. Stewards, bailiffs, and constables were put on oath to enforce the statute, and judges were directed to jail first offenders for forty days, and then to double the punishment for every subsequent conviction. For a time this deterrent sufficed to check the rise in wages, but eventually economic laws proved stronger than the statute. In 1359 the government used the new quarter sessions in a fresh endeavour to keep the law effective, but employers and employed were increasingly prepared to ignore its precepts. The merchants and other employers in the towns, the bigger landholders, the church, and even the king's officers, all wanted more hands to serve, farm, and build. If they were to hire as much labour as they needed, they had to offer attractive wages, and this meant that, despite the laws of 1349, 1361, and 1383 against vagrancy, men were tempted to take their families away from their traditional homes and set out in search of these reported better conditions.

Travellers upon those fourteenth-century roads were a mixed crew. Most of them, freemen and runaway villeins alike, were honestly seeking good jobs; others, natural rogues or disbanded soldiers often still wearing the livery of their ex-captains, were out to pillage and live off the countryside. Such conditions led to frequent frustrations and spasmodic outbursts of violence and destruction. The peasants blamed the tyranny and greed of many landholders, and the employers, especially the poorer ones, petitioned the authorities to enforce the law. This politically combustible material sparked into the flame of the Peasants' Revolt when the tax-gatherers, forcefully and often brutally, began to collect the poll tax which the commons had reluctantly granted in December 1380. In Kent, Essex, Suffolk, and Norfolk – all four relatively prosperous counties – the rebels aired a string of grievances and voiced a number of brave demands, but they had not the material resources to do more than make their protest. The government dispersed the rank and file and hanged the leaders, but it could not halt or turn aside the indomitable march of economic change. Throughout the next century England continued its steady transformation from a traditional feudal society into a three-decker society of landholders living chiefly off rents, freehold or tenant farmers actively engaged in agriculture, and virtually landless labourers selling their labour. The gap between the standards of living of the rich and the poor tended to widen, so that by the late sixteenth century, stimulated and strengthened by the division and redistribution of monastic lands, a squirearchy was ruling the English countryside. It continued to do so for the next three centuries.

The new Poor Law, or revised Statute of Labourers, which the Cambridge parliament approved in the autumn of 1388, can be dismissed as yet another abortive, backward-looking attempt to keep society static. After all, its endeavour to peg wages and restrict the movement of workmen met with as little success as the 1351 statute had done. But in its bid to cure vagrancy, the Cambridge parliament established two principles upon which successive Tudor governments were later to build their poor law administration, which, in spirit if not in letter, persisted until 1929. First, it made a clear distinction between 'sturdy beggars' capable of work and beggars who were incapacitated by age or infirmity – the future 'sick poor' of the Elizabethan Poor Law. Secondly, by forbidding servants to move out of their hundred without legal authority, it made each hundred responsible for housing and keeping alive its own paupers, and thus pointed the way towards the Tudor and Stuart policies of settlement. But, like the early Tudor parliaments, the Cambridge parliament made no provision for maintaining the sick poor. For more than two centuries ahead, nothing but charity could prevent the old and the infirm from starving or freezing to death.

One further aspect makes the statute of 1388 historically important: it assumed, almost naturally, that the justices of the peace would enforce it. This was not the beginning of the justices; their office had developed logically from that of the keepers of the peace, who, since Richard I's reign, had been used by the crown for special administrative tasks. Edward II had given them the responsibility of enforcing the reissued Statute of Winchester, and Edward III had empowered them to carry out commissions of array and to see that in their counties men observed the provisions of the 1351 Statute of Labourers. Eventually in 1368, after a vacillating policy which reflected its indecision about their suitability for the work, the crown permanently upgraded the keepers into justices of the peace.

It is granted and agreed that the statute and ordinance concerning labourers and artificers shall be kept and observed and duly enforced, and for these matters there shall be issued in each county commissions to justices of the peace to hear and settle cases arising from the said statute, and to award appropriate damages to the plaintiff.

By an earlier statute, passed in 1361, Edward III had first authorized justices of the peace, but three years later he had virtually withdrawn their authority. This 1361 statute had laid it down that there should be no more than five justices in each county – 'a lord together with three or four of the most worthy men in the county' – but the Cambridge statute of 1388 raised the number to six, and only two years later eight justices became permissible. From the first, the crown enjoined justices of the peace to maintain law and order, and especially to deal with 'those pillagers and thieves' who had returned from abroad and 'who wander about and do not work as they used to do'. This commission was often beyond the capabilities of these newly-fledged justices, but the act of 1388 gave them a task which they could do and which they made peculiarly their own. From 1388 until the Poor Law Amendment Act of 1834 had created boards of guardians, justices of the peace administered the poor law. Tudor acts steadily increased and more carefully defined their powers and responsibilities, and from the Elizabethan Poor Law of 1601 onwards, they controlled houses of correction, heard countless petitions for relief, and kept a keen eye on the activities of the parish overseers of the poor. In addition, the crown piled on their wide shoulders a heavy burden of other executive and judicial duties. They became the 'great unpaid', the solid basis which bore the weight of English local government.

\*

The Norman-French text of this statute of Richard II is printed in *Statutes of the Realm*, Record Commissioners (1810–28), vol. II, 56–9. Edward III's Ordinance of Labourers (1349) and Statute of Labourers (1351) are printed in *Statutes of the Realm* (op. cit.), vol. I, 307–9 and 311–13; and also in B. H. Putnam, *The Enforcement of the Statutes of Labourers, 1349–59* (1908), 8\*–17\*, Appendix.

For the developing role of the justices of the peace and their part in enforcing the labour laws, see B. H. Putnam, *The Enforcement of the Statutes of Labourers* (op. cit.), and more especially her article, 'Transformation of the Keepers of the Peace into Justices of the Peace', in *Trans. Royal Hist. Soc.*, 4 ser., XII (1929), 19–48, and the introduction to her edition of *Proceedings before the Justices of the Peace in the Fourteenth and Fifteenth Centuries* (1938), xvi–cxxxii. C. A. Beard, *The Office of Justice of the Peace in England* (1904), 11–71, is also useful for the early history of the justices.

For economic conditions generally, see E. Lipson, *Economic History of England*, 12th ed. (1959), vol. I; and for the structure of agrarian society in particular, Sir Paul Vinogradoff, *Villeinage in England* (1892), and H. S. Bennett, *Life on the English Manor, 1100–1400* (1937). Three useful articles conveniently collected together by E. M. Carus-Wilson (ed.), *Essays in Economic History*, vol. II (1962), are by R. H. Hilton, 'Peasant Movements in England Before 1381', *Econ. Hist. Rev.* (1949); Nora Ritchie, 'Labour Conditions in Essex in the Reign of Richard II', *Econ. Hist. Rev.* (1934); and F. G. Davenport, 'The Decay of Villeinage in East Anglia', *Trans. Royal Hist. Soc.* (1900).

A. Steel, *Richard II* (1941), is useful for the political background of the reign and for a good chapter, pp. 58–91, on the Peasants' Revolt of 1381. J. J. Jusserand, *English Wayfaring Life in the Middle Ages*, 4th ed. (1950), is a vivid and very readable account of the different kinds of movement along the medieval roads which the authorities were so anxious to control.

## 12. The Statute of Cambridge, 1388: Labourers and Servants, Beggars and Vagrants
### 12 Richard II

For the common profit and universal good of all the realm, our lord the king, at his parliament held at Cambridge on the day after the Nativity of Our Lady [9 September] in the twelfth year of his reign, has made certain statutes and ordinances in the following form, with the agreement of the lords and commons there assembled. . . .

(3) It is granted [by the king] and agreed [by the lords and commons] that all the statutes of artificers [craftsmen], labourers, servants, and victuallers [provisions merchants], both those made in the time of our present lord the king, and those which date and are still effective from the time of his grandfather, on whose soul may God have mercy, shall be strictly observed and kept and duly enforced. Artificers, labourers, servants, and victuallers [who offend against these statutes] shall be duly brought before the justices of the peace, at the king's suit as well as at the suit of the plaintiffs, in accordance with the requirements of the statutes. Mayors, bailiffs, the stewards of lords, and town constables, shall carry out the duties of their offices which relate to such artificers, servants, labourers, and victuallers; and there shall be stocks in each town for the punishment of these servants and labourers, as is ordained in the statutes.

It is further granted and agreed that no servant or labourer, male or female, when his or her term of service expires, may leave the hundred, rape, or wapentake where he is living, to take up residence or service elsewhere, or with the professed intention of going on a far pilgrimage, unless he has a letters patent under the king's seal, which states the purpose of his journey and the time appointed for his homecoming, if he is to return. The king's seal to be used for this purpose shall be supplied to some reliable man of the hundred or hundreds, or of the rape, wapentake, city, or borough, and entrusted to his safekeeping, for him to draw up such letters as may be necessary and issue them at the discretion of the justices of the peace, in the manner required by law; and not to issue them otherwise, upon his sworn oath. Seals shall have the name of the county inscribed around the rim, and the name of the hundred, rape, wapentake, city, or borough inscribed across the face.

If any servant or labourer is discovered in a city, borough, or elsewhere as a vagrant from some other place, without a letters patent in his possession, the mayors, bailiffs, stewards, or constables shall immediately arrest him and put him in the stocks, and keep him prisoner until he finds surety to return to his [bound] service in the town from which he has come, or to go back there and be a servant or labourer, until for some good reason he has a letter to depart.

Let it be noted, however, that a servant or labourer is free to leave his service at the end of his time and enter into service elsewhere, provided that he has some definite employer and has been issued with the necessary letter.

Similarly, it is not the intention of this statute that servants who ride or otherwise travel upon the business of their lords or masters shall be included within the terms of this ordinance during the period whilst they are so engaged.

If anyone carries a letter which can be shown to be forged or false, he shall be imprisoned for forty days because of this deception; and he shall stay in prison beyond the forty days if need be, until he has found surety to return [to his place of origin] and be a servant or labourer there, as in the former case [of a servant or labourer without a letter].

No one shall receive a servant or labourer who leaves his hundred, rape, wapentake, city, or borough without a letter to warrant him; and even if he has a letter, he shall not be received for longer than one night, unless he is ill or has some other good excuse for staying longer; or unless he is prepared, and the letter which he carries shows that he is authorized, to stay there in service or as a labourer. If anyone receives him except on one or other of these conditions, he shall be punished, and his punishment shall be determined by the justices of the peace.

Artificers and craftsmen, together with their servants and apprentices, who are of no great substance and for whose artifice or craft there is no great demand, shall be bound at harvest time to help with the harvest, by cutting, gathering, and bringing in the grain.

Mayors, bailiffs, stewards, and town constables shall duly enforce this statute, or else they shall undergo such punishment as the justices of the peace in their sessions shall fix and determine.

No one shall charge more than 1d. for drawing up, sealing, and issuing a letters patent.

(4) Furthermore, since servants and labourers are unwilling, and have been for a long time unwilling, to provide their service and labour except for an outrageous and excessive hire, which is greater than any paid to such servants and labourers in any time past, so that, in consequence of the high cost of their labour and service, the farmers and estate tenants [who employ them] cannot pay their rents and are hardly able to make a living from their holdings, to the very great loss and damage of their lords and of all the commonalty besides; and because the rates of hire to be paid to such labourers and servants have not been definitely established up to this present time, it is therefore granted and agreed that the following rates of wages shall be paid:

| | |
|---|---|
| Farm bailiffs, by the year, with one suit of clothes a year, at the most | 13s. 4d. |
| Master hinds [farm workers with some responsibility], carters, and shepherds | 10s. 0d. |
| Oxherds and cowherds | 6s. 8d. |
| Swineherds, women labourers, and dairymaids | 6s. 0d. |
| Ploughmen, at most | 6s. 0d. |

Every other labourer and servant shall be paid according to the nature of his work; and in districts where lower rates have customarily operated, they shall continue to be paid at these lower rates, with no additional benefits in the way of clothing or other allowances and perquisites under their contracts of service.

No servant of an artificer or victualler in a city, borough, or other town shall be paid at higher rates than those set out above for labourers and servants, but they shall be paid at these rates appropriately to the work which they do, with no extra benefits by way of clothing or other allowances and perquisites under their contracts of service, as was before provided.

If anyone is convicted on a charge of giving or receiving, under a contract of service, more than is specified above, both donor and recipient, for a first offence, shall be fined the amount of the excess: but if convicted for a second time, they shall each pay double the excess; and if the recipient has not the means of paying, he shall be imprisoned for forty days.

(5) It is granted and agreed that any male or female person who works steadily as a carter or at the plough or at some other agricultural labour or service until he or she is twelve years of age shall work only in this employment from that time forward, and shall not be put to a trade or craft. Any contract of service or articles of apprenticeship made for the future in breach of this provision shall be held to be null and void.

(6) It is granted and agreed that no servant of an artificer or victualler shall in future wear a baselard [short sword or hanger], dagger, or sword, on pain of forfeiting these arms, except in wartime for the defence of the realm, and then only under the supervision of the arrayers [organizers of the militia] for the time being; or when they are travelling about the country in attendance on their masters or engaged upon their masters' business: but servants and labourers shall have bows and arrows, with which they shall practise on Sundays and holidays; and they shall take no part in ball games, whether played with the hand or with the foot, nor in the other games known as quoits, dice, stone-throwing, and skittles, nor in other such useless sports.

The sheriffs, mayors, bailiffs, and constables shall be empowered, and shall duly exercise their power, to arrest all offenders against this provision, and to confiscate their baselards, daggers, and swords. They shall seize these weapons and keep them until the justices of the peace are in session, when they shall bring the weapons before the justices, at the sessions, together with the names of those who carried them.

The king does not intend by this to encroach upon the rights of local lords to have the possession of such confiscated weapons.

(7) It is granted and agreed that anyone who takes to the road as a beggar, although able to serve and labour, shall be dealt with as in the former case of a man who leaves his hundred, or other place or district before-mentioned, without a letter to warrant him; except for people of religion and true hermits who have warrants from their superiors. Beggars who are unfit for service shall remain resident in the cities and towns where they are living at the time when this statute is proclaimed, unless the inhabitants of these cities and towns are unwilling, or unable, to find[for?] them; in which event, they are to betake themselves to other towns of the same hundred, rape, or wapentake, or to the towns where they were born, within forty days after the statute is proclaimed, and remain there in fixed residence for the rest of their lives.

All those who go on pilgrimage as beggars, although fit to work, shall be dealt with in the same way as the servants and labourers before mentioned, unless they have letters patent under seal to show that they are pilgrims.

Clerks [students] of universities who go on pilgrimage as beggars in this way shall obtain letters from their chancellor to show that they are pilgrims, or else they shall be punished in the same way [as servants and labourers].

(8) It is ordained and agreed that those persons who claim to have been travelling outside the country and to have been detained there shall obtain letters to support their stories either from the authorities of the places abroad where they were living or from the local mayors and bailiffs when they first re-enter the country. The mayors and bailiffs shall inquire of such travellers where they have been living, and with whom, and the where-

abouts of their home in England, and shall issue them with letters patent under their official seal, attesting the date of their arrival and the places where, according to their own statements, they have been. They shall swear an oath, administered to them by the mayors and bailiffs, that they will go straight back to their own districts, unless they have a letters patent under the king's great seal which allows them to do otherwise. If any of these persons is found without such a letter in his possession, he shall be treated in the same way as the servants and labourers before mentioned.

This ordinance shall be understood as applying to those who have been abroad and who go begging through the country on their return.

(9) It is ordained and agreed that these ordinances and statutes of servants and labourers, beggars and vagrants, shall apply and be enforced in cities and boroughs, as well as in other towns and places within the kingdom; in franchises, as well as outside them. Sheriffs, and mayors and bailiffs, and the keepers of jails, shall be bound under instructions to receive the said servants, labourers, beggars, and vagrants, into their custody, and to detain them in prison, in the way already prescribed, without releasing them to mainprize [into the hands of sureties] or bail, and without taking a fee or any other consideration from them, or from others acting on their behalf, either when they enter or leave prison, or during the term of their imprisonment, on penalty of paying a fine of 100s. to the king.

(10) It is ordained and agreed that only six justices, apart from the justices of the assizes, shall be assigned to any commission of the justices of the peace. These six justices shall hold their sessions at least once a quarter, for three days at a time if the business in hand demands it; and if they fail to do this, they shall be punished accordingly as the king's council, at the suit of anyone who chooses to lodge a complaint, shall advise. Beside their other official duties, they shall make careful inquiry whether the mayors, bailiffs, stewards, constables, and jailers have properly enforced the ordinances and statutes of servants and labourers, beggars and vagrants, and they shall punish those

who have incurred the fine of 100s. by imposing this fine upon them; and if anyone has offended, but not by an offence to which this penalty attaches, they shall punish him at their discretion.

The justices shall each receive 4s. a day in wages whilst they are sitting, and their clerk 2s., out of the fines and other sums paid and falling due at the sessions; these sums shall be dispensed to them by the sheriffs. The lords of the franchises [within the area of the sessions] shall contribute towards the wages of the justices and their clerk, in proportion to the share which they receive of the fines and other sums mentioned above.

No steward of a lord shall be appointed to serve on any of these commissions, and no new members shall be added to a commission of the justices of the peace, when once it has been issued.

It is not the intention of this statute that, where the justices of either bench, or the serjeants at law, are named in such commissions, they should be required, under the provisions of the statute, to hold sessions four times a year in the same way as other commissioners who are permanently resident in their districts, but that they should hold these sessions at such times as they can properly attend to them.

# 13. The Act of Supremacy, 1534

'THE King's Majesty justly and rightfully is and ought to be the Supreme Head of the Church of England.' With these words the Act of Supremacy of 1534 put a formal end to the medieval church in England. It set aside the centuries-old concept of ecclesiastical and temporal administrations sharing power as twin authorities, and established in England the Erastian church which has been so prominent a feature of the country ever since. In retrospect we can see the act as an expression of the nationalism which in the sixteenth century was growing rapidly in many parts of Europe. We can compare it with the eager way in which some contemporary German princes were adopting Lutheranism in order to govern the church within their boundaries, or with the later insistence of such outstanding Catholic kings as Philip II and Louis XIV that they should have effective control of the appointment of Spanish and French bishops. Yet, however justified such comparisons might be and however true it is that in sixteenth-century Europe the new idea of absolute monarchy was militating against the traditional Christendom-wide authority of Rome, there is no denying that it was more accidental than planned that the Act of Supremacy should have been passed in the thirties. The act signified the logical end of a remarkable sequence of events, but chance rather than logic determined the route those events should take. Had Princess Mary been a boy, or had Charles V invaded Italy in 1528 instead of 1527, or had pestilence not dispersed a French army south of Rome, the Act of Supremacy would never have been passed in 1534. Whether it, or something like it, would have become law later in the century is an open speculation.

The sequence of events began in 1525 when for the first time Henry VIII became seriously concerned about not having a son to succeed him. Queen Catherine, then turned forty, had been pregnant at least half a dozen times, but she had had only one child – and that a girl, Mary – who had grown to maturity. King Henry had no pretenders to contend with: from his father he had inherited the Lancastrian claim, and from his mother the Yorkist. But if he were compelled to leave Mary as his heir, this newly found unity would be in jeopardy: England would run the risk, if Mary married a nobleman, of suffering a new dynastic struggle, or, if she married a foreign prince, of losing her national independence. No true patriot could countenance either prospect, but the only alternative was for the king to have a son. For some time Henry had been earnestly searching his conscience to find out why God had denied Catherine a son. Bessie Blount had demonstrated that he could father a male child, and Catherine was far from being barren. In the end Henry convinced himself that God was showing his displeasure because he had married his brother's widow. *Leviticus* explicitly stated that any couple who broke this law should be childless. By the end of 1525 Henry was certain that Julius II had exceeded his authority when, twenty years before, he had granted a dispensation for him to marry Catherine.

During the next year, Henry's new infatuation for Anne Boleyn strengthened this conviction. For her part, Anne had no intention of satisfying the king's desires and within a few months becoming, like her sister Mary, or Bessie Blount, an abandoned and forgotten royal mistress. She appears from the beginning both to have realized that Henry would be compelled to put aside Catherine, and to have foreseen that if she, Anne, played her cards circumspectly, the queen's crown could be hers. Henry's greatest difficulty was to explain his beliefs and hopes to Catherine, for he had a sincere respect for her, and wished to spare her all possible sorrow. Moreover, he feared the scorn which he knew she would pour on his theories and explanations. Yet his desire for Anne and his need for a son spurred on his resolution. 'Henceforward my heart shall be yours alone,' he wrote to Anne, 'would that my body could be yours too, as God can bring about if He so wishes.'

Henry put off taking any action until May 1527. He then arranged that Cardinal Wolsey and Archbishop Warham should summon him to appear before them on a charge of having lived incestuously with his brother's widow. Both judges hesitated to do the king's will and declare him guilty. They preferred that the whole bench of bishops should share the responsibility of asking the pope to confirm so momentous a decision. But while they were in the process of canvassing their colleagues, they and the king were devastated to hear that Emperor Charles V, Queen Catherine's nephew, had invaded Italy, sacked Rome, and virtually imprisoned the pope. When the Westminster court had first sat, it had seemed unlikely that Clement VII, Henry's ally in the recently signed League of Cognac, would seriously oppose the king's wishes. But now that he was a political prisoner, the pope could hardly be expected gratuitously to insult his jailer's aunt. To make matters worse Catherine showed that she had not the slightest intention of accommodating her husband in any way. She refused to leave court, or to listen to his point of view.

More than a year went by before Henry could see another chink of hope. In the summer of 1528, Clement agreed that Cardinal Campeggio should come to England and, with Wolsey's help, try 'the king's great matter'. The court wasted weeks in fruitless attempts to argue away Henry's convictions, and in laboriously listening to evidence, but at last, on 23 July 1529, Henry came to Blackfriars full of expectation that Campeggio would that day declare in his favour. Instead, disappointed and angry, he heard the cardinal adjourn the court until October. Campeggio could do nothing else, for Clement had secretly instructed him, whatever the evidence, to come to no definite decision. The pope had set up the court only to buy time, and by the late summer of 1529 time had not worked in Henry's favour. Plague had devastated the French army, which had temporarily forced Charles V to relax his grip on Rome. This had led the French king to make his peace with the emperor, and so destroy any lingering hopes of a political change which would leave Clement free to help Henry. During the summer adjournment of the Blackfriars court, Clement recalled the case to Rome. The angry and frustrated Henry vented his wrath on Wolsey. He charged him with breaking the Statute of Praemunire by holding a papal court in England. Wolsey had no practical alternative but to plead guilty. He surrendered his office of lord chancellor, transferred much of his treasure to the king, and was gratified to find that Henry allowed him to retire to his archbishopric at York.

Another full year passed without progress. Henry's appeal to the universities of Europe for a legal decision on his 'great matter' only brought contradictory opinions. The parliament which met in November 1529 offered neither sympathy nor helpful suggestions, and Wolsey's death a year later robbed the king of the chance of recalling his old, faithful adviser. But towards the end of 1530, Henry became increasingly aware of the potentialities of Thomas Cromwell, a recent recruit to his administration. Cromwell seemed to be as shrewd a politician as ever Wolsey had been, and since he enjoyed the advantage of not being a cleric, he ran no danger of encountering divided loyalties: he would be the king's man all the time. He began by showing Henry how to put pressure on the church, and how to exploit the anti-clericalism of the commons.

In December 1530 Henry charged the whole of the church of England with having broken the Statute of Praemunire, because, as a body, it had condoned and abetted Wolsey's offence. The convocation of Canterbury, thinking it largely a matter of money, admitted the technicality and offered to pay the crown £40,000. Henry demanded £100,000, and, more significantly, the recognition of himself as *Sole Protector and Supreme Head of the Church and clergy of England*. The clergy showed genuine alarm. It seemed impossible to acknowledge such a title without diminishing traditional papal authority, and equally impossible to refuse to consider it without incurring the heavy penalties that the king could legally exact under the dreaded statute. Both the convocations of Canterbury and York proposed alternative forms of wording. Tunstal of Durham suggested *Only and Supreme Lord after Christ in temporal matters*, but Henry, anxious, as he said, to control spiritual persons not spiritual things, would not accept the implied restriction. Over temporal matters, he argued, he had supreme power already. In the end both convocations agreed on *Singular Protector, Only and Supreme Lord, and, as far as the law of Christ allows, even Supreme Head*. This title represented a partial victory for the king, but its real meaning, still unresolved, lay in the interpretation of *as far as the law of Christ allows*. Parliament, the commons especially, enthusiastically recorded this clerical discomfiture by passing the bill 'concerning the pardon granted to the king's spiritual subjects', but when Henry tried to go further by asking the lords to discuss the legality of his marriage to Catherine, his spokesmen were heard in silence. Rather than attempt to force the issue at that moment, Henry prorogued parliament.

Parliament did not meet again until January 1532. During the previous months the king's cause had made no further progress at Rome, but Henry was obviously determined to marry Anne somehow. In July he had compelled Catherine both to leave court and to be separated from their daughter Mary. Anne, flushed with pride, was beginning to assume the queen's place. Few people liked these changes, and lords and commons openly showed sympathy for Catherine and hostility to the Boleyn faction. Cromwell, however, steered parliamentary discussion away from the subject of the 'divorce' towards the ever popular one of clerical abuses, with the result that before midsummer both houses had approved Henry's claim to license all canons (that is, all legislation passed by convocation), had made legal the appointment of English bishops without papal approval, and, in anticipation of retaliation, had denounced excommunication and interdict should the papacy seek to use these weapons against the English crown. All this action was one-sided. Rome would claim that it had no effect upon the rights of the papacy, but henceforward it was going to be most difficult for any of the king's subjects to disobey these new acts. Thomas More, Wolsey's successor as chancellor, saw the imminent danger. He resigned office as soon as convocation, with hardly a struggle, had thrown away its independence by recognizing the crown's right to approve or disallow its decisions. From many eyes this vital step was screened by the fuss over the unimportant Act of Annates, which proposed holding back payments which each bishop at his consecration traditionally made to Rome. Henry had to force this bill through both houses, but in Rome he pretended that, since he had so far not consented to put the bill into operation, he was defending papal rights against a critical and clamouring parliament. When parliament adjourned in the early summer of 1532, Cromwell must have felt satisfied with its work. The preliminaries of the anti-clerical campaign had been completed. All must now await the death of Warham, the aged archbishop of Canterbury.

Warham died on 23 August 1532. A week or so later, on 1 September, Henry created Anne marchioness of Pembroke in her own right, and henceforward, on formal as well as informal occasions, openly treated her as if she were queen. He also sent envoys to bring back Thomas Cranmer from his diplomatic work at the Imperial court, and by the end of the year Cranmer was dutifully petitioning Rome for the papers necessary to confirm his appointment as the new archbishop. Clement was glad to be able to do something uncontroversial for Henry. He, like many others, assumed that Anne's new title signified that she had reduced her price for becoming Henry's mistress, and that Henry would probably soon abandon his plans to free himself from Catherine. It was a fatal assumption. Very secretly indeed Henry and Anne went through a service of marriage at the end of January 1533. By the time Clement was sealing Cranmer's papers in Rome, and parliament was prohibiting any appeals to Rome in 'causes testamentary and causes of matrimony and divorce', Anne was telling Henry that she was pregnant. Both had to keep their secret until after Cranmer had been created archbishop on 30 March. After that nothing but formality remained.

On 11 April the new archbishop requested the king's permission to settle the king's 'great cause of matrimony'. Henry, after some pretended hesitation, empowered Cranmer to judge the case. The archbishop's court sat at Dunstable towards the end of May, and, after painstakingly but unnecessarily re-examining the evidence, delivered the expected verdict. Five days later Cranmer announced that since Henry had never been legally married to Catherine, his secret marriage to Anne Boleyn must be valid. On Whit Sunday in Westminster Abbey, Cranmer publicly demonstrated this verdict by crowning Anne queen in the presence of nobles, clerics, and people. There could be no appeal. The recent act forbade it. Irrevocably the decision had been made, and convocation, unable to initiate any canon without royal permission, had to accept it.

When parliament met again in January 1534, it completed the subjugation of the English church by strengthening the act against annates, forbidding the payment of the traditional Peter's pence to Rome, and declaring that the court of chancery, a secular court, should hear appeals from the archbishop's court. It also passed the Act of Succession which declared not only that 'all the issue had and procreate . . . between your Highness and your said most dearly and entirely beloved wife Queen Anne shall be your lawful children, and be inheritable and inherit . . .' but also that 'if any person or persons . . . maliciously and obstinately publish, divulge, or utter anything . . . to the slander or prejudice of the said matrimony solemnized between your Highness and the said Queen Anne . . . every such offence shall be taken and adjudged for misprision of treason'. With such legislation already on the statute book, the Act of Supremacy, passed in the following November, was almost superfluous. It merely highlighted the significance of the previous acts. In unmistakable language it proclaimed what had already been achieved – that, although the king had no theological quarrel with the pope and still professed to be the defender of the faith, the church *in* England had been transformed into the church *of* England, subject, like all other national institutions, to the will of the crown.

\*

The Act of Supremacy is printed in *Statutes of the Realm*, Record Commissioners (1810–28), vol. III, 492, as the first of several miscellaneous enactments of 26 Henry VIII, including one for the Oath to the Act of Succession. The act appears here in its original form, except for minor changes in spelling and capitalization.

For the constitutional issues involved, see K. Pickthorn,

*Early Tudor Government*, vol. II, *Henry VIII* (1934), and G. R. Elton, *England under the Tudors* (1955). F. M. Powicke, *The Reformation in England* (1941), is useful for its insistence on regarding the Henrician Reformation as representing a natural development of the relations between church, king, and people.

There are very many good biographies of the personalities involved in the church reforms of the period, and particular reference should be made to those by R. W. Chambers, *Thomas More* (1935); A. G. Dickens, *Thomas Cromwell and the English Reformation* (1959); and the series of works by A. F. Pollard, *Thomas Cranmer and the English Reformation* (1904), *Henry VIII* (1913), and *Wolsey* (1929). More recent biographies of Henry VIII are by J. J. Bagley (1962) and John Bowles (1964).

For the social, economic, and political background of the reformation movement generally over the thirty years 1529–59, the reader will be well served by the recent work of A. G. Dickens, *The English Reformation* (1964).

## 13. THE ACT OF SUPREMACY, 1534
### 26 Henry VIII, c. 1

*An Act concerning the King's Highness to be Supreme Head of the Church of England and to have authority to reform and redress all errors, heresies, and abuses in the same.*

Albeit the King's Majesty justly and rightfully is and ought to be the Supreme Head of the Church of England and so is recognized by the clergy of this realm in their Convocations; yet nevertheless for corroboration and confirmation thereof, and for the increase of virtue in Christ's religion within this realm of England, and to repress and extirp all errors, heresies, and other enormities and abuses heretofore used in the same, Be it enacted by authority of this present Parliament that the King our

Sovereign Lord, his heirs and successors kings of this realm, shall be taken, accepted, and reputed the only Supreme Head in earth of the Church of England called *Anglicana Ecclesia*, and shall have and enjoy annexed and united to the imperial Crown of this realm as well the title and style thereof, as all honours, dignities, pre-eminences, jurisdictions, privileges, authorities, immunities, profits, and commodities to the said dignity of Supreme Head of the same Church belonging and appertaining : And that our said Sovereign Lord, his heirs and successors kings of this realm, shall have full power and authority from time to time to visit, repress, redress, reform, order, correct, restrain, and amend all such errors, heresies, abuses, offences, contempts, and enormities, whatsoever they be, which by any manner spiritual authority or jurisdiction ought or may lawfully be reformed, repressed, ordered, redressed, corrected, restrained, or amended, most to the pleasure of Almighty God, the increase of virtue in Christ's religion and for the conservation of the peace, unity, and tranquillity of this realm : any usage, custom, foreign laws, foreign authority, prescription, or any other thing or things to the contrary hereof notwithstanding.

## 14. The Act for the Dissolution of the Greater Monasteries, 1539

THE monasteries and friaries of medieval England were doomed several years before they were dissolved. Once Henry VIII's campaign against papal authority had reached the point of no return, and certainly once parliament had formally endorsed the breach with Rome by passing the Act of Supremacy, it became evident that Christendom-wide orders could not continue to live inside a national church. The first crisis occurred in 1534–5 when Henry insisted that all abbots, priors, and other heads of religious houses should take an oath accepting the Act of Succession. This meant acknowledging the validity of the king's marriage to Anne Boleyn, declaring the baby Elizabeth to be the true heir to the throne, and denying that Catherine had ever been Henry's wife. The king and his ministers argued that such an oath presented no difficulty to loyal subjects. But any Englishman who acknowledged that he had a further loyalty to Rome could not take the king's oath without defying or ignoring the pope's order. For in Rome on 23 March 1534 Clement VII had at length clearly given his verdict that Henry's marriage to Catherine was lawful. In doing this he had implicitly denounced both Anne's claim to be queen and the recognition of Elizabeth as heir to the throne. For the moment, most English monks and friars attempted to reconcile two incompatibles. Their very membership of an order implied acceptance of the spiritual leadership of the pope, yet all but a handful of them took the required oath. They asserted their obedience to the crown, the more menacing of their two masters, and refused to recognize that this implied any disloyalty to the papacy.

The few regular clergy who declined to take the oath of succession were the Carthusian monks, the nuns and priests of the Bridgettine house at Syon near Isleworth, and the Observant Franciscan friars, who at Greenwich explained to the king's visitors that to deny papal supremacy would be 'clearly against their profession and the rules of St Francis'. The visitors tried to meet their objection with 'reasonable argument'. They maintained that St Francis had required his original followers to be obedient to the 'bishop of Rome' because the first friars had lived in his diocese, and, they continued, if English friars were logical, they would realize that they could only carry out St Francis's will and intent by obeying their own bishop. The practice of having a cardinal as 'governor, protector, and corrector of their brotherhood' had been instituted not by St Francis himself but after his death by 'some ambitious friar', and, furthermore, as religious they knew full well that 'God's law' required them to obey their king. Neither the pope nor St Francis nor any 'previous vows, oaths, or professions' could take away 'one jot of the obedience which they owed to the king by God's law'. The consciences of most monks and friars gratefully accepted such reasoning, but a resolute few went into exile or suffered torture and the gallows rather than deny, implicitly or explicitly, the supreme authority of Rome in all spiritual matters.

During the previous four centuries, first the monasteries and then, to a lesser extent, the friaries had grown rich. Rents, tithes, voluntary offerings, fines, and fees provided most of their wealth, but the riches were so unevenly distributed that some communities were outstandingly prosperous and some comparatively poor. Less than half a dozen monks or friars lived in the smallest houses, and they had little influence on the life or economy of their area. Most laity and secular clergy had thought for years that these houses did not justify their existence. Already they had tacitly approved when Wolsey dissolved St Frideswide's Abbey and another score of smaller houses in order to endow Cardinal's College at Oxford, and later suppressed a further group in order to found his college at Ipswich. It was natural enough, therefore, that once he had become head of the Church, Henry should turn envious eyes towards this source of wealth. He had to get money quickly from somewhere. Long ago he had exhausted his inheritance from his father. Inflation was steadily nibbling away his own inadequate income, and parliament, which he needed to keep as cooperative as possible, seemed to think that granting a paltry £200,000 over four years was giving him a fortune.

No one knew how rich the English church was. Therefore, in January 1535, Sir Thomas Audley, the chancellor, sent out commissioners to value all ecclesiastical property in the kingdom. Parliament's recent grant to the crown of an annual tax of a tenth on the net incomes of all spiritual benefices made the survey an urgent one. The commissioners worked rapidly and well, so that by June most of the field reports on some 650 monasteries and nunneries and 200 friaries and hospitals were being fashioned into the uniform schedules required by the exchequer. This information, now available in print in the six folio volumes of the *Valor Ecclesiasticus*, reveals that the contemporary annual value of the total possessions of the religious houses easily exceeded £200,000, and long before the official report had been completed, Cromwell resolved that some of this wealth should be transferred to the crown. In August 1535 he sent out visitors to bring back evidence which would justify the imminent attack he proposed to make on the monasteries and friaries. Unlike the commissioners of the *Valor Ecclesiasticus*, these visitors did not set out with open minds to record facts. They knew what they wanted to find, and they were determined to find it. They reported dozens of houses for being slack in the observance of the offices, recorded many examples of superstition and the worship of false relics, and unearthed scandals which shocked the devout. Such irregularities undoubtedly existed, but the visitors emphasized and exaggerated them to make them serve Cromwell's purpose. They formed the basis and justification of the preamble – the *apologia* – of the bill which members of parliament were invited to debate in February 1536:

> For as much as manifest sin, vicious, carnal, and abominable living, is daily used and committed among the little and small abbeys, priories, and other religious houses of monks, canons, and nuns, where the congregation of such religious persons is under the number of twelve persons, whereby the governors of such religious houses and their convent spoil, destroy, consume, and utterly waste, as well their churches, monasteries, priories, principal houses, farms, granges, lands, tenements, and hereditaments, as the ornaments of their churches and their goods and chattels, to the high displeasure of Almighty God, slander of good religion, and to the great infamy of the King's Highness and the realm. . . .

The bill proposed to suppress the lesser monasteries, and defined a lesser house not as one which had fewer than twelve in its community, but as one which had an income of less than £200 a year. Both lords and commons passed the bill without offering any serious opposition. Politically it was a clever bill. It brought the crown property which would yield a modest but useful £20,000 a year. Most people accepted its moderate proposals as a beneficial and overdue pruning, and it silenced any protest from the larger monasteries by its flattery. It proposed to transfer the inhabitants of the suppressed houses 'to divers and great solemn monasteries of this realm wherein, thanks be to God, religion is right well kept and observed'. It did not specify which monasteries the king and Cromwell had in mind, but every self-respecting community with more than £200 a year could do no other than assume that it figured among the righteous. For a large house to protest against the 1536 act on the assumption that it was the first stage of a wider suppression would be to run the risk of condemning itself. It could be made to appear that, for dark reasons unknown outside the community, it did not consider itself among the 'divers and great solemn monasteries'.

When, in the autumn of 1536, the royal officers began to put the act into operation, they sparked off revolt first in Lincolnshire and then in the whole of the northern counties. In these areas where tradition died hard, administrative changes, enclosures, and government interference in the cloth industry had already roused widespread anger. Sympathy for Queen Catherine and dislike of the recent religious changes piled more fuel on the bonfire of revolt: the suppression of local communities and the destruction of familiar buildings set it alight. The protests were too spontaneous to be well organized. The Lincolnshire rising, which first flared up with a riot at Louth on 1 October, burnt itself out within three weeks, and Robert Aske and the other leaders of the more serious Pilgrimage of Grace were too trusting and too sincere about their aims to exploit strength when they had it. Norfolk and the king succeeded in dispersing the rebel army by promises, and then arrested and executed the leaders and many others for alleged breaches of the truce. By the spring of 1537 they had reduced the north to a sullen silence.

The government achieved the suppression of the lesser monasteries without serious opposition from the rest of the church. In the southern counties there was no protest to speak of; in the north a few of the seculars and of the inhabitants of the larger abbeys supported the Pilgrimage, so that in the eventual reckoning the abbots of Jervaulx, Whalley, Kirkstead, and Barlings, the prior of Bridlington, and more than a score of monks died on the scaffold. The humiliating defeat of the Pilgrimage speedily convinced most religious that further protest was impossible, and that nothing could prevent the crown from swallowing the major monasteries as soon as it had digested the revenues of the minor. Abbot Pyle of Furness saw no advantage in postponing the inevitable, and, early in 1537, readily accepted a suggestion of the earl of Sussex that he should voluntarily surrender his abbey to the king. The monks of Furness consented, and buildings, lands, rights, and privileges passed to the crown. This eager yielding of a major house set a precedent. Lewes and Titchfield followed in similar fashion in November, and during the early weeks of 1538, one royal commissioner, Dr Legh, was busy receiving surrenders in the south-west, and another, Dr Layton, was equally active in East Anglia. Many communities, seeing nothing ahead but a short, troublesome future, were anxious to be gone; in other places the commissioners won over a hesitating abbot or prior with promises and blandishments. And everywhere local laymen were hovering like vultures to purchase any monastic lands which might become available. The friaries did not offer anything like the same pickings as the monasteries, but during 1538 Richard Ingworth, once a leading Dominican but now suffragan bishop of Dover, worked hard carrying out Cromwell's orders to suppress the friaries. Much was done in doubtfully legal form, but the act passed in May 1539 ratified and legalized all the surrenders that had been made as well as the seizure of any more houses 'which hereafter shall happen to be dissolved'. In 1539 a few abbots and monks tried, far too late, to resist events – the abbots of Glastonbury, Colchester, and Reading were executed for treason – and by March 1540 the last house, Waltham Abbey, had surrendered. Monks and friars, so important a part of medieval life, were no longer active in England.

At first sight it seems surprising that this revolution occasioned so little contemporary regret, but the explanation lies in the advantages it offered to so many different groups of men. That the dissolution more than doubled the crown's revenue gratified not only Henry and his ministers but also members of parliament and tax-payers in general. Advocates of the national church considered that the dissolution strengthened its independence, and those who wanted doctrinal as well as administrative changes were of the opinion that it brought England nearer to Protestantism. The six new dioceses centred on transformed houses at Gloucester, Bristol, Peterborough, Chester, Oxford, and Westminster pleased the secular church, and pensions or alternative work mollified the majority of monks and monastic servants. Above all, however, the surrendered property and lands gave existing and would-be landowners unprecedented chances of growing rich. Even before a community had surrendered its house to the crown, the speculators were jostling for advantages. The large, estab-lished landowners sought opportunities to acquire a fat abbey or a rich shrine. The lesser men hoped to buy an extra manor or a coveted field or two, and there was no lack of customers to purchase furniture, tiles, metals, glass, and faced stone when the royal commissioners began to dismantle the churches and cloister buildings. These up-and-coming men and women had few disturbing, nostalgic regrets for the past. Their eyes were on the beckoning future, rather than on the architectural beauties of the doomed buildings, and they thought as little of robbing deserted monasteries for stone, timber, and lead as our generation does of pulling down Georgian and Victorian buildings that have served their purpose or stand in the way of lucrative development. We justify our depredations by our need for new town centres, flats, offices, and car-parks. The Tudors used their new wealth to raise their standard of living, to finance trade ventures, to improve harbours and bridges and provide amenities in the towns, and, after a few years, to build themselves stone houses which flaunted the importance of their family. Fountains Hall near Ripon, Sir John Tregonwell's house at Milton Abbas, and Richard Assheton's house at Whalley were obvious results of the dissolution of Fountains, Milton, and Whalley Abbeys respectively, but many of the Elizabethan and early Stuart houses, from large imposing mansions to far more humble halls and manor houses, were financed in part from revenues which once had been monastic.

During the last five years of his reign, Henry VIII fought expensive and fruitless campaigns against Scotland and France. To raise his fighting funds he sold far more monastic estates than he would have done in times of peace, so that when he died hundreds of men and women had important financial interests vested in the dissolution of the monasteries. Edward VI's reign consolidated this revolution. Therefore when Mary succeeded to the throne she had no real chance of undoing what her father had done. Most of her subjects were prepared to accept the restoration of papal supremacy, but too many of them stood to lose valuable possessions if she attempted to restore the monasteries of England.

*

The Act for the Dissolution of the Greater Monasteries and Abbeys is printed in *Statutes of the Realm*, Record Commissioners (1810–28), vol. III, 733–9, as one of the several miscellaneous acts which make up the statute 31 Henry VIII. It is given below in its original form, except that some archaic spellings and obsolete forms of auxiliary verbs have been silently modernized; repetitive formulas are indicated by [etc.] . . . after their first appearance.

The Act of 1536 for the Dissolution of the Lesser Houses is printed in *Statutes of the Realm* (op. cit.), vol. III, 575–8, as 27 Henry VIII, c. 28, and, in part, by G. R. Elton, *The*

*Tudor Constitution: Documents and Commentary* (1960), 374–8.

The best modern account of monastic life before the dissolution, and of the dissolution itself and its effects, is by Dom David Knowles, *The Religious Orders in England*, vol. III, *The Tudor Age* (1959). Classic earlier treatments are by F. A. Gasquet, *Henry VIII and the English Monasteries* (1906), written from the Catholic point of view; and by G. Baskerville, *English Monks and the Suppression of the Monasteries* (1937), from a viewpoint much less sympathetic towards the monks. G. C. Coulton, *Five Centuries of Religion*, vol. IV (1950), writes well of the period, but with a Protestant bias. There is a good short account by Rose Graham, *An Essay on the English Monasteries* (1939), reprinted by G. Barraclough (ed.) in *Social Life in Early England* (1960); and a recent book, *The Dissolution of the Monasteries* (1966) by G. W. O. Woodward.

For the extent of the monastic holdings, see J. Caley and J. Hunter (eds.), *Valor Ecclesiasticus*, 6 vols., Record Commissioners (1810–34); and the definitive analysis by A. Savine, 'The English Monasteries on the Eve of the Dissolution', in *Oxford Studies in social and legal history*, ed. P. Vinogradoff, I (1909).

T. Wright (ed.), *Three Chapters of Letters relating to the suppression of the monasteries*, Camden Society, XXVI (1843), prints some of the highly entertaining reports which his agents made to Thomas Cromwell during the general visitation of the monasteries. There is also the modern compilation by G. H. Cook, *Letters to Cromwell and Others on the Suppression of the Monasteries* (1965).

*English Historical Documents*, vol. V (1967), ed. C. H. Williams, prints documents relating to the dissolution of the monasteries and the confiscation of church wealth on pp. 761–94, with introductory material and full bibliography on pp. 635–51.

## 14. THE ACT FOR THE DISSOLUTION OF THE GREATER MONASTERIES, 1539
### 31 Henry VIII, c. 13

Where divers and sundry abbots, priors, abbesses, prioresses, and other ecclesiastical governors and governesses of divers monasteries, abbeys, priories, nunneries, colleges, hospitals, houses of friars, and other religious and ecclesiastical houses and places within this our Sovereign Lord the King's realm of England and Wales, of their own free and voluntary minds, good wills and assents, without constraint, coaction, or compulsion of any manner of person or persons, since the fourth day of February, the twenty-seventh year of the reign of our now most dread Sovereign Lord [1536], by the due order and course of the common laws of this his realm of England, and by their sufficient writings of record under their convent and common seals, have severally given, granted, and by the same their writings severally confirmed all their said monasteries, abbeys [etc.] . . . and all their sites, circuits, and precincts of the same, and all and singular their manors, lordships, granges, meses [messuages], lands, tenements, meadows, pastures, rents, reversions, services, woods, tithes, pensions, portions, churches, chapels, advowsons, patronages, annuities, rights, entries, conditions, commons, leets [courts leet], courts, liberties, privileges, and franchises appertaining or in any wise belonging to any such monastery [etc.] . . . by whatsoever name or corporation they or any of them were then named or called, and of what order, habit, religion, or other kind or quality soever they or any of them were then reputed, known, or taken; to have and to hold all the said monasteries [etc.] . . . sites, circuits, precincts, manors, lands, tenements, meadows, pastures, rents, reversions, services, and all other the premises to our said Sovereign Lord, his heirs and successors forever; and the same their said monasteries [etc.] . . . sites, circuits [etc.] . . . and other the premises voluntarily as is aforesaid have renounced, left, and forsaken . . . : Be it therefore enacted by the King our Sovereign Lord and the lords spiritual and temporal and the commons in this present Parliament assembled, and by authority of the same, that:

(1) The King our Sovereign Lord shall have, hold, possess, and enjoy to him, his heirs and successors forever, all and singular such late monasteries [etc.] . . . which since the said fourth day of February, the twenty-seventh year of the reign of our said Sovereign Lord, have been dissolved, suppressed, renounced, relinquished, forfeited, given up, or by any other means come to his Highness; and by the same authority and in like manner shall have, hold, possess, and enjoy all the sites, circuits, precincts, manors, lordships, granges, meses, lands, tenements, meadows, pastures, rents, reversions, services, woods, tithes, pensions, portions, parsonages appropriate, vicarages, churches, chapels, advowsons, nominations, patronages, annuities, rights, interests, entries, conditions, commons, leets, courts, liberties, privileges, franchises, and other whatsoever hereditaments which appertained or belonged to the said late monasteries [etc.] . . . in as large and ample manner and form as the late abbots [etc.] . . . had, held, or occupied, or of right ought to have had, held, or occupied in the rights of their said late monasteries [etc.] . . . at the time of the said dissolution, suppression, renouncing, relinquishing, forfeiting, giving up, or by any other manner of means coming of the same to the King's Highness, since the fourth day of February above specified.

(2) And it is further enacted by the authority abovesaid that not only all the said late monasteries [etc.] . . . sites [etc.] . . . and all other the premises forthwith, immediately and presently, but also all other monasteries [etc.] . . . which hereafter shall happen to be dissolved, suppressed [etc.] . . . and also all the sites [etc.] . . . and other hereditaments whatsoever they be, belonging or appertaining to the same or to any of them, whensoever and as soon as they shall be dissolved [etc.] . . . shall be vested, deemed, and adjudged by authority of this present Parliament in the very actual and real seisin and possession of the King our Sovereign Lord, his heirs and successors forever, in the state and condition as they now be, and as though all the said late monasteries [etc.] . . . as also the said monasteries [etc.] . . . which hereafter shall happen to be dissolved, sup-

pressed, renounced, relinquished, forfeited, given up, or come unto the King's Highness, sites, circuits, precincts, manors, lordships, granges, lands, tenements, and other the premises whatsoever they be, and every of them, were in this present Act specially and particularly rehearsed, named, and expressed by express words, names, titles and faculties, and in their natures, kinds, and qualities.

(3) And . . . that all the said late monasteries [etc.] . . . and all the manors, lordships, granges, lands, tenements, and other the premises, except such thereof as have come to the King's hands by attainder or attainders of treason, and all the said monasteries [etc.] . . . which hereafter shall happen to be dissolved [etc.] . . . and all the manors [etc.] . . . and other hereditaments, whatsoever they be, belonging to the same or to any of them, except such thereof which shall happen to come to the King's Highness by attainder or attainders of treason, shall be in the order, survey, and governance of our said Sovereign Lord the King's Court of Augmentations of the Revenues of his Crown, and of the chancellor, officers, and ministers of the same; and all the farms, issues, revenues, and profits coming and growing of the premises and every part thereof, except before excepted, shall be ordered, taken, and received to the King's use by the said chancellor, ministers, and officers of the same court, in such and like manner and form as the monasteries, priories, sites, circuits, manors [etc.] . . . and other hereditaments late appertaining or belonging unto the monasteries, abbeys, priories, or other religious houses, late by authority of Parliament suppressed, have been ordered, surveyed, and governed.

(4) Saving to all and every person and persons and bodies politic and their heirs and successors, and the heirs and successors of all and every of them (other than the said late abbots [etc.] . . . and their successors, and the successors of every of them, and such as pretend to be founders, patrons, or donors of such monasteries [etc.] . . . or of any manors, messuages, lands, tenements, or other hereditaments belonging to the same or to any of them, their heirs and successors and the heirs and suc-

cessors of every such founder, patron, or donor, and their now abbots [etc.] . . . of such monasteries [etc.] . . . which hereafter shall happen to be dissolved, suppressed, renounced, relinquished, forfeited, given up, or come to the King's Highness, and such as pretend to be founders, patrons, or donors of such monasteries [etc.] . . . or of any manors, messuages, lands, tenements, or other hereditaments to the same belonging, or to any of them, their heirs and successors and the heirs and successors of every of them) all such right, title, claim, interest, possession, rents, charges, annuities, leases, farms, offices, fees, liveries and livings, portions, pensions, corrodies, commons, synods, proxies, and other profits which they or any of them have, claim, ought, may, or might have had, in or to the premises or to any part or parcel thereof, in such like manner, form, and condition to all intents, respects, constructions, and purposes as if this Act had never been had nor made; rent-services, rent-secks, and all other services and suits only excepted.

(5) Provided always . . . that if any late abbot, prior, prioress, abbess, or other ecclesiastical governor or governess abovesaid, within one year next before the dissolution [etc.] . . . or coming to the King's Highness of his late monastery [etc.] . . . hath made any lease or grant under his convent or common seal or otherwise, for term of life or for term of years, of the site, circuit, and precinct of his said late monastery [etc.] . . . or of any part thereof, or of any manors [etc.] . . . or other hereditaments which belonged or appertained to his said late monastery [etc.] . . . which manors [etc.] . . . or other hereditaments were not before the same lease commonly used to be set nor let to farm, but were kept and reserved in the manurance, tillage or occupation of the said governor or governess for the maintenance of hospitality and good housekeeping; or within one year as is abovesaid has made any lease or grant for term of life or for term of years of any manors [etc.] . . . or other hereditaments whatsoever they be, whereof or in the which any estate or interest for term of life, year or years at the time of the making of any such grant or lease then had its being or continuance, and then was not determined, finished, or expired; or within the time of one year as is abovesaid has made any lease or grant for term

of life or for term of years of any manors [etc.] . . . or other
hereditaments whatsoever they be, upon the which leases and
grants the usual and old rents and farms accustomed to be
yielded and reserved by the space of twenty years next before the
first day of this present Parliament is and be not thereupon
reserved and held; or if any such governor or governess has made
any bargain or sale of his woods within one year as is afore
limited, which woods be yet growing and standing; that then all
and every such lease, grant, bargain, and sale of wood or woods
shall be utterly void and of no effect.

(6) And . . . that all feoffments, fines, and recoveries had,
made, knowledged, or suffered by any governor or governess
without the King's licence under his Great Seal, within one year
next before the dissolution [etc.] . . . or coming unto the King's
Highness of his said monastery [etc.] . . . or any manors, meses,
lands, tenements, or other hereditaments whatsoever they be,
which the said late abbot, prior, abbess, prioress, and other
ecclesiastical governors and governesses or any of them, or any
of their predecessors, had or held of the gift, grant, or confirmation of our said Sovereign Lord or of any of his Highness's
progenitors, or of the which monasteries [etc.] . . . our said
Sovereign Lord was founder or patron, or which manors, meses,
lands, tenements, or other hereditaments were of the ancient or
old foundation or possession of the said late monasteries [etc.]
. . . shall be utterly void and of no effect.

[Clauses 7 and 8 repeat 5 and 6 for monasteries about to be
dissolved.]

(9) Provided always . . . that if any abbot, prior, abbess or
prioress, or other governor or governess abovesaid, within one
year next before the first day of this present Parliament, or if any
late abbot [etc.] . . . within one year next before any such
dissolution, suppression, renouncing, relinquishing, forfeiting,
giving up, or coming to the King's Highness of the premises or
of any parcel thereof as is aforesaid, has made any demise, lease,
or grant to any person or persons for term of years of any manors
[etc.] . . . or other hereditaments aforesaid, which person or
persons at the time of the said demise, lease, or grant, had and

held the same to farm for term of years not then expired, that then the said person or persons to whom any such demise, lease, or grant has been so made, shall have and hold the same for the term of twenty-one years only from the time of the making of the said demise, lease, or grant, if so many years be by the said demise, lease or grant specified, limited, and expressed, or else for so many years as in such demise, lease, or grant are expressed; so that the old rent be thereupon reserved, and the same lease or leases exceed not twenty-one years; this Act or anything therein contained to the contrary notwithstanding.

[Clauses 10 and 11 reserve the rights of life tenants and copyhold tenants of monastic lands.]

(12) Provided always . . . that all leases heretofore made of any of the premises by authority of our Sovereign Lord the King's Court of Augmentations of the Revenues of his Crown, and all such leases, feoffments, and wood sales made by the said governors and governesses or any of them under their convent seals or under the convent or common seal of any of them, within one year next before the dissolution [etc.] . . . of the said monasteries [etc.] . . . which said leases, grants, feoffments, and wood sales have been examined, enrolled, decreed, or affirmed in our said Sovereign Lord the King's Court of Augmentations, and the decree of the same put in writing sealed with the seal of the said Court of Augmentations, shall be good and effectual according to the same decree; any clause or act heretofore in this present Act to the contrary notwithstanding.

(13) Provided always . . . that if any person or persons have justly and truly, without fraud or covin [deceit], paid or given any sum or sums of money to any of the said late governors or governesses for the bargain and sale of any woods, being and growing in or upon any manors, lands, tenements, or hereditaments which appertained or belonged to the said late monasteries [etc.] . . . or unto any of them, which bargain and sale by authority of this Act is made void and of no effect, and by means thereof the King's Highness may have and take the commodity and profit of such woods so bargained and sold, that then the chancellor and other officers of our said Sovereign Lord the King's Court of Augmentations, or three of them whereof the

chancellor for the time being shall be one, [out] of our said Sovereign Lord the King's treasure remaining in the treasury of the same court shall satisfy and recompense every such person and persons such sum of money or other recompense as the same chancellor and officers or three of them, whereof the said chancellor shall be one, shall think meet and convenient; and if any other person or persons shall happen to take profit and commodity by reason of avoiding of such wood sales by authority of this Act, that then every person and persons which may or shall take such profit shall be ordered for satisfaction to be made to the parties that shall happen to be grieved by this Act, by the said chancellor and other the officers of the same court.

(14) Provided also . . . that all and every person and persons, their heirs and assigns, which since the said fourth day of February, by licence, pardon, confirmation, release, assent, or consent of our said Sovereign Lord the King, under his Great Seal heretofore given, had or made, or hereafter to be had or made, have obtained or purchased by indenture, fine, feoffment, recovery, or otherwise of the said late abbots [etc.] . . . any monasteries, priories, colleges, hospitals, manors, lands, tenements, meadows, pastures, woods, churches, chapels, parsonages, tithes, pensions, portions, or other hereditaments, shall have and enjoy the same according to such writings and assurances as have been thereof, before the first day of this present Parliament or hereafter shall be, had or made; Saving to all and every person and persons and bodies politic, their heirs and successors, and to the heirs and successors of every of them (other than the said late abbots [etc.] . . . and their successors and the successors of every of them, and such as pretend to be founders, patrons, or donors of the said monasteries [etc.] . . . or any of them, or of any manors, messuages, lands, tenements or other hereditaments late belonging to the same or to any of them and their heirs and successors, and the heirs and successors of every such founder, patron, or donor) all such right, title, interest, possession, rents, annuities, commodities, offices, fees, liveries and livings, portions, pensions, corrodies, synodies, proxies, and other profits which they or any of them have, ought or might have had in or to any of the said monasteries, abbeys [etc.] . . . at any time

before any such purchase, indentures, fines, feoffments, recoveries, or other lawful means between any such parties had or made as is abovesaid; this Act or anything therein contained to the contrary notwithstanding.

(15) And where our said Sovereign Lord since the fourth day of February the said twenty-seventh year of the reign of our said Sovereign Lord, has obtained and purchased, as well by exchanges as by gifts, bargains, fines, feoffments, recoveries, deeds enrolled, and otherwise, of divers and sundry persons many sundry and divers honours, castles, manors, lands, tenements, meadows, pastures, woods, rents, reversions, services, and other hereditaments, and has not only paid divers and sundry great sums of money for the same, but also has given and granted for the same unto divers and sundry persons divers and sundry manors, lands, tenements, and hereditaments and other recompenses in and for full satisfaction of all such honours [etc.] . . . and other his hereditaments by his Highness obtained or had as is abovesaid; Be it therefore enacted by the authority abovesaid that our said Sovereign Lord the King, his heirs and successors, shall have, hold, possess, and enjoy all such honours [etc.] . . . and other hereditaments as his Highness since the said fourth day of February, the twenty-seventh year abovesaid has obtained and had by way of exchange, bargain, purchase, or other whatsoever mean or means, according to the true meaning and intent of his Highness's bargain, exchange or purchase. . . .

(16) And where it has pleased the King's Highness of his abundant grace and goodness, as well upon divers and sundry considerations his Majesty specially moving, as also otherwise, to have bargained, sold, exchanged, or given and granted by his Grace's several letters patent, indentures, or other writings as well under his Highness's Great Seal as under the seal of his Highness's Duchy of Lancaster and the seal of the office of the augmentations of his crown, unto divers and sundry of his loving and obedient subjects, divers and sundry honours, castles, manors, monasteries, abbeys, priories, lands, tenements, rents, reversions, services, parsonages appropriated, advowsons, liveries, tithes, oblations, portions, pensions, franchises, privileges,

liberties and other hereditaments, commodities and profits, in fee simple, fee tail, for term of life or for term of years; for avoiding of which said letters patent and of the contents of the same, divers sundry and many ambiguities, doubts and questions might hereafter arise, be moved and stirred . . . albeit the words in effect contained in the said letters patent be according to the true intent and meaning of his most royal Majesty; Be it therefore enacted by the authority of this present Parliament, that as well all and every the said letters patent, indentures, or other writings and every of them, under the seal or seals abovesaid or any of them, made or granted by the King's Highness since the said fourth day of February, the said twenty-seventh year of his most noble reign, as all and singular other his Grace's letters patent, indentures, or other writings to be had, made, or granted to any person or persons within three years next after the making of this present Act, of any honours, castles, manors, monasteries [etc.] . . . and all other hereditaments and possessions of what kind, nature, or quality soever they be, or by whatsoever name or names they or any of them be named, known or reputed, shall stand and be good, effectual, and available in the law of this realm. . . .

(17) And where divers and sundry abbots, priors, abbesses, prioresses, and other ecclesiastical governors and governesses of the said late monasteries [etc.] . . . have had, possessed, and enjoyed divers and sundry parsonages appropriated, tithes, pensions, and portions, and also were acquitted and discharged of and for the payment or payments of tithes to be paid out [of] or for their said monasteries [etc.] . . . manors, messuages, lands, tenements, and hereditaments; Be it therefore enacted by the authority abovesaid that as well the King our Sovereign Lord, his heirs and successors, as all and every such person and persons, their heirs and assigns, which have or hereafter shall have any monasteries [etc.] . . . sites, circuits, precincts of the same, or any of them, or any manors, messuages, parsonages appropriate, tithes, pensions, portions, or other hereditaments, whatsoever they be, which belonged or appertained or which now belong or appertain unto the said monasteries [etc.] . . . or unto any of them, shall have, hold, retain, keep and enjoy, as well the said

parsonages appropriate, tithes, pensions, and portions of the said monasteries [etc.] . . . sites, circuits, precincts, manors, meses, lands, tenements, and hereditaments whatsoever they be, and every of them, according to their estates and titles, discharged and acquitted of payment of tithes as freely and in as large and ample manner as the said late abbots [etc.] . . . had, held, occupied, possessessed, used, retained, or enjoyed the same or any parcel thereof, at the days of their dissolution [etc.] . . . or coming to the King's Highness of such monasteries [etc.] . . . ; this Act or anything therein contained to the contrary notwithstanding. Saving to the King's Highness, his heirs and successors, all and all manner of rents, services, and other duties whatsoever they be, as if this Act had never been had nor made.

(18) And that . . . such of the said late monasteries [etc.] . . . and all churches and chapels to them or any of them belonging, which before the dissolution [etc.] . . . were exempted from the visitation or visitations and all jurisdiction of the ordinary or ordinaries within whose diocese they were situate or set, shall from henceforth be within the jurisdiction and visitation of the ordinary or ordinaries, within whose diocese they or any of them be situate and set, or within the jurisdiction and visitation of such person or persons as by the King's Highness shall be limited or appointed; this Act or any other exemption, liberty, or jurisdiction to the contrary notwithstanding.

(19) And where before this time it hath pleased the King's Majesty at the contemplation and humble petition of the right noble Thomas, Duke of Norfolk, to give his royal assent of licence by his Grace's word, without any manner of letters patent or other writing, to purchase and retain to him and to his heirs forever of William Flatbery, late abbot of the monastery of Sipton in the county of Suffolk and convent of the said late monastery now being dissolved, all the same monastery together with all and singular manors, lordships, lands, tenements, woods, waters, commons, courts, leets, advowsons, patronages, parsonages, vicarages, chantries, free chapels, tithes, portions of tithes, pensions, annuities, rents, suits, services, reversions, remainders, and all other things which were the hereditaments or the possessions of the said late monastery, wheresoever they lay

or were within the realm of England; and in likewise our said Sovereign Lord gave like licence by his Grace's word unto the right honourable George, Lord Cobham, to purchase and receive to him and to his heirs forever, of the late master and brethren of the college or chantry of Cobham in the county of Kent now being utterly dissolved, the site of the same college or chantry, and all and singular their hereditaments and possessions, as well temporal as ecclesiastical wheresoever they lay or were within the realm of England; Be it therefore enacted by the authority of this present Parliament that the Act above written or anything therein contained shall not be in any wise prejudicial or hurtful to the said Duke and Lord Cobham or to either of them or to the heirs or assigns of either of them; but that the same Duke and Lord Cobham and either of them sundrily and the heirs and assigns of either of them, shall and may have, hold, retain, and enjoy the premises by them sundrily purchased or received according to the purports and effects of such evidences, writings, and conveyances as they or any of them sundrily have caused to be devised and made to them or to their uses for the same. Saving always and reserving to all and singular persons and bodies politic and to their heirs and successors (other than the said late abbot and convent and their successors and the said late master and brethren and their successors and the founders of the same monastery or of the said college or chantry and the heirs of either of them, and all donors, grantors, or augmentors of them or either of them, and the heirs and assigns of either of them) all such rights, titles, possessions, rents, services, fees, offices, annuities, corrodies, liveries, leases, and all other their such interests, profits, and commodities as they or any of them had, should or ought to have of, to or in any of the premises sundrily purchased or received by the said late Duke or Lord Cobham if this present Act had never been had or made; anything in the same Act to the contrary being in any wise notwithstanding.[1]

1. This confirmation in favour of the duke of Norfolk and Lord Cobham is annexed as a schedule to the original act.

# Glossary of Archaic and Technical Words
## Used in the Text

ADVOWSON. The right of patronage or of presenting a clergyman to a living

AID. A periodic payment made by a feudal vassal to his lord

ALIENATION. The transference of land from one holder to another

AMERCEMENT. A fine levied by a court

APPEAL. A formal accusation of treason or felony made by a private individual. In Norman times the matter was usually settled by trial by battle, later by a jury

APPROPRIATE. The term used when a monastery or other religious body took over the temporalities of a benefice

ASSART. An area of arable land won from the forest or waste

ASSIZE. A statutory regulation or law; or legal proceedings

ATTACH. To seize a man's person or his goods as security for a debt

BENEFIT OF CLERGY. Exemption of the clergy from the jurisdiction and sentence of ordinary courts of law

BURGAGE. Lands or tenements held in a borough by payment of a yearly rent to the lord

CALENDAR. A list of documents with summaries of their contents. Usually arranged in chronological order

CANON. Originally a secular priest, but after the Norman Conquest an increasing number of canons (canons regular) lived monastic lives, e.g. Augustinian and Premonstratensian canons. A second, quite different, meaning is a church decree

CARTULARY. A list or record of lands and privileges granted by charters

CHANCELLOR. The head of the CHANCERY (q.v.). Eventually the king's chief minister

CHANCERY. The royal secretariat

CHAPTER. The chapter of a religious house consisted of all the full members. The part of the Rule, read daily in the chapter house, was also called the chapter

CLERK. A word of several meanings in the Middle Ages: any clergyman; a man in minor orders; one in charge of accounts or records; a scholar

COMMISSION OF ARRAY. Instruction addressed by the king to a group of local gentlemen to call out the SHIRE LEVY (q.v.)

CONSTABLE. The captain of a royal estate, having the custody of prisoners and some limited judicial authority

CORONER. A county official appointed from 1194 onwards to supervise the financial and legal interests of the crown. He combined the present-day functions of a coroner with the wider duties of an examining magistrate

CORRODY. A pension or annuity which monasteries often exchanged for a substantial single payment

COURT LEET. A local court authorized by royal grant to hear cases of petty jurisdiction. Courts leet were often responsible for the view of FRANKPLEDGE (q.v.)

COURT OF AUGMENTATIONS. A court of record with its own chancellor and officials established in 1536 to administer the estates of dissolved monasteries

COURT ROLL. The record of a court's activities, so called because the parchment on which the record was written was filed as a roll

COVIN. Deceit

DANEGELD. A direct tax on land for defence against the Danes. It was continued by Canute and the Normans, but became obsolete in Henry II's reign

DARREIN PRESENTMENT. Judicial cases concerned with ADVOWSON (q.v.)

DEMESNE. Part of the manor land which the lord farmed directly. The 'home-farm'

EPICYCLE. A small circle with its centre on the circumference of another circle

ESCHEAT. The reversion of land to the feudal overlord, usually either through lack of an heir or because the tenant had committed a felony

ESQUIRE or SQUIRE. A knight's 'apprentice'

ESSOIN. An excuse for non-attendance at a court

EXCHEQUER. The royal counting house

EXTENT. A detailed valuation of land and property

FARM. The rent or service paid for landholding; or a fixed sum paid to the exchequer by a county or borough which collected its own taxes

FEE or FIEF. A KNIGHT'S FEE (q.v.) was a unit of land, varying in extent, charged with the provision of one knight for the lord's service. An estate might be made up of several fees

FEE-FARM. Holding land by a fixed monetary rent

FEE SIMPLE. Land held in fee simple was held without restriction on inheritance

FEE TAIL. Land held in fee tail was entailed or settled upon a succession of persons, none of whom could treat it as absolute owner

FEODARY. One who holds lands on condition of homage and service to an overlord. Also an officer concerned with inheritance of land

FEOFFMENT. A method of conveying freehold land; delivery of possession by handing over keys, etc.

FEUDAL HOST. The army which assembled when the king required his tenants in chief to support him in war

FEUDALISM. Social organization based on holding land in feud or fief, i.e. from a superior on specified terms of service

FINAL CONCORD. A legal agreement or settlement

FINE. Two meanings – a fee or an end (*finis*). Often applied to a final agreement or decision concerning landholding. Such fines were written in triplicate. Copies went to the disputants, and the third copies, feet of fines, were filed in the records of the court of common pleas. AMERCEMENT was used for the modern meaning of *fine*

FINE ROLLS. Records of payments made for writs issued by the crown

FOREST. Area reserved for game and hunting. Special laws, forest laws, governed these areas, which were far from being all woodlands

FORESTER. Officer in charge of the king's (or his lord's) forest lands and game

FRANCHISE. An immunity or exemption: a LIBERTY (q.v.)

FRANKPLEDGE. The system by which the householders of a manor or village were grouped into TITHINGS (q.v.), in order that each tithing could be held corporately responsible for the good behaviour of its members. Cases of lawbreaking were heard twice a year at a view of frankpledge

GAGE. A pledge (*vadium*), i.e. anything given as security for an act or payment

GELD. A tax. Particularly associated with English and Norman taxes of the tenth and eleventh centuries

GILD. A corporation of merchants or craftsmen inside a borough

GRAND ASSIZE. A group of neighbours sworn to give evidence and judgment concerning disputed land-holding. In Henry II's reign this was an alternative method of settlement to ORDEAL by combat (q.v.)

GREAT SCHISM. Division in the papacy, which began in 1378 and ended with the election of Martin V as pope in 1417

HANSE. Probably the entrance fee to join a merchant gild, and therefore the treasury of the gild; but also used of the gild itself and its trading monopoly, and of its place of meeting

HIDE. An area of land, which differed considerably in size in different counties. By 1086 it had become a tax assessment unit rather than a measurement

HOLDING LAND. Since all land belongs to the crown, no subject can *own* it. Tenants in chief *held* it directly from the crown; subtenants *held* from a superior lord. *Teneo*: I hold

HOMAGE. Acknowledgement of allegiance to a superior

HUNDRED. An administrative subdivision of a county with its own court

HUSTINGS. The chief assembly and law court of the City of London

INDENTURE. An agreement written two, three, or more times on a single parchment. To insure against forgery, the copies – one for each party to the agreement – were separated by irregular, wavy cuts

INFANG[EN]THIEF. The right sought by borough and manor courts to apprehend and punish anyone caught thieving within the boundaries of their jurisdiction

INQUISITION. An inquiry. Inquisition *post mortem* was an inquiry into the holdings, services, and succession of a deceased person, who held land of the king. Writ of inquisition of life and limbs was a chancery writ, instituted by Henry II, enabling the defendant against a charge of homicide to avoid trial by combat and refer the case to a local jury

INVESTITURE. Putting a priest or deacon in possession of a benefice. The Investiture Dispute in the eleventh and twelfth centuries concerned the right of lay rulers to receive homage from ecclesiastics

ITINERANT JUSTICE. A royal judge who moved from centre to centre hearing pleas of the crown

JUSTICE IN EYRE. A judge commissioned by the crown to undertake a journey, or eyre, in order to hear all pleas at certain county centres

JUSTICIAR. The king's chief minister and regent during the late twelfth and early thirteenth centuries

KNIGHT'S FEE. Originally a grant of land in exchange for undertaking to supply a lord with the services of a fully armed knight and his necessary servants for forty days each year. Eventually, payment was made by rent, and knight's fees were often divided among several tenants

LASTAGE. Charges for lading, i.e. putting goods on board ship. The charges constituted a national tax collected locally

LETTERS CLOSE. Private letter or letters

LETTERS PATENT. Open letter or letters

LIBERATE ROLLS. Records of writs which authorized the spending of the king's money

LIBERTY. An area made free from specified restrictions, e.g. from shrieval control. Also a grant to an individual or corporation of special privilege, such as rights of jurisdiction

LIVERY. A provision or allowance made to support an office; payment for services rendered

MANOR. A feudal freehold estate. Manors varied considerably in size, but usually the lord of the manor, or his deputy, presided over a manor court, which administered the manor lands and controlled the manor tenants. Since manors were held in FEE

SIMPLE (q.v.), they passed automatically from the lord to his heir

MANURANCE. Occupation and management of land

MARCH. Border territory

MARK. A German coin introduced into England in the twelfth century. Its value was 13s. 4d.

MERCY. To be in mercy was to be liable to punishment for an offence

METES. Boundaries

MINTAGE. A tax levied on towns and counties whenever a new coinage was introduced

MISKENNING. A penalty for not stating a legal case in the correct form

MOIETY. One of two parts into which an estate was divided: not necessarily a half

MORT D'ANCESTOR. Judicial cases concerned with claims of inheritance

MOTTE-AND-BAILEY CASTLE. A Norman castle, built of wood on an artificial mound of earth (the motte) and adjoining a stockaded living area (the bailey)

MURAGE. The right granted by the crown to a community to exact tolls. Also, the name of the tax itself

MURDER-FINE. A corporate fine levied on the inhabitants of an area in which a murder had taken place, when the culprit could not be found and when the victim could not be proved not to be of Norman blood

NOVEL DISSEISIN. Judicial cases concerned with dispossession of land

NOVICE. A probationary member of a monastic community

OBEDIENTIARY. A monk in charge of an administrative department inside a monastery

OBLATION. An offering to the church in honour of God

ORDEAL. A means of submitting a case to 'divine judgement'. The English and the Normans both used the ordeals of fire and water. The Normans added ordeal by combat for knights

OUTFANG[EN]THIEF. The right to pursue a thief outside a person's or corporation's territorial jurisdiction and bring him back for punishment

OYER ET TERMINER. To hear and give judgment. A court of oyer et terminer was one of final judgment usually held by one of the king's judges

PANNAGE. The right to feed pigs in the woods. Also the payment made to hold that right

PASSAGE. Tolls on passengers or goods

PETTY ASSIZES. Legal proceedings which originated from a royal writ granted at the request of the plaintiff and which posed certain questions of fact. Cases were decided by a local jury

PETTY SERGEANTY. Holding land in return for a small specified personal service to the king

PIPE ROLL. Record of payments made to the EXCHEQUER (q.v.)

PLEA. Action at law. Pleas of the crown were cases reserved for the king's justices. The court of common pleas heard civil actions only

PONTAGE. A tax or toll for the maintenance and repair of bridges

PRAECIPE. A royal writ, *praecipe quod reddat*, which removed cases of disputed holding of land from the court baron of a feudal lord to the king's court

PROXY. The entertainment provided for a church visitor or an annual money payment to commute this provision

PURPRESTURE. An encroachment, especially on to deer pastures in the forest

QUADRIVIUM. The four more advanced subjects taught in medieval schools – arithmetic, music, geometry, and astronomy

QUIT RENT. Money payment made by a small landholder in place of traditional services

RAPE. A subdivision of a county

RECOVERY. Originally a collusive transfer of entailed property from one person to another; but later a regular form of conveyance

REEVE. A deputy. The shire reeve (sheriff) was the king's deputy in the county: the manor reeve the lord's deputy in the manor court

REGULAR CLERGY. Clergy living according to a religious rule. Monks and friars were regulars

RELIEF. A payment made to the overlord by an heir succeeding to a feudal estate

RENT-SECK. A rent fixed by deed but without a clause of distraint in case of arrears

RENT-SERVICE. Personal service in addition to, or in lieu of rent

SAC AND SOC or SAKE AND SOKE. The right to hold a court and require tenants to attend it. The territorial area over which the rights were held

SCAVAGE. A national tax, locally collected and often farmed, paid on imported goods by foreign merchants for the privilege of displaying them for sale

SCOT. A local tax paid by inhabitants to the sheriffs and town officials

SCUTAGE. A money payment made to the king instead of personal military service. Scutage became increasingly usual from the reign of Henry II onwards

SECULAR CLERGY. Priests who live among laymen and not in a religious order. Bishops, parish priests, and curates are all seculars

SEIGNIORIAL BOROUGH. A borough which received its charter from an earl, baron, or local landholder, i.e. not from the crown

SEIZE. Possess. A freeholder was said to be *seized* of his land. To be *disseized* was to be dispossessed. *Seisin* was legal possession or tenure

SENESCHAL. Steward

SERF. An unfree servant: a slave

SERJEANTY. To hold land by serjeanty was to hold it in exchange for an agreed service other than military duties

SHIRE LEVY. The defence force provided for by the Assize of Arms, 1181

SOCAGE. Tenure without servile obligation; the tenant usually paid a rent

SOKE or SAKE. See SOC or SAC

SOKEMAN or SOCMAN. A free tenant, who came under the lord's jurisdiction

SPIRITUALITIES. Tithes, gifts, and other ecclesiastical sources of income belonging to a bishop or religious house

STALLAGE. A tax on stall-holders in markets and fairs

SYNOD. An ecclesiastical council or assembly

SYNODY. A payment made by lesser clergy at the synod, or to their church visitor

TALE. Count or total

TALLAGE. A tax, usually levied arbitrarily by a lord on his vassals

TEMPORALITIES. Lands, buildings, and other secular sources of income belonging to a bishop or religious house

TENANT IN CHIEF. One who held land directly from the crown

THEAM or TEAM. In the phrase *toll, theam, sake, and soke,* is a right of jurisdiction, probably over cases of theam, i.e. claims for recovery of stolen property where the defendant pleaded a guarantee of title from some third person

THEGN. An Anglo-Saxon retainer of noble birth. By 1086, however, many thegns owned little land and enjoyed few privileges

TITHE. Payment to the church of a tenth of the produce of the land. In a parish the great tithes, i.e. tenths of the main products, went to the rector, and the small tithes to the vicar

TITHING. A group of householders in the FRANKPLEDGE system (q.v.). Originally a tithing had ten members, but eventually numbers varied considerably

TOLL. The right granted in most borough charters to exact toll from strangers bringing goods to the market

TRIVIUM. The three basic subjects taught in medieval schools – grammar, rhetoric, and logic

VAVASOUR. A feudal tenant of high standing but below the rank of baron

VIEW OF ARMS. A six-monthly inspection of the arms held by the SHIRE LEVIES (q.v.)

VILL. A settlement: a hamlet

VILLEIN. An unfree peasant or villager, who usually farmed

strips in the common fields, and, therefore, was better off than a serf

WAPENTAKE. Another name, Norse in origin, for a HUNDRED (q.v.)

WARDROBE. The more personal household administration developed by Henry II and Edward I to by-pass the heavy administrative machine of the CHANCERY and EXCHEQUER q.v.). Edward III used the wardrobe, by then a subsidiary of the exchequer, as his war treasury overseas

WARRENER. An officer employed by king or tenant to safeguard game other than deer

WER. The price for which a man's death could be legally atoned in Anglo-Saxon times. The *wer* or *wergild* varied according to the victim's social rank

WITAN or WITENAGEMOT. The king's council in Anglo-Saxon England. The Norman kings transformed it into the Great Council, the assembly of feudal magnates

# Index

Dates following names of monarchs and popes are dates of their reign.
Dates following other names are of birth and death, or death alone,
or period when most active.

## MORE ABOUT PENGUINS
## AND PELICANS

*Penguin Book News*, which appears every month, contains details of all the new books issued by Penguins as they are published. From time to time it is supplemented by *Penguins in Print*, which is a complete list of all books published by Penguins which are in print. (There are nearly three thousand of these.)

A specimen copy of *Penguin Book News* will be sent to you free on request, and you can become a subscriber for the price of the postage – 3s. for a year's issues (including the complete lists). Just write to Dept EP, Penguin Books Ltd, Harmondsworth, Middlesex, enclosing a cheque or postal order, and your name will be added to the mailing list.

The second volume of *A Documentary History of England* is described overleaf.

Note: *Penguin Book News* and *Penguins in Print* are not available in the U.S.A. or Canada

# A DOCUMENTARY HISTORY
## OF ENGLAND
### Vol. 2 (1559–1931)

This second volume covers thirteen key documents, from the Act of Uniformity 1559 to the Statute of Westminster 1931, and includes the Bill of Rights 1689, the Reform Act 1832, and the Chadwick Report on the Sanitary Condition of the Labouring Population 1842.

# TELEVISION
# IN THE MAKING

*Edited By*

## Paul Rotha

THE FOCAL PRESS
London and New York

OTHER BOOKS BY PAUL ROTHA

**The Film Till Now**
(*1930, and with Richard Griffith, 1949*)

**Celluloid:**
*The Film Today (1931)*

**Documentary Film**
(*1936, 1939 and with Richard Griffith and Sinclair Road, 1952*)

**Movie Parade:**
*A Pictorial Survey of the Cinema (1936, and with Roger Manvell, 1950*)

**Portrait of a Flying Yorkshireman**
(*the letters of Eric Knight to Paul Rotha, 1952*)

Printed 1956 in Great Britain by Billing and Sons Ltd., Guildford and London,
for Focal Press Ltd., Fitzroy Square, London, W.1.